Lumber Widths and Thicknesses

Lumber is ordered by thickness, width, and length. When you order in U.S. or imperial measurements (2 inches x 4 inches x 8 feet, for example), the thickness and width figures (in this instance 2x4) refer to nominal size—the dimensions of the piece as it left the saw. But what you get is the smaller, actual size remaining when the piece has been planed smooth; in actual fact, a piece $1^1/_2$ inches x $3^1/_2$ inches x 8 feet. (Length is not reduced by the processing.)

Metric measurements, on the other hand, always describe the actual dimensions of the processed piece.

Nominal size in inches	Actual size in inches	Actual size in millimeters
1x3	$^3/_4$ x $2^1/_2$	16 x 64
2x2	$1^1/_2$ x $1^1/_2$	38 x 38
2x4	$1^1/_2$ x $3^1/_2$	38 x 89
2x6	$1^1/_2$ x $5^1/_2$	38 x 140
2x8	$1^1/_2$ x $7^1/_4$	38 x 184
2x10	$1^1/_2$ x $9^1/_4$	38 x 235
4x4	$3^1/_2$ x $3^1/_2$	89 x 89
4x6	$3^1/_2$ x $5^1/_2$	89 x 140

Tiles and Tiling

This formula (based on 23-centimeter square tiles and a room 5 meters long by 4 meters wide) will help you to determine how many tiles you need to cover a room:

1. Divide 100 centimeters (1 meter) by 23 (100 ÷ 23 = 4.35 tiles per meter).

2. Find the number of tiles per side by multiplying length and width respectively by tiles per meter (5 x 4.35 = 21.75; 4 x 4.35 = 17.4).

3. Calculate the area in tiles (21.75 x 17.4 = 378.45, or about 380 tiles).

4. Add 10% for fitting (380 + 10% = 418).

Sheet Vinyl Flooring and Carpeting

To estimate your sheet vinyl flooring and carpeting needs in square meters:

1. Measure the room's longest and widest wall (include doorways and alcoves in the measurements), adding 7.5 centimeters to each wall for good measure. Your calculation will be something such as:

    5.18 meters + 7.5 centimeters = 5.26 meters (width)
    5.79 meters + 7.5 centimeters = 5.87 meters (length)

2. Calculate the area of the room (5.26 meters x 5.87 meters = 30.87 square meters). You will need 31 m² to cover the room.

Metric Plywood Panels

Plywood panels generally come in two standard metric sizes: 1,200 millimeters x 2,400 millimeters and 1,220 millimeters x 2,400 millimeters (the equivalent of a 4 foot x 8 foot panel). Other sizes are available on special order. With sheathing and select sheathing grades, metric and inch thicknesses are generally identical. The metric sanded grades, however, come in a new range of thicknesses.

Metric thicknesses

Sheathing and Select Grades		Sanded Grades	
7.5 mm	$(^5/_{16}$ in.)	6 mm	$(^4/_{17}$ in.)
9.5 mm	$(^3/_8$ in.)	8 mm	$(^5/_{16}$ in.)
12.5 mm	$(^1/_2$ in.)	11 mm	$(^7/_{16}$ in.)
15.5 mm	$(^5/_8$ in.)	14 mm	$(^9/_{16}$ in.)
18.5 mm	$(^3/_4$ in.)	17 mm	$(^2/_3$ in.)
20.5 mm	$(^{13}/_{16}$ in.)	19 mm	$(^3/_4$ in.)
22.5 mm	$(^7/_8$ in.)	21 mm	$(^{13}/_{16}$ in.)
25.5 mm	(1 in.)	24 mm	$(^{15}/_{16}$ in.)

THE FAMILY
Handyman ®

Home Storage Projects

Home Storage Projects

A Room-by-Room Guide to Practical Storage Solutions

THE READER'S DIGEST ASSOCIATION, INC.
Pleasantville, New York/Montreal

A READER'S DIGEST BOOK

Produced by Roundtable Press, Inc.
Directors: Susan E. Meyer, Marsha Melnick
Executive Editor: Amy T. Jonak
Project Editor: David R. Hall
Editor: David A. Kirchner
Assistant Editor: Abigail A. Anderson
Design: Sisco & Evans, New York
Editorial Production: Steven Rosen

For The Family Handyman
Editor in Chief: Gary Havens
Special Projects Editor: Ken Collier
TFH Books Editor: Spike Carlsen

Library of Congress Cataloging in Publication Data
The family handyman home storage projects: a room-by-room guide to practical storage
    solutions.
           p.   cm.
           Includes index.
           ISBN 0-89577-889-0
           1. Cabinetwork—Amateurs' manuals. 2. Shelving (furniture)—
Amateurs' manuals. 3. Storage in the home—Amateurs' manuals.
I. Reader's Digest Association. II. Family handyman.
TT197.H654   1997
684.1'6—dc20   96-12462

A Note from the Editor

The dream home that most people write books about has neat features like hardwood floors throughout, ceramic tile entry halls, zoned heating and cooling, triple-glazed no-maintenance windows, a brick driveway, automatic lawn sprinklers, a greenhouse and sunroom . . . the list could go on.

But what people really dream about—and what we've put in this book—is lots and lots of storage. Time and again, homebuilders are told what their customers really want is plenty of closet space, handy cubbyholes, space for desks and cabinets, shelves where they need them, and other kinds of places to simply put their stuff.

If you're one of those folks, this book will be the answer to your dreams. Over the years, the editors of *The Family Handyman* magazine have devised dozens of storage solutions for every room in the home, ranging from simple shelf systems to attractive cabinets and clever built-ins that look like they've always been there. You'll find the very best right here.

Like all projects developed by *The Family Handyman*, every one of these has actually been built by our editors. This means that the inevitable design flaws have been fixed and the construction procedures simplified. The plans are accurate and complete; the step-by-step instructions will yield the best possible results with the least difficulty. You'll also find accurate shopping lists for the projects, with tips on where to find any of the hard-to-locate items.

We've tried to make this book the key to achieving the *real* home of your dreams. The editors and I hope it works for you. Happy building!

Gary Havens
Editor in Chief
The Family Handyman

Home Storage Projects

Contents

Introduction

There's something indefinably soul satisfying about increasing your home's storage capacity. Perhaps it's the promise of organizing all that clutter you've been meaning to sort through, or the immediate gratification of completing a one-weekend project.

Shelves are at the heart of the more than thirty storage projects you'll find in *The Family Handyman Home Storage Projects*. Whether they're for CD players, clothes, or kitchen overflow—not to mention books—these storage solutions can work wonders all through your house, from top to bottom.

Most of these projects are perfect for beginning and intermediate do-it-yourselfers. Many are modular in design, so you can build only the components you really need or adapt the projects shown here to your available space.

Outfitting your home with functional storage projects should be fun, so don't spoil it with an accident. Wear eye protection whenever you use power tools—and even when you work with hand tools, if there's a possibility that material may become airborne. Always follow your power-tool manufacturers' safety precautions to the letter, and keep all your tools clean, sharp, and well maintained. And if by chance your workshop itself could use a bit of organizing, by all means build the project we show here and on page 172 first!

Home Storage Projects

Living Room & Dining Room

Choose from a wide range of projects—from
simple shelves to window seat cabinets—that
add attractive storage options to your living
and dining areas.

Fast, Flexible Bookcases

Adapt these handy universal plans to
assemble handsome bookcases to suit a
variety of situations.

12

Easy Display Shelving

Create display space to suit any decor with three simple weekend shelf projects.

Built-in Library Shelves

Add built-in shelving that won't look like an afterthought. Use modular design to transform a room or create a beautiful shelving system.

Window Seat Cabinets

Add both storage and seating with this easy, inviting window seat and cabinet combination piece.

Dinnerware Rack

Show off your dinnerware. This open rack stows twelve place settings of plates, platters, saucers, bowls, and cups.

Fast, Flexible Bookcases

Adapt these handy universal plans to assemble handsome bookcases to suit a variety of situations.

Step-by-step instructions for building a versatile "Built-in" Bookcase

Plus adaptable designs for four more projects:

- **Modern Bookcase**
- **Stained Oak Entertainment Center**
- **Wall-Mounted Desktop Hutch**
- **Child's Book and Toy Shelves**

A well-designed bookshelf system should be simple enough that you can build sturdy shelves in just a few hours. And, like the one at right, it should be adaptable, so that you can create attractive shelves that are at home in a living area or a dining room.

All the designs in this chapter satisfy both of these requirements. They avoid complicated joints so that even a novice can quickly assemble bookshelves like the ones shown here.

You'll find described here the tools and techniques needed to make the versatile "Built-in" Bookcase (opposite). You can use the same techniques to create the shelving designs on pages 26–29. Follow the designs as they are, change the dimensions to suit your particular needs, or just let the drawings stimulate your imagination.

You can produce most of the shelves from these designs by using just a circular saw, a 1/4-inch or 3/8-inch variable-speed drill, and a few hand tools. Additional tools and accessories that can make your work even easier appear in the Tools and Materials lists on the facing page.

Despite its easy-to-build design, this elegant bookcase—with its room-matching base trim and solid oak top—looks like an expensive built-in. Best of all, the plans are easy to adapt to your specific space for that same custom-built look.

TOOLS

HAND TOOLS

Clamps

Drill with depth stop

Earplugs

Framing square

Hammer

Level

Pry bar

Roller or wood block

Safety goggles

Screwdriver

Steam iron

Utility knife

Wood file

POWER TOOLS

Circular saw; 40-tooth carbide-tip blade

Jigsaw

Miter box

Variable-speed drill; 1/4" brad-point bit; combination bit for No. 6 screws; adjustable drill stop

OPTIONAL

Handsaw

Reciprocating saw

Table saw

MATERIALS

Qty.	Size and Description
24	Pin-type shelf clips
24	No. 6 x 2-1/2" drywall screws
6	No. 6 x 1-3/4" drywall screws
	1-lb. box 6d finish nails
	1-lb. box 4d finish nails
	3/4" birch plywood
	Birch-veneer edging
	1/4" dowel stock
	Yellow woodworker's glue
	Sandpaper
	Furniture shims
	Stain
	Clear finish
	Pine boards and moldings
	Oak boards and moldings
	Wood shims

Plan Your Shelf System

There's more than one good way to build a shelf system. Because you may want to adapt these designs to your own special needs, you'll find several alternative construction techniques here that will increase your options. Use these hints to make your shelving unit stronger, more attractive, or more economical to build.

Most importantly, a shelf system should be practical. The shape your system takes will depend on where you want to place it and what you plan to put on it. With practicality in mind, let your imagination go to work. Use a pad of paper and a pencil to sketch some rough shelf-system designs in their actual room settings. Then use the following guidelines to put preliminary dimensions on your plans.

Choosing the Right Depth

Bookcases don't just hold books. Plan your shelf depth—the front-to-back measurement—to fit the largest objects you'll want to hold: books, photo albums, stereo gear, toys, or whatever. The box here lists the standard dimensions for various common household objects, but be sure to measure everything you plan to store on these shelves, especially oversize items such as TV sets.

The shelves on the previous page were designed primarily for books of all sizes, but their 11-1/4 inch depth also worked well to display photos, ceramic bowls, and flowers. Additional shelf-system plans on pages 26–29 show how you can adapt standard shelf sizes for other purposes.

Additional shelf-system plans on pages 26–29

Selecting the Correct Length

Well-designed shelves shouldn't sag, so plan their length to support the heaviest objects you're likely to set on them without causing a noticeable dip. Although you probably won't call upon your shelves to hold excessive weights, they should at least be strong enough to support a heavy load of books.

Using books as a standard, follow this rule of thumb: if 3/4-inch thick wood shelves are 10 to 12 inches deep, they should span no more than 32 inches between supports. (This figure is a conservative average span for a variety of wood species as well as plywood.) Although stronger boards, such as the best-quality 3/4-inch oak and maple, may be able to span an additional foot, it's still best to limit your shelf spans to 32 inches. Refer to the table on the facing page to help determine standard lengths for unbraced shelves in various materials.

You can design shelves that are longer or stronger in three different ways: either reinforce 3/4-inch shelves with 1x2 strips glued and nailed to their front and/or back edges, simply use thicker wood, or nail the shelves to the back of the cabinet if they're not adjustable.

All these shelf systems were designed to use 3/4-inch thick wood, because standard 1x8's, 1x10's, and 1x12's are all 3/4 inch thick. Although other materials, like 3/8-inch glass, would also work, 3/4-inch wood is one of the best shelving choices available. Whether solid boards or plywood, wood is strong, easy to work with, and readily available. And because there is such a range of types of wood, you can choose one that's as economical or elegant as your budget and the project warrant.

Calculating the Best Height

You can build your shelf system as tall as you like, but remember that the taller it is, the more prone it will be to tipping over. Unless it has a wide, stable base, a shelf system more than 3 feet tall should be screwed directly to the wall framing. You can always remove the screws if you need to move the unit.

Design Tip

Build your bookcase low enough to provide a suitable display surface on top or extend it to the ceiling. Don't leave an awkward, unusable space between the ceiling and the top.

Standard Shelf Depths

To house the items listed below, make sure your shelves meet the minimum depth requirements shown.

Item	Depth (Front to back)	Item	Depth (Front to back)
Compact disks	6 in.	Record albums	14 in.
Paperback books	10 in.	Sound equipment	18–20 in.
Hardcover books	11 in.	Television set	24 in. +
Magazines	11 in.	(Measure oversize items)	
Art books	11–14 in.		

Choosing the Material

With the dimensions of your projected bookshelf system in mind, consider how you'd like it to look. Do you plan to paint the shelves to match the room, or will you leave them unfinished? Are you after a formal look? Does your home have an overall traditional feel, or is your style more clean and contemporary?

Much of what you decide now will determine the material you choose. The box at the right lists the advantages and disadvantages of common shelving materials. Refer to it in choosing your materials.

As you consider what material to use for your own shelving, keep in mind the selection process that occurred for the shelving project that begins on the next page.

The bookcase described on the following pages looks virtually built-in, because after it was installed it was painted to match the woodwork and embellished with a decorative oak top stained to complement the floor.

The height of the top strikes a comfortable balance: it provides a display surface low enough to avoid the wall sconces but still high enough to supply the maximum amount of cabinet space below. The depth of these shelves, 11-1/4 inches, is sufficient for all but oversize books and record albums. For greater depth to accommodate a sound system or television set, you might prefer to consider the Stained Oak Entertainment Center shown on page 27.

Choices like these will present themselves as you adapt the following projects to your own space and budget.

Types of 3/4-inch Shelving

All shelving is 3/4-inch material except as noted.

Material	Pros	Cons
No. 2 Pine boards	Easy to cut and assemble; takes paint well except for rough knots; good rustic appearance	Quality varies, so select boards carefully; look for straight, flat boards; you often will have to fill and seal knots before painting; accepts stain poorly
Clear Pine	Same as for No. 2 pine boards, except free of knots or flaws	Stains poorly; expensive
Oak, Birch, and Maple boards	Attractive; usually stained or given a natural finish; birch and maple take paint well	More difficult to cut, nail, and sand than pine; oak does not paint smoothly; expensive
Birch Plywood	Attractive, smooth, flat boards; easy to cut and nail; accepts paint or a natural finish well	Difficult to stain; exposed edges must be covered for a finished look; must saw boards from 4x8-foot sheets
Oak Plywood	Attractive, smooth, flat boards; easy to cut and nail; accepts stain well	Takes paint poorly; exposed edges must be covered for a finished look; must saw boards from 4x8-foot sheets
Fir Plywood	Flat boards; easy to cut and nail; sanded smooth grades (coded AB) accept paint and stain fairly well; rougher grades (coded CD) are inexpensive	Rougher grades (CD) finish poorly; exposed edges must be covered for a finished look; must saw boards from 4x8-foot sheets
Particleboard (not recommended)	Flat; inexpensive	Weaker than solid wood or plywood (maximum shelf length 26 in.); difficult to nail or screw together or paint; rapidly deteriorates when moist
Glass	Excellent for displaying collectibles, especially when combined with spotlights or undershelf lighting	Limited strength (maximum length 18 in.)
Precut Stair Treads	Extra-strong, 1 inch or more thick; bullnose molding; hardwoods	Expensive; oak does not take paint smoothly

Versatile "Built-in" Bookcase

The birch plywood selected for this versatile "Built-in" Bookcase shelf system provided a perfectly flat, smooth surface for painting at a moderate price. However, the choice of plywood rather than pine shelving meant that more time had to be spent cutting the shelving to width. If you have a table saw, this task will go quickly. A circular saw guided by a straightedge will take longer but will also yield good results.

A solid oak board was chosen for the decorative top, for several reasons:

▶ A surface of solid wood is more attractive and longer-lasting than one of oak-veneer plywood.

▶ Wide, solid hardwood boards that have been glued together from narrower boards provide as much warp protection as plywood does.

▶ It's easier to apply edge molding to solid wood than to plywood. There's no worry about ruining a thin plywood veneer when you sand the molding joints smooth.

▶ A solid-oak top will cost less than an oak-veneer plywood one because you'll normally need to buy an entire 4x8-foot sheet of plywood just to obtain the one piece you need.

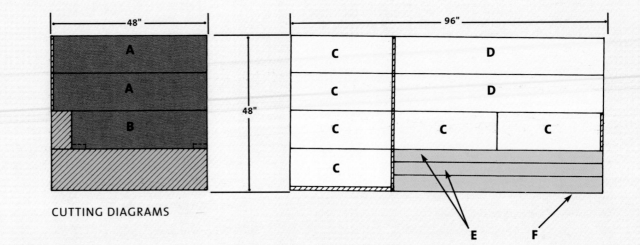

CUTTING DIAGRAMS

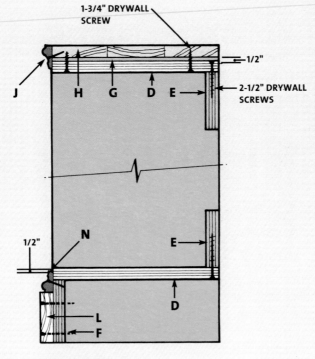

CROSS SECTION

CUTTING LIST

Key	Qty.	Size and Description
A	2	3/4" x 11-1/4" x 47-7/8" plywood
B	1	3/4" x 11-1/4" x 42" plywood
C	6	3/4" x 11-1/4" x 31-1/2" plywood
D	2	3/4" x 11-1/4" x 64" plywood
E	2	3/4" x 4" x 64" plywood
F	1	3/4" x 4-3/8" x 64" plywood
G	3	1/2" x 4" x 11-1/4" plywood
H	1	3/4" x 11-1/4" x 65-1/2" oak
J	1	3/4" x 1-1/4" x 66-1/4" oak trim
K	1	3/4" x 1-1/4" x 12-1/4" oak trim
L	1	3/4" x 3-1/2" x 66-1/4" pine
M	1	3/4" x 3-1/2" x 12-1/4" pine
N	1	3/4" x 1-3/8" x 66-1/4" pine trim
P	1	3/4" x 1-3/8" x 12-1/4" pine trim

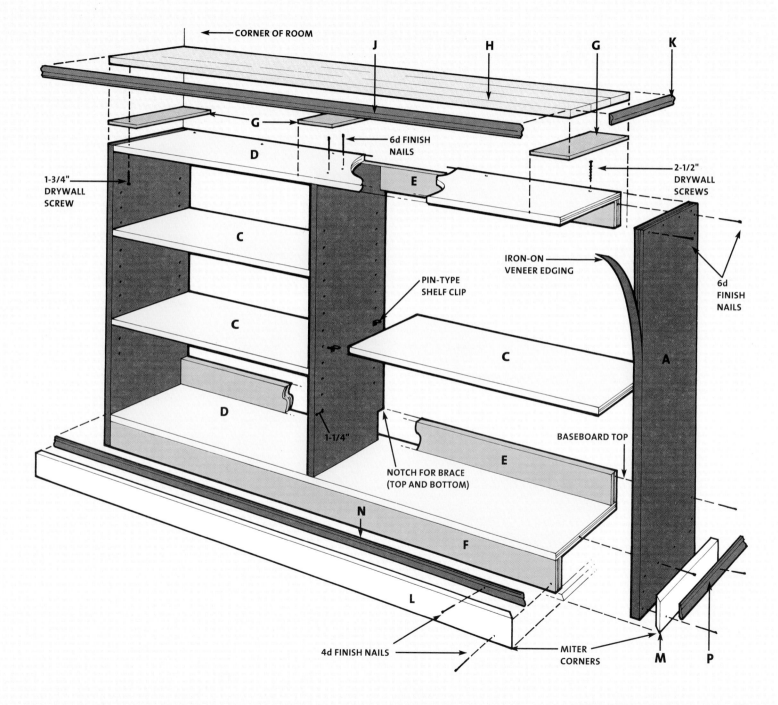

CORNER OF ROOM

J

H

G

K

G

6d FINISH
NAILS

D

2-1/2"
DRYWALL
SCREWS

1-3/4"
DRYWALL
SCREW

E

C

IRON-ON
VENEER EDGING

6d
FINISH
NAILS

PIN-TYPE
SHELF CLIP

C

C

A

D

1-1/4"

E

BASEBOARD TOP

NOTCH FOR BRACE
(TOP AND BOTTOM)

N

F

L

4d FINISH NAILS

MITER
CORNERS

M

P

Cut Out the Parts

Start this project by cutting the plywood pieces to size. Cutting plywood takes a bit more time than cutting 1x12 boards, but the extra time will be offset by the advantages of using plywood. For one, by using the factory edge as an 8-foot long saw guide, you can cut your shelving perfectly straight, using a circular saw (Photo 1). And, if you can use a factory corner as a guide for crosscuts, later when you cut the parts to length you can trim each piece perfectly square. Plan to spend at least two hours cutting the shelves. Be sure to wear eye and ear protection while using all power tools.

You can simplify your finish work by making the saw cuts as smooth as possible. Use a sharp 40-tooth carbide-tip blade rather than a 20- to 24-tooth standard blade (Photo 2). The smoother edge will cut down on sanding time.

If you don't have an extra sheet of plywood on hand to use as a cutting guide, trim a 12-inch strip off one side of the birch plywood panel. (Later you can convert this guide into a shelf by making its other edge straight.)

Clamp the guide you have just cut to the plywood sheet so that the saw base slides along the factory edge (see Photo 1). If you set your saw blade to cut only 1 inch deep, you can saw right across the 2x4's used to support the plywood.

The old saying "measure twice and cut once" remains good advice. Slide your saw

---

CUT OUT THE PARTS

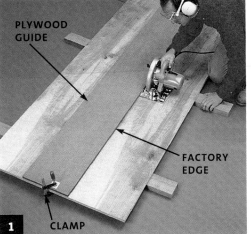

1 Cut shelving components with a circular saw, using the factory edge of a clamped length of plywood as a guide. Wear eye and ear protection, and if possible work on the floor for stability.

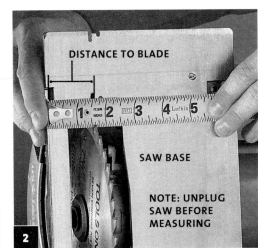

2 Unplug the saw, then measure the distance between the edge of the saw base and the blade. Adjust the plywood guide accordingly. Use a sharp, 40-tooth carbide blade, not a standard blade.

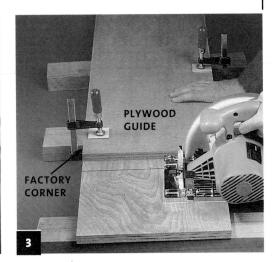

3 Clamp the factory corner of a sheet of plywood to the shelves for a perfect right angle along which to make the crosscut guide when cutting shelves to length. The saw base will slide along the edge.

along the guide until the blade just nicks the plywood. Then stop the saw and check your measurement to make sure the kerf will fall exactly where it should.

After cutting out the 11-1/4 inch shelves from the panel, trim them to length. This step, called crosscutting, can be tricky with plywood and solid wood alike. The top surface of both kinds of wood tends to splinter when you saw across the grain. The box at the right describes how to achieve the best results with crosscuts in plywood. These cuts are more difficult to make than the same cuts in solid wood. If you master these techniques, you should be able to adapt them readily to hardwoods or softwoods.

This time, use one factory corner of the plywood for a guide, which will provide you with an exact right angle. Clamp the guide so that the long factory edge is even with one edge of the shelf (Photo 3).

Making Clean Crosscuts

To avoid splintering the surface of veneered plywood, slice 1/16 inch into the top layer with a utility knife run along a metal straightedge (right). Since the teeth are pushing into the wood from the bottom, splintering is not a problem. Applying masking tape to the bottom along the cutting line will help reduce splintering there.

Because of the direction in which the saw's teeth cut, place the good surface facing up if you are using a bandsaw or radial arm saw. If you are cutting with a circular saw or a hand-held jigsaw, place the good surface down. In any case, remember to make the cut just on the waste side of your cutting line, to allow for the kerf, the material removed by the blade.

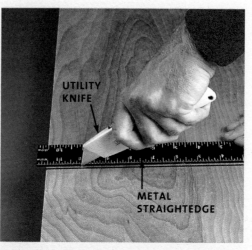

Score with a utility knife along a metal straightedge to prepare the crosscut lines and prevent splintering the top surface of veneered plywood.

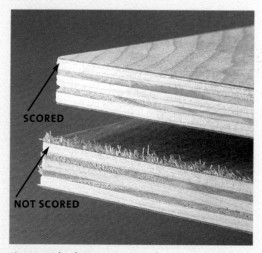

The scored (top) piece cut cleanly, but the unscored (bottom) piece splintered badly when sawed.

Make the Shelves Adjustable

The ability to make adjustments lets you customize your shelves to accommodate everything from tall coffee-table books to compact disks. The system shown here is easy to make, and nearly invisible.

The simplest but most visible types of shelf support are metal standards and wooden cleats (see Shelf Support Techniques, opposite). Pin-type shelf supports, shown on the opposite page, each have their own strengths and weaknesses.

Drilling the many shelf-support holes can admittedly be monotonous, but there is little room for carelessness. If all four holes that support a shelf don't line up exactly, the shelf will have an annoying wobble. Using a simple homemade jig can improve your accuracy and speed the job considerably (Photo 4).

You can make a jig like the one shown below from a piece of 1/4-inch plywood cut to the exact width of the shelving. Drill the holes 1-1/4 inches in from each edge

and 1-1/4 inches apart. After clamping the jig in place and drilling one set of holes, simply slide the jig up the board, align it by shoving a 1/4-inch dowel into the last hole drilled, and then reclamp the jig and drill another set of holes.

It's easy to make a mistake on alignment if you begin drilling the holes at different levels or accidentally flip the jig over from top to bottom when you start to drill another board. Unfortunately, you won't discover your error until the end of

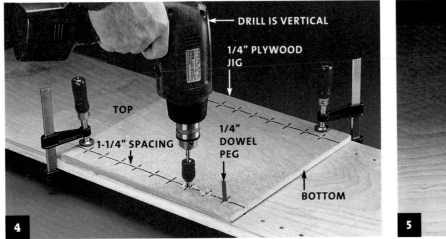

4

Drill holes for shelf supports to make the shelves adjustable, using a plywood jig. Clamp it, drill the holes, and move it along the shelf. Use a 1/4-in. dowel peg to hold the jig in alignment.

5

A brad-point bit cuts cleaner holes than a regular twist bit. Use an adjustable stop like the one shown here to set the right hole depth. Both are available at home centers and woodworking supply stores.

the project, when you try to install the shelves. So label the top and bottom edges of the jig and mark the locations of the starting holes accurately on each piece.

Two tools are essential for accurate drilling. An adjustable drill stop will control the hole depth and, more importantly, keep your drill bit from breaking through the other side of the board (Photo 5). A brad-point drill bit like the one in Photo 5 will cut a cleaner hole than a regular twist bit and won't chip the edges of the hole. However, a brad-point bit doesn't always cut a perfect hole. Experiment first on scrap wood to find the combination of drill speed and pressure that gives you the cleanest cut.

The simple pin-type shelf supports that fit into the 1/4-inch holes in this unit are functional and unobtrusive. See the box at the right for various shelf support options.

Shelf Support Techniques

This project uses unobtrusive and sturdy pin-type shelf clips to support the shelves. There are several styles of pin-type supports to choose from (top, right).

Other options for supporting shelving are more visible but offer their own advantages of ease and sturdiness. Metal standards (bottom, left) and wooden cleats (bottom, right) are two practical alternatives to the pin-type shelf clips used in this project.

Metal standards are the quickest and easiest to install. This hardware is available in gold, chrome, and brown finishes. Before you install the standards, stand them side by side on a flat surface to make sure that their holes line up with each other, to avoid wobbly shelves later. Then simply attach the standards to the sides of the shelf system with the special short nails supplied with the standards and snap the adjustable clips into place.

Cleats nailed or screwed in pairs to the sides of the shelf system provide the strongest support and are particularly useful for utility shelves, where appearance is not of primary importance. Space the cleats to allow for a range of placement options. You can improve their appearance by using strips of molding as shown. Just be sure to mount the cleats at a perfect right angle to the front edge of the sides, to prevent wobbling.

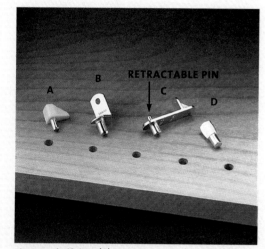

Pin-type shelf clips: (A) European style (requires a 5 mm drill bit); (B) angle style, available with a plastic button or coating for glass shelves; the hole allows you to screw the shelf on tightly; (C) locking style, in which a pin holds the 3/4-in. shelf in place so it doesn't wobble; (D) spoon-shaped style.

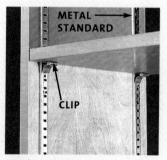

Metal standards

Wooden cleats

Assemble the Frame

If you've cut all of the pieces accurately, assembling the shelf frame will be simple. The trick is to work on a flat floor or table with a helper to hold the pieces in place. Professional carpenters can work alone by using long clamps to hold joints together. (For more information on various types of clamps, see the box Woodworking Clamps on page 81.) You probably won't have clamps long enough for this project, so recruit a helper to hold the sides exactly on your layout marks while you predrill 3/32-inch holes through the sides (Photo 6). Predrilling isn't always absolutely necessary, especially with plywood, but it will help you drive the fastener perfectly straight so that it hits the center of the board on the other side. Predrilling also makes the wood less likely to split.

Draw a line with a framing square to mark the center of the joining board so you can drill the holes accurately (Photo 7). This line was darkened to make it more visible in the photo; you should draw a light pencil line you can easily erase.

Screws or Nails?

You have the option of predrilling pilot holes and driving screws instead of nails. Although screws hold better, there are several reasons you might prefer nails.

▶ You're primarily relying on glue to strengthen the joints.

▶ This shelf system was anchored in place with no expectation of having to move it, so there was no need for the extra strength of screws.

▶ Screwheads leave larger holes than finish nails, making them more difficult to conceal. (This system used screws to attach the braces to the shelf frame, where the screwheads are out of sight.)

Gluing the Frame

After predrilling all four sides, spread yellow woodworker's glue on each end of the horizontal frame pieces and drive the nails home (Photo 7). Punch them below the wood surface with a nail set. You'll need two pairs of hands—one to hold the boards in line, the other to drive the nails.

Work quickly, because you don't want the glue to set until you're able to square up the frame. You'll know the frame is square when the diagonals are equal. Measure across each diagonal, nudging the corners in or out until the two measurements are the same. Then nail a temporary brace to the frame to keep it rigid and square (Photo 8).

At this point, let the glue dry for about two hours. Keep the temporary brace in place until you've completed all the work on the frame. While the glue dries, you can begin covering the plywood edges.

Covering the Plywood Edges

Plywood has one disadvantage that solid boards don't—its edges are unsightly. Even a thick coat of paint can't hide the layered pattern of the wood plies. The shelves made for this project expose a lot of plywood edges, but you can dress them up quickly with veneer edging.

These shelves used a thin birch-veneer edging that was factory coated on one side with hot glue. To apply this type of self-adhesive edging, cut a piece to length, hold it in place, and run a hot iron over it to heat the glue (Photo 9). Then use a roller or a wood block to press the edging down until the glue cools and hardens.

Veneer edging is 7/8 inch wide, so you'll have to use a file, sandpaper, or utility knife to trim the excess (Photo 10). Work carefully, especially if you plan to apply a natural or stain finish; you don't want to cut through the thin surface of the veneer. Iron the veneer onto all the visible plywood edges so they'll appear identical to the sides once they're finished.

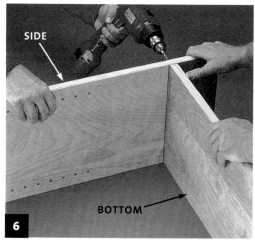

6

Predrill all four corners of the frame with a 3/32-in. bit. This is a two-person job; you'll need a helper to position the parts.

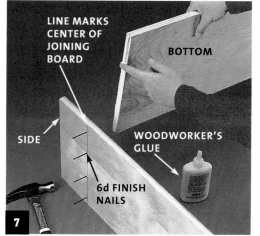

7

Spread glue evenly across the ends and nail all four corners. Wipe off excess glue with a screwdriver and a damp cloth. Work quickly, then square up the frame.

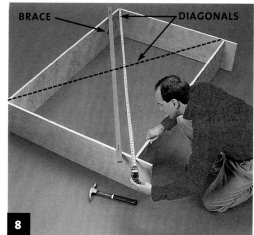

8

Square up the frame by measuring across the two diagonals, adjusting the frame until the measurements are equal. Then tack on a brace and let the glue dry.

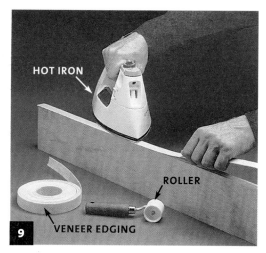

9

Use a hot iron to press iron-on veneer edging onto all exposed plywood edges. Then roll the edging down firmly as the glue cools and sets.

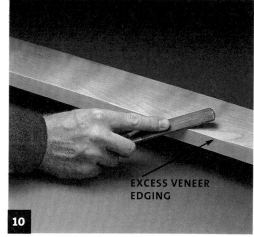

10

File the excess veneer edging flush with the plywood surfaces. Push the file—don't pull it—so you won't chip the thin veneer.

Complete the Assembly

Prepare the center divider by using a jigsaw to cut 3/4-inch notches to accommodate the top and bottom braces (Photo 11). Predrill pilot holes, then glue and nail the divider to the frame (Photo 12). You may need to bow the frame's top and bottom outward slightly to slip in the divider without smearing the glue. Finally, glue and screw the top and bottom braces in place using 1-3/4 inch No. 6 drywall screws (see Photo 13 and the drawings on pages 16–17). Predrilling with a combination bit will make quick, clean holes for the screws. The screwheads will fit flush with or slightly below the surface of the wood. Use 6d finish nails to fasten the ends of the braces to the sides of the frame. Nails will leave smaller holes than screws in these highly visible areas.

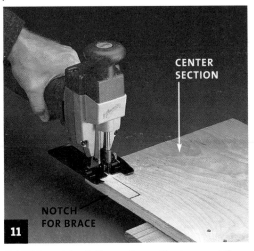

11

Cut 3/4-in. notches in the center section to accept the top and bottom braces, using a jigsaw, as shown here, or a handsaw to cut the notches.

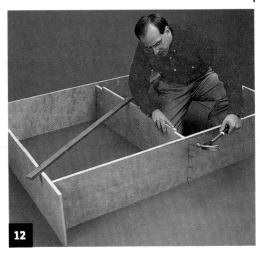

12

Glue and nail the center section in place. Flex the frame members outward slightly to let you slip in the center piece without smearing the glue.

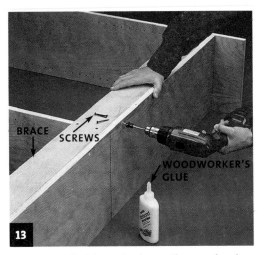

13

Screw the two back braces in place so the screwheads won't show and drive 6d finish nails where the heads will. Nail on the front bottom board (part F, page 17).

Install the Shelf System

This shelf system was designed to fill a specific wall section in a living room. To help it blend with the room's decor and give it a permanent, built-in look, the unit was wrapped with base trim that matched the trim in the rest of the room, then it was screwed to the wall and fitted with a decorative oak top.

Adding Base Trim

Wrapping the system with base trim not only adds a touch of style but also gives the base more visual weight, making the system appear better proportioned from top to bottom. Plan this step in advance by locating the bottom shelf 1/4 inch higher than your room's base trim. This 1/4-inch reveal also serves nicely to hide any small variations in floor height.

Attaching the System to the Wall

Begin the installation by removing the base trim so you can butt the system directly up against the wall (Photo 14). If you think that you're going to damage the wall when you remove the base trim, cut the trim with a jigsaw or reciprocating saw and remove only the section that is covered by the unit. Although new trim will cover any rough-sawn edges, be warned that the cuts themselves aren't easy to make.

Another method for dealing with base trim is to leave the old trim in place and notch the sides of the shelf system, and the bottom shelf, to fit around it. This trick wouldn't have worked for the installation shown on these pages, however, because one entire side of this system had to fit into a corner.

Now position the system tight against the wall, level it with shims, and screw it to the wall through the braces. Test-fit the shims and mark a cutoff line flush with the plywood surface. Then remove the shims and trim them to size with a utility knife. Put a few drops of glue on the shims when you reinstall them so they won't slip out later (Photo 15). Then measure, cut, and install the base, mitering the outside corners for a clean appearance (Photo 16).

Finally, assemble and fit the top. This one was made from a solid 3/4-inch oak board with 1-1/4 inch decorative oak molding tacked onto its edge to give it a more substantial look (Photo 17). Before screwing the top down, add 1/2-inch spacers to raise it slightly and maintain the illusion of greater mass. Attach the screws from underneath, out of sight.

INSTALL THE SHELF SYSTEM

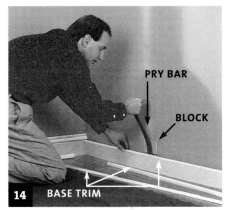

14 PRY BAR / BLOCK / BASE TRIM

Remove the base trim so the shelf system sits flush against the wall. Use a pry bar and wood block to protect the wall and trim.

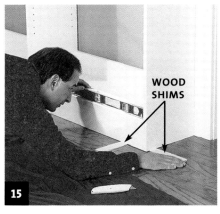

15 WOOD SHIMS

Level the shelf system with thin wood shims. Cut the shims off with a utility knife, then apply dabs of glue when you refit them.

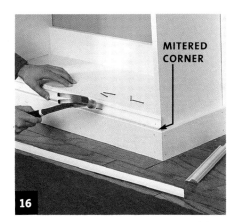

16 MITERED CORNER

Reinstall the base trim, wrapping it around the shelf system. You won't have enough of the old material, so plan to use additional trim.

17 STAINED OAK TOP

Assemble the oak top, stain it, and apply a clear finish. Then screw it to the shelving from below so the screws will be hidden.

Modern Bookcase

This Modern Bookcase and the bookcase and shelving designs on the following pages are all unique in appearance and function. Nevertheless, each uses the same principles of design and construction presented in the instructions for the versatile "Built-In" Bookcase on the preceding pages. To adapt these designs to fill your storage needs, follow the step-by-step process you have just seen on pages 18–25. From a rough sketch of your project draw up a materials list, then cut and assemble the pieces and install them as described.

In adapting the design of this Modern Bookcase, or any other project here, feel free to apply what works best for you. For instance, you could use plywood or hardboard sliding doors to cover the entire front of this bookcase and hide the shelf support system. In that case, you might find it easier to use the metal standard or cleat supports shown in the box on page 21 instead of the pin-type supports, for ease of installation.

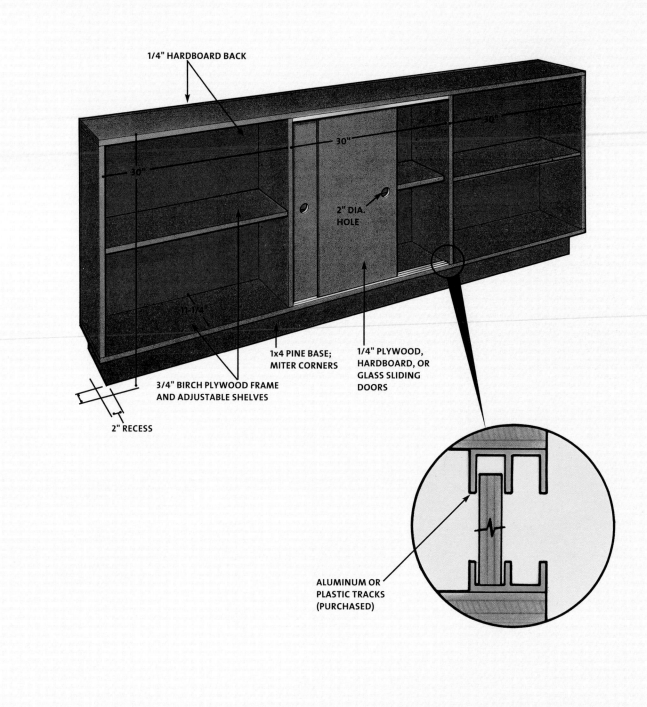

1/4" HARDBOARD BACK

30"

30"

30"

2" DIA. HOLE

11-1/4"

1x4 PINE BASE; MITER CORNERS

1/4" PLYWOOD, HARDBOARD, OR GLASS SLIDING DOORS

3/4" BIRCH PLYWOOD FRAME AND ADJUSTABLE SHELVES

2" RECESS

ALUMINUM OR PLASTIC TRACKS (PURCHASED)

Stained Oak Entertainment Center

This three-in-one center for all your entertainment equipment can be sized to house your television, VCR, and sound system, along with their associated tapes, CDs, books, and stuff. (For a related project, see High-Tech Entertainment Center, page 84.) Cross-braces top and bottom on the back keep the equipment from working its way back on the shelves, and openings midway provide air circulation to prevent heat build-up. The measurements shown here are typical for the items likely to be stored in this cabinet, but be sure to measure your individual pieces and allow for wiring and plugs before you decide on your unit's final dimensions.

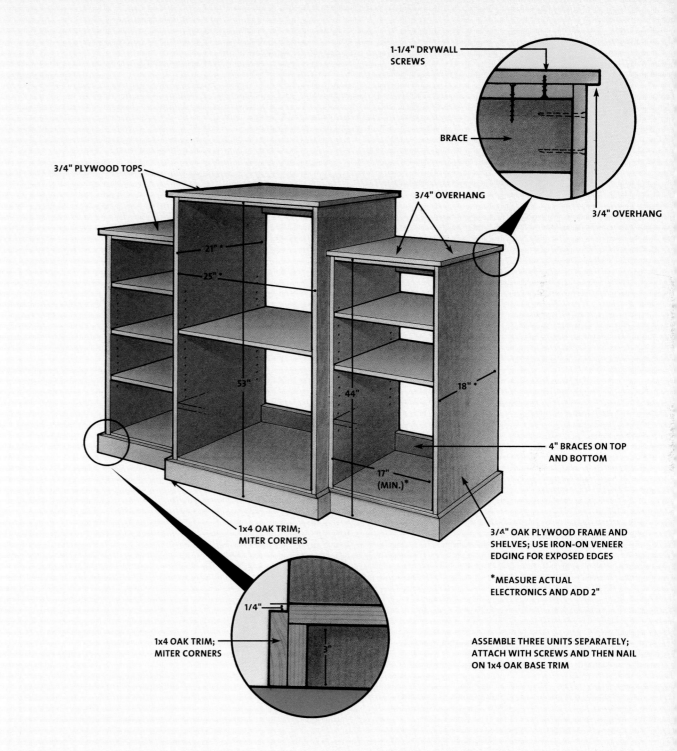

1-1/4" DRYWALL SCREWS

BRACE

3/4" OVERHANG

3/4" PLYWOOD TOPS

3/4" OVERHANG

21"

25" *

53"

44"

18" *

4" BRACES ON TOP AND BOTTOM

17" (MIN.)*

1x4 OAK TRIM; MITER CORNERS

3/4" OAK PLYWOOD FRAME AND SHELVES; USE IRON-ON VENEER EDGING FOR EXPOSED EDGES

*MEASURE ACTUAL ELECTRONICS AND ADD 2"

1/4"

3"

1x4 OAK TRIM; MITER CORNERS

ASSEMBLE THREE UNITS SEPARATELY; ATTACH WITH SCREWS AND THEN NAIL ON 1x4 OAK BASE TRIM

Wall-Mounted Desktop Hutch

This wall-mounted hutch can be dressed up with cove molding around the top and an undershelf light as shown at right. Or it can be left unadorned if that suits your decor better. The shelf-support system can likewise be adapted to the setting, and you might want to apply a full hardboard back instead of the 4-inch combination brace and hanging rail shown.

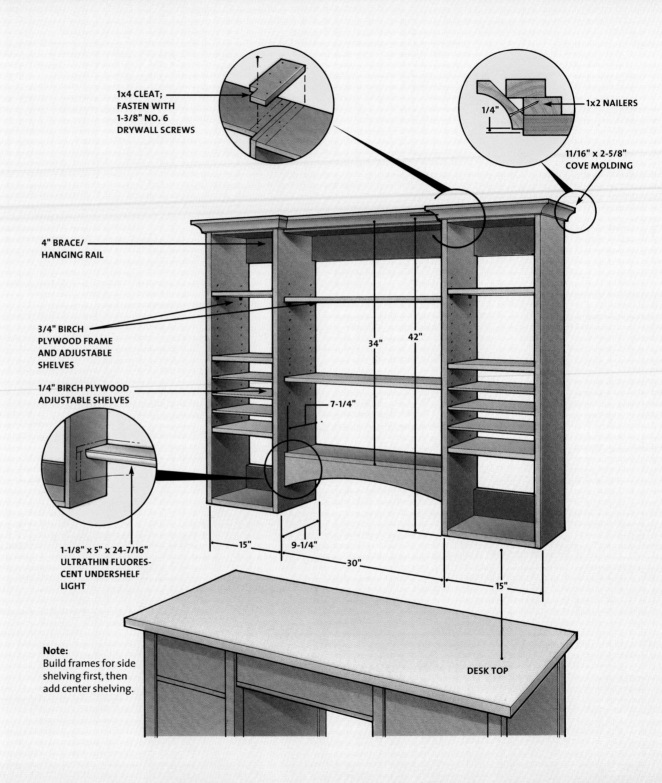

1x4 CLEAT; FASTEN WITH 1-3/8" NO. 6 DRYWALL SCREWS

1x2 NAILERS

1/4"

11/16" x 2-5/8" COVE MOLDING

4" BRACE/ HANGING RAIL

3/4" BIRCH PLYWOOD FRAME AND ADJUSTABLE SHELVES

1/4" BIRCH PLYWOOD ADJUSTABLE SHELVES

7-1/4"

34"

42"

1-1/8" x 5" x 24-7/16" ULTRATHIN FLUORES-CENT UNDERSHELF LIGHT

15"

9-1/4"

30"

15"

DESK TOP

Note:
Build frames for side shelving first, then add center shelving.

Child's Book and Toy Shelves

Of all the simple shelving systems suggested in this chapter, the modular box units here provide the most design flexibility. These unattached boxes may be rearranged or added to in any way to fit growing needs for space. They can also be made to fit into odd-shaped corners.

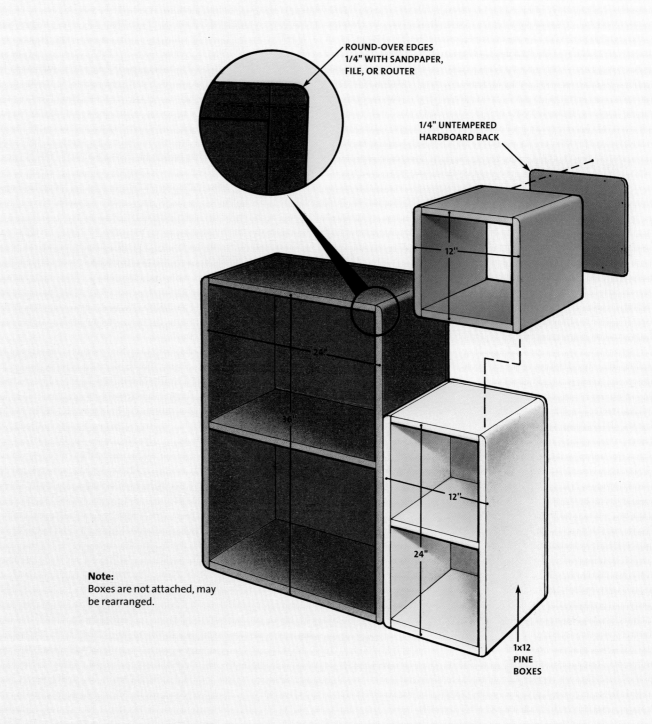

ROUND-OVER EDGES 1/4" WITH SANDPAPER, FILE, OR ROUTER

1/4" UNTEMPERED HARDBOARD BACK

12"

24"

36"

12"

24"

Note:
Boxes are not attached, may be rearranged.

1x12 PINE BOXES

Easy Display Shelving

Create display space to suit any decor with three simple weekend shelf projects.

No matter what your decorating style, one of these shelving units should fill the bill. The Glass Wall Unit is perfect for a contemporary scheme, the Dowel-Rod Display Shelves look great in a traditional decor, and the Stacking Shelves are right at home in an eclectic, casual enviroment.

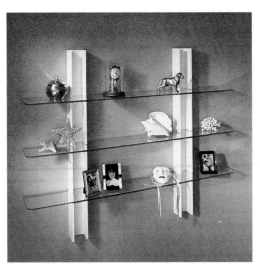

This glass wall unit is an attractive setting for your family treasures. You can highlight them even better with display lights above or below.

The open construction of this dowel-sided, two-section shelving system works particularly well to make the most of smaller areas.

The stacking shelves shown here in a natural finish could also be painted bright colors for use in a child's room or playroom.

Glass Wall Unit

You can build this elegantly simple glass shelf system with a minimum of time and effort. The three 1/4-inch tempered plate-glass shelves, which feature polished edges and rounded front corners, should be available from a local glass supplier.

▶ Start by building the two upright supports from 1/2-inch birch-veneer plywood. First cut the four side pieces and the two backs to width and length. Then assemble them with glue and 6d finish nails, butting the side pieces against the backs. Countersink the nail holes and fill them with a matching wood filler.

▶ Next, cut three double slots for the shelves in each upright. To be safe, make them 1/16 inch wider than the thickness of the glass, which may not be exactly 1/4 inch thick. You can cut these slots with a handsaw and a large miter box. Or clamp the two uprights together along with a guide and make the cuts using a circular saw. Finish off with a handsaw.

▶ Drill three evenly spaced mounting holes in each upright, countersunk to accommodate the screwheads and wood buttons that will cover them.

▶ Sand the uprights thoroughly, then prime and paint them. Mount them 32 inches apart, screwed firmly into wall studs. Make sure they're plumb vertically and level them so they are aligned horizontally with each other. Finally, glue the wood buttons over the screwheads and slide the shelves into place.

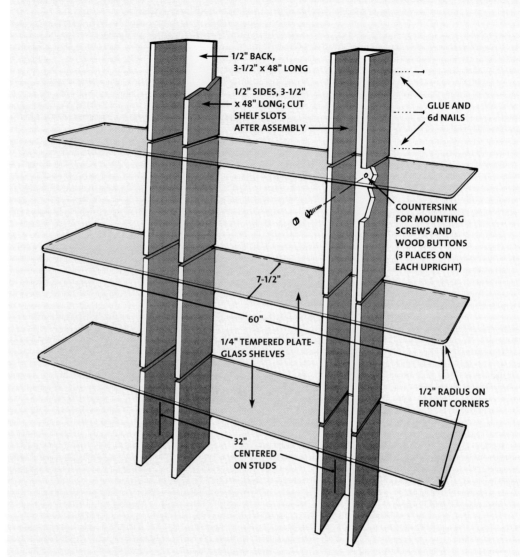

1/2" BACK, 3-1/2" x 48" LONG

1/2" SIDES, 3-1/2" x 48" LONG; CUT SHELF SLOTS AFTER ASSEMBLY

GLUE AND 6d NAILS

COUNTERSINK FOR MOUNTING SCREWS AND WOOD BUTTONS (3 PLACES ON EACH UPRIGHT)

7-1/2"

60"

1/4" TEMPERED PLATE-GLASS SHELVES

1/2" RADIUS ON FRONT CORNERS

32" CENTERED ON STUDS

HAND TOOLS

Hammer

Handsaw

Level

Miter box

Nail set

Tape measure

POWER TOOLS

Circular saw

Drill; countersink bit

OPTIONAL

Clamps

MATERIALS

3 1/4" tempered plate-glass shelves, 7-1/2" x 60," with smoothed edges and rounded front corners

1/4 sheet 1/2" birch plywood

6 2-1/2" drywall screws

6 wood buttons

Woodworker's glue

6d finish nails

Sandpaper

Wood filler

Primer and paint

Paintbrush

Dowel-Rod Display Shelves

This decorative dowel-sided shelving unit requires precise drilling and cutting, but otherwise it is easy to build.

You can assemble this system either as a seven-shelf-high stack, as shown in the photograph, or as two freestanding, four-shelf sections, as illustrated in the plans at right. The two-section arrangement requires you to build one additional shelf.

▶ First cut 22 pieces of 1-1/2 inch x 1-1/2 inch birch 16 inches long for the top and bottom members and the spacer blocks. (Cut two more pieces if you're building two separate units.) If you can't find 1-1/2 inch x 1-1/2 inch birch or you don't want to cut it yourself, ask your lumberyard to rip the birch to size for you.

▶ Locate and drill 1/2-inch diameter holes for the 1/2-inch dowels 3/4 inch deep into the top and bottom members and all the way through the spacer blocks. Use a drill-guide attachment to keep the holes straight and to the proper depth.

▶ Assemble the four side sections by gluing the 36-inch long dowels into the top and bottom members. Then cut the shelves to size and glue and screw on the 1/4-inch x 3/4-inch birch edging.

▶ Drill and countersink holes in the spacer blocks for the joint-connector bolts that will secure the adjustable shelves to the dowels. (You can save a bit of work later by using a combination drill-and-countersink bit now, as shown on page 42.) Then cut the spacer blocks in half lengthwise along the centers of the holes drilled earlier for the dowels. Glue and screw spacer-block halves to each shelf end with 1-3/4 inch drywall screws. Countersink the screwheads, unless you used a combination bit earlier to do this.

▶ Loosely assemble the unit now with the joint connectors to make sure that everything fits properly. Then disassemble the shelves from the dowels and finish-sand all the parts, first with medium-grit (60–100) and then with fine-grit (120–180) sandpaper. Finish the edges, spacer blocks, and top and bottom members with stain and an oil finish. You can leave the dowels unfinished or, if you like, apply a clear oil finish. Once the finish is dry, reassemble the unit.

This shelf can be assembled either as two stacking units with a total of seven shelves, as shown, or as two separate, matching four-shelf units.

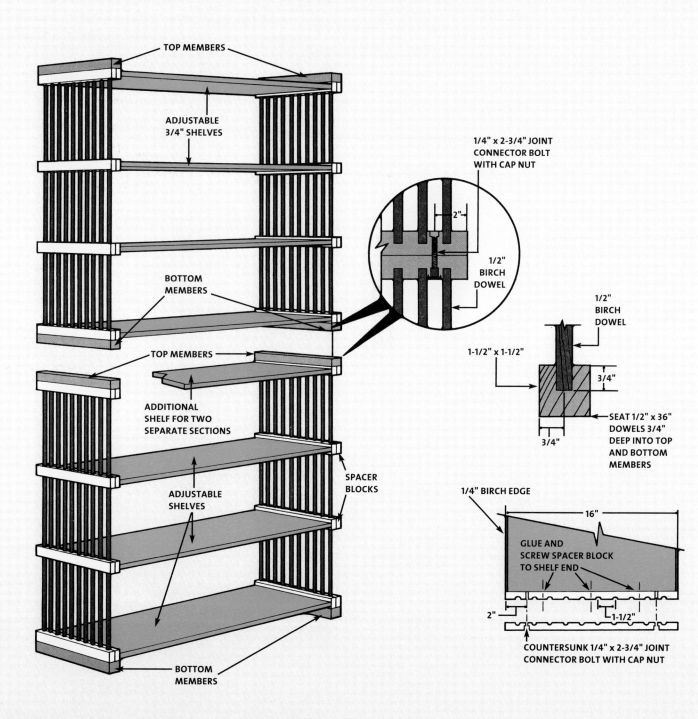

TOP MEMBERS

ADJUSTABLE
3/4" SHELVES

BOTTOM
MEMBERS

TOP MEMBERS

ADDITIONAL
SHELF FOR TWO
SEPARATE SECTIONS

ADJUSTABLE
SHELVES

SPACER
BLOCKS

BOTTOM
MEMBERS

1/4" x 2-3/4" JOINT
CONNECTOR BOLT
WITH CAP NUT

2"

1/2"
BIRCH
DOWEL

1/2"
BIRCH
DOWEL

1-1/2" x 1-1/2"

3/4"

3/4"

SEAT 1/2" x 36"
DOWELS 3/4"
DEEP INTO TOP
AND BOTTOM
MEMBERS

1/4" BIRCH EDGE

16"

GLUE AND
SCREW SPACER BLOCK
TO SHELF END

2"

1-1/2"

COUNTERSUNK 1/4" x 2-3/4" JOINT
CONNECTOR BOLT WITH CAP NUT

HAND TOOLS

Screwdrivers

Tape measure

POWER TOOLS

Circular saw

Drill; drill guide

OPTIONAL

Drill press

MATERIALS

40 1/2" birch dowels
36" long

34 ft. of 1-1/2" x 1-1/2"
birch

1-1/2 sheets 3/4" birch
plywood

48 1-3/4" drywall screws

36 joint-connector bolts
2-3/4" long, with cap
nuts

50 ft. of 1/4" x 3/4" birch
edging

Clear oil finish

Fine- and medium-grit
sandpaper

Stain

Woodworker's glue

Stacking Shelves

These adaptable stacking shelves were built with 3/4-inch oak-veneer plywood, then given a stain and oil finish. If you prefer, you could use less-expensive birch plywood and paint the shelves.

Since this system was intended to be given a natural finish, dowels were used to attach the sides so that nailheads or screwheads wouldn't show. However, you can simplify the construction by gluing and nailing the joints or by screwing them together and filling the countersunk screwhead holes with wood plugs.

▶ Begin construction by cutting the plywood to the proper widths for the ends, backs, and shelves. Then trim these pieces to length. Next, notch out the rounded interlocking ends with a jigsaw. Glue the oak-veneer edging to the fronts of the shelves and sides, then to the top edges of the upper shelf before putting together the unit.

▶ Start assembling the shelves by gluing and nailing the backs to the shelves. Then drill dowel holes for mounting the ends, using a doweling jig and dowel centers. This tool enables you to drill the holes perfectly straight and exactly aligned with each other. Take care to make all of the shelf modules exactly the same size and precisely square so they will stack smoothly.

▶ If you decide to assemble the shelves with dowels, use bar clamps to draw all the glued joints tightly together. Clamps will also help if you choose instead to secure the shelves with nails and screws, but they aren't absolutely necessary.

▶ After assembly, sand the units thoroughly with medium (60–100 grit) and fine (120–180 grit) sandpaper, then apply the stain and oil finish of your choice.

This interesting freestanding system features stacking shelves that interlock to form a sturdy yet easy-to-move unit.

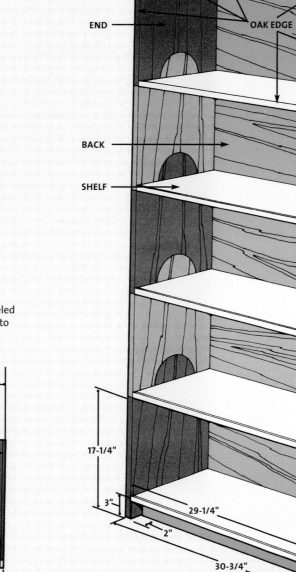

TOOLS

HAND TOOLS
Bar clamps
Compass
Doweling jig; dowel centers
Hammer
Screwdriver
Tape measure

POWER TOOLS
Circular saw
Jigsaw

MATERIALS

(For five-section shelf system)
1-1/2 sheets 3/4" oak plywood
28 ft. of 1/4" x 3/4" oak edging
80 1/4" x 1-1/4" dowels
Oil finish
Stain
Woodworker's glue

Note:
Ends are glued and doweled with 1/4" x 1-1/2" dowels to shelves and backs.

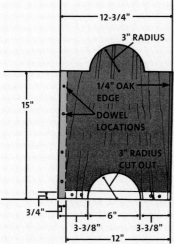

END
OAK EDGE
BACK
SHELF

77-1/4"
17-1/4"
3"
29-1/4"
2"
30-3/4"

12-3/4"
3" RADIUS
1/4" OAK EDGE
DOWEL LOCATIONS
3" RADIUS CUT OUT
15"
3/4"
6"
3-3/8"
3-3/8"
12"

Built-in Library Shelves

Add built-in shelving that won't look like an afterthought. Use modular design to transform a room or create a beautiful shelving system.

You won't need cabinetmaking skills to adapt this design to your own needs, because these shelves are built from standard boards, plywood, and molding.

Design Considerations

This system is modular, so you can build all or part of it to fit your space. For instance, the plate rail and mantel shown on page 45 may not suit the room you are working in. The modular design lets you do the messy cutting, sanding, and finish work in your shop and then assemble the finished pieces at the installation site. The picture at the right will help you visualize the modular elements that would work best in your own plans.

Materials Considerations

Instead of using plywood to build this shelving system, you can substitute medium-density fiberboard, or MDF (Photo 1). Although MDF isn't as strong as plywood, it's smoother, it won't warp if you store it flat, and it cuts without chipping the thin layer of veneer oak glued to the fiber core. It's also usually less expensive than veneered plywood. Professional cabinetmakers often use MDF in place of plywood, so call a cabinetmaker for a source if you can't find it at your lumberyard.

This project utilized rift-sawn or quarter-sawn oak boards and rift-sawn oak-veneered MDF, for its straight, tight grain lines. You could substitute less-expensive plain-sawn oak, however, which has a more varied grain.

Buy your solid wood in standard cabinet widths, precut and smooth, from lumber-yards that serve cabinetmakers. If you were to try to rip these pieces yourself from wider boards, they'd be likely to warp and twist.

Tool and Skill Considerations

The simplicity of this design means that you won't need a shop full of expensive stationary power tools to achieve first-rate results. You won't even need a table saw unless you add cabinet doors. However, a power miter box is essential to make clean, square cuts, and using an air-powered finish nailer will speed your work. Both tools are available at rental centers.

If you lack extensive woodworking experience, you can scale this project back to make it more manageable. You might, for example, initially build just one or two sections of shelving to familiarize yourself with the techniques.

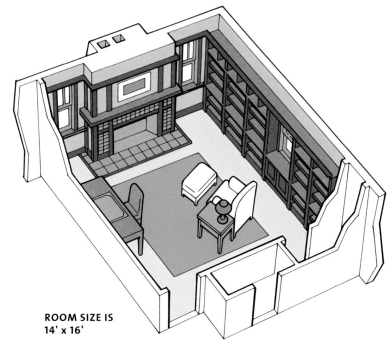

ROOM SIZE IS 14' x 16'

Refer to this schematic drawing in deciding which modular elements to adapt for your shelving system.

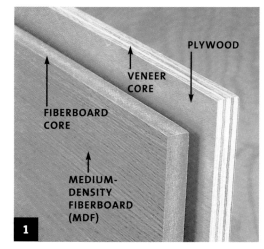

PLYWOOD

VENEER CORE

FIBERBOARD CORE

MEDIUM-DENSITY FIBERBOARD (MDF)

1

Plywood is stronger and lighter, but medium-density fiberboard (MDF) is smoother, more stable, easier to cut without chipping the veneer, and less expensive.

Construction Plan: Shelving

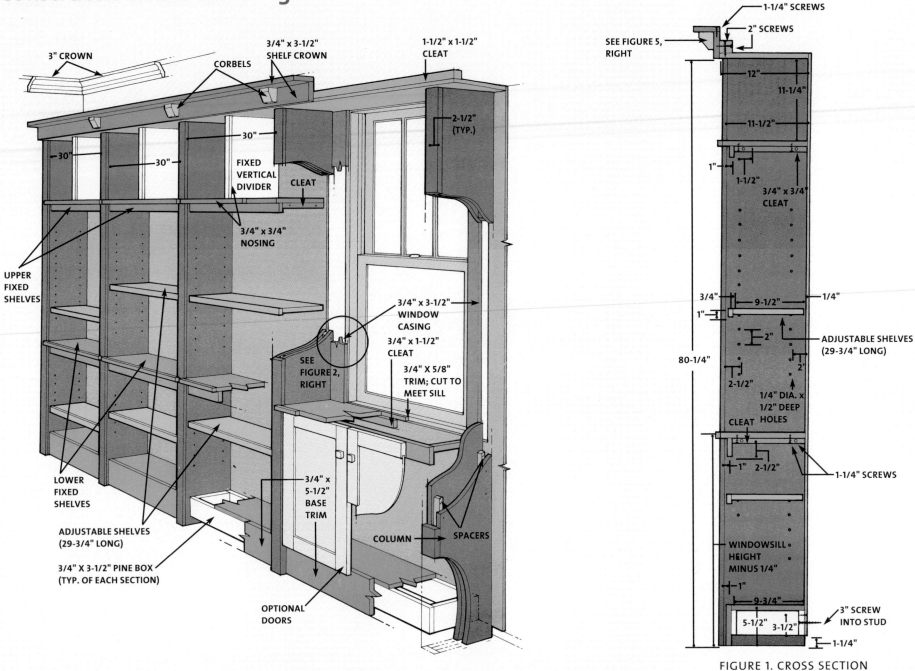

3" CROWN

CORBELS

3/4" x 3-1/2" SHELF CROWN

1-1/2" x 1-1/2" CLEAT

30"

30"

30"

FIXED VERTICAL DIVIDER

CLEAT

3/4" x 3/4" NOSING

2-1/2" (TYP.)

UPPER FIXED SHELVES

SEE FIGURE 2, RIGHT

3/4" x 3-1/2" WINDOW CASING

3/4" x 1-1/2" CLEAT

3/4" X 5/8" TRIM; CUT TO MEET SILL

LOWER FIXED SHELVES

3/4" x 5-1/2" BASE TRIM

ADJUSTABLE SHELVES (29-3/4" LONG)

3/4" X 3-1/2" PINE BOX (TYP. OF EACH SECTION)

COLUMN

SPACERS

OPTIONAL DOORS

SEE FIGURE 5, RIGHT

1-1/4" SCREWS

2" SCREWS

12"

11-1/4"

11-1/2"

1"

1-1/2"

3/4" x 3/4" CLEAT

3/4"

9-1/2"

1/4"

1"

2"

ADJUSTABLE SHELVES (29-3/4" LONG)

2-1/2"

2"

80-1/4"

1/4" DIA. x 1/2" DEEP HOLES

CLEAT

1-1/4" SCREWS

1"

2-1/2"

WINDOWSILL HEIGHT MINUS 1/4"

1"

9-3/4"

5-1/2"

3-1/2"

3" SCREW INTO STUD

1-1/4"

FIGURE 1. CROSS SECTION

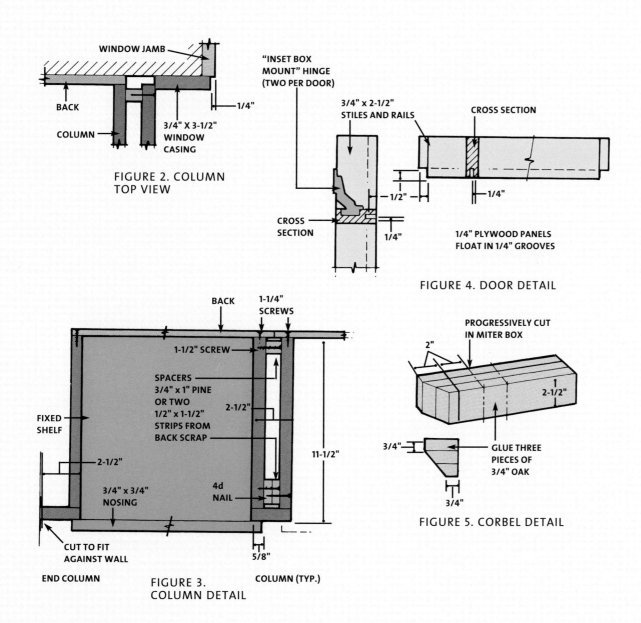

WINDOW JAMB

BACK

COLUMN

1/4"

3/4" X 3-1/2"
WINDOW
CASING

FIGURE 2. COLUMN
TOP VIEW

"INSET BOX
MOUNT" HINGE
(TWO PER DOOR)

3/4" x 2-1/2"
STILES AND RAILS

CROSS SECTION

1/2"

1/4"

CROSS
SECTION

1/4"

1/4" PLYWOOD PANELS
FLOAT IN 1/4" GROOVES

FIGURE 4. DOOR DETAIL

BACK

1-1/4"
SCREWS

1-1/2" SCREW

SPACERS
3/4" x 1" PINE
OR TWO
1/2" x 1-1/2"
STRIPS FROM
BACK SCRAP

2-1/2"

11-1/2"

FIXED
SHELF

2-1/2"

3/4" x 3/4"
NOSING

4d
NAIL

CUT TO FIT
AGAINST WALL

5/8"

END COLUMN

FIGURE 3.
COLUMN DETAIL

COLUMN (TYP.)

PROGRESSIVELY CUT
IN MITER BOX

2"

2-1/2"

3/4"

GLUE THREE
PIECES OF
3/4" OAK

3/4"

FIGURE 5. CORBEL DETAIL

TOOLS

HAND TOOLS

Hammer

Nail set

Screwdriver

Tape measure

Utility knife

POWER TOOLS

Circular saw and saw guides

Drill; 1/4" brad-point bit, countersink bit, depth stop

Finish nailer (rented)

Miter box (rented)

OPTIONAL

Air-powered finish nailer

Pegboard for shelf peg template

Table saw

MATERIALS

4d and 6d finish nails

1-1/4" screws

Clear finish

Oak-veneer medium-density fiberboard or plywood: 3/4" for columns and shelves, 1/2" for backs

Rift-sawn oak and 3/4" oak veneer for trim, door frame, cleats

1x4 pine for base

Sandpaper

Stain

Wood putty

Wood sealer

Woodworker's glue

OPTIONAL

1/4" plywood for cabinet doors

3/4" x 3-1/2" oak for plate rail

Draw Up Your Plan

Even though this project was designed to fit into an extra bedroom, you can adapt it to any room. It's easy to flow the shelving and trim around existing windows and doors, because builders usually install these openings so that their tops align, about 80 inches above the floor. The trim at the top of the shelves matches the plate rail above the mantel, which also serves as the top window casing (see page 45).

The ceilings in the room shown are 8 feet 6 inches high. If you have an 8-foot ceiling, you may want to run the shelving all the way up to it. The lower, fixed shelf meets the bottom of the window to become an extension of the sill (see Construction Plan: Shelving on page 38).

▶ To decide how wide to make your shelves, begin with the fixed features of the wall—a door or window, in this case—and divide the wall spaces into equal parts. Limit the shelves' width to about 36 inches, which is the maximum length they can span without sagging under a load of books. For guidelines on weight limits and standard shelf sizes for books, records, disks, and so on, see the table on page 14. Lay out your design first with masking tape to show the size and spacing of the

shelves and trim. Then, if you like, actually draw your plan on the walls, so you can visualize it more easily and measure the dimensions precisely (Photo 2). If your floor is more than 1/4 inch out of level, make sure you take your measurements from the highest point.

▶ Now sketch your plan on paper and add the necessary lumber dimensions, using the diagrams on pages 38–39 as a guide.

Then make up a cutting list for your particular design and buy your materials.

▶ Use the step-by-step photos that follow and the construction plan on page 38 to prepare the pieces and assemble the units. The following procedures will help you through some of the more difficult steps. These guidelines are adaptable to the wall units, fireplace shelving and mantel, or other areas.

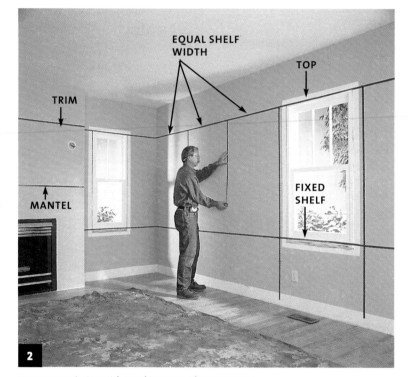

Lay out your design with masking tape, then measure and draw your plan directly onto the wall to find the exact locations of windows and doors.

Cut and Assemble the Columns

Install the 3-inch crown molding at the ceiling first. Then paint it and the walls before you proceed.

Next, cut the sheets of medium-density fiberboard (MDF) to length and width for the columns with a circular saw and saw guides. Score cutting lines with a utility knife first, to prevent chipping (Photo 3). (For more information on crosscutting in paneling, see Making Clean Crosscuts on page 19.)

Rather than trying to make perfectly smooth joints between the MDF and the solid-oak fronts, which is a difficult job even for a professional carpenter, slightly round the edges of each piece with sandpaper. This technique leaves a tiny groove at the joints that will be barely noticeable but make your work much easier.

Cut the solid oak for the column fronts and shelf nosings to length in a power miter box. Sand this oak smooth with 120-grit sandpaper and a wood block. Then round the edges slightly with the sandpaper (Photo 4).

It's a lot easier—and a good deal less messy—to finish the parts before you assemble them. Apply the stain of your choice and one coat of sealer.

Assemble the columns, using 1-inch spacers. Apply a bead of carpenter's glue to the MDF, then secure the oak edging with 6d finish nails. Use a power nailer and 2-inch nails, or predrill the solid oak pieces with a 3/32-inch bit for the 6d nails. Apply the glue sparingly so that it won't squeeze out into the rounded grooves (Photo 5). Most glues specify a minimum clamping time.

Keep nails and screws at least 3 inches from the fragile corners of the MDF.

CUT AND ASSEMBLE THE COLUMNS

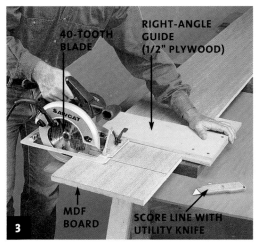

Score cutting lines with a utility knife to prevent chipping, then cut the sheets of MDF to length and width with a circular saw and saw guides.

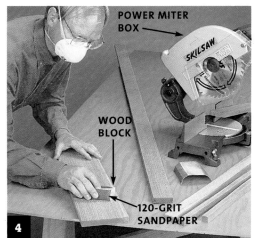

Cut the solid oak for shelf nosings to length with a power miter box, sand the pieces with 120-grit sandpaper, and round their edges slightly by sanding.

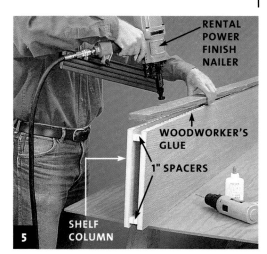

Assemble the columns using 1-in. spacers. Fasten the oak edgings over a bead of glue with 6d finish nails, after predrilling the edging with a 3/32-in. bit.

Make the Shelves and Assemble the Units

Cut the MDF paneling to size for the shelves in the same way you did on the previous page for the columns.

Assemble the shelves, fastening cleats to the stationary shelves with 1-1/4 inch screws (Photo 6).

Predrill pilot holes and countersink them for the screwheads. You'll be able to drive the screws more quickly if you use a special countersink bit and a power screwdriver (Photo 7).

Set the shelf-system backs out of the way for the time being.

Referring to your own sketch and the construction plan on page 38, mark, cut, and assemble the pine bases from 1x4 pine stock. Then stand the columns upright, set the pine bases between them on 1-1/4 inch spacers, and fasten the columns and bases together with three 1-1/4 inch screws per joint (Photo 8).

Assemble the units about 18 inches out from the wall, laying them on stiff cardboard to avoid damaging the floor or carpet when you slide them back.

MAKE THE SHELVES AND ASSEMBLE THE UNITS

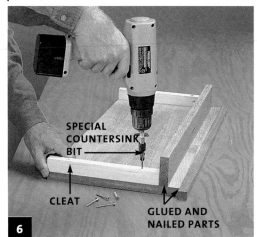

Assemble the fixed shelves, fastening cleats to them with 1-1/4 in. screws.

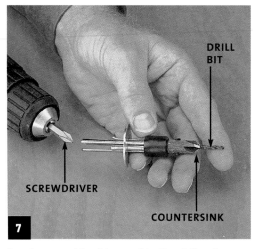

Speed up assembly with a combination drill and countersink bit and a power screwdriver.

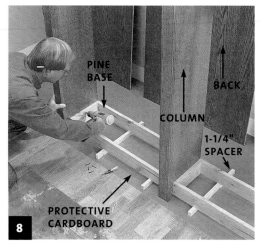

Stand the columns up and set the bases between them. Screw the columns and bases together.

Complete the Shelf Units

Screw the fixed shelves to the columns by driving two 1-1/4 inch screws through each cleat (Photo 9). Use two spacers to temporarily support the shelves. Then screw on the top, leaving it 1/4 inch short on each end so it won't rub against the side walls when you slide the unit back into position.

Drill holes 1/2 inch deep for the shelf supports with a 1/4-inch brad-point bit. Space these holes 2 inches apart. To achieve this spacing, clamp a section of pegboard to the columns as a drill guide, and attach a depth gauge to the bit so you don't drill too deep (Photo 10). If you don't want to invest in a depth gauge for your drill bits, just temporarily wrap a piece of masking tape around the bit at the depth to which you want to drill.

Shim and level the shelves temporarily, then install the 1/2-inch MDF backs with 1-1/4 inch screws. Predrill and countersink the screw holes.

If you're building wall-to-wall shelves like this system, leave off for now the nosings for the fixed shelves at each end and the solid-oak fronts on the end columns (Photo 11). You'll have to shave one edge of these column fronts to fit tightly against irregular side walls after you have the shelf system in its final location. The sometimes tricky business of fitting a unit against an end wall can be solved in the worst cases by scribing and custom fitting a loose stile, or panel, to fill an uneven space (see page 73).

COMPLETE THE SHELF UNITS

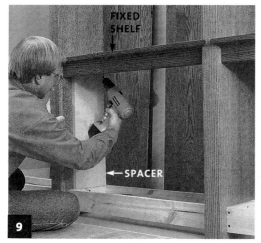

Screw the fixed shelves to the columns with 1-1/4 in. screws through the cleats. Screw on the top, leaving its ends 1/4 in. short so it won't rub the walls.

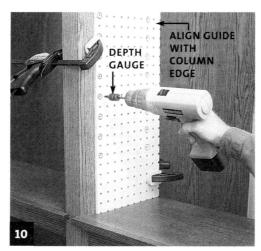

Drill holes 1/2 in. deep for the shelf supports with a 1/4-in. brad-point bit. Clamp pegboard to the columns as a drill guide. Use a depth gauge for uniformity.

Shim and level the shelves temporarily, then install the backs with 1-1/4 in. screws. Predrill and countersink the screw holes.

Install the Shelf System

Move the shelf system back against the wall, using two helpers to maneuver these heavy MDF units. Align the pieces with the window, then shim and level them if necessary. Add the fronts to the columns at each end, trimming them so they fit tightly against the side walls. Now add the nosings to the fixed shelves on each end, which you left off earlier.

The shelf-system backs will square up the unit once they are attached, so be sure to shim and level the shelves again before you screw on the backs. After sliding the units against the wall, level them one last time (Photo 12). If shimming leaves a crack at the bottom that's larger than 1/4 inch, nail on a small piece of base-shoe molding to conceal it. Carpeting may also be used to cover the gap.

Make cutouts in the back for electrical receptacles and switches, being sure to add metal extension collars as required by code (Photo 13). Extend floor ducts through elbows out the base, then attach the vent grilles.

For safety, it's important to fasten this shelf system to wall studs with screws driven through the back near the top of each column.

After the shelves are in place, install the rest of the trim throughout the room.

Use the construction plan on page 38 as a guide for building the optional base-cabinet doors. If you add this feature, you'll need a table saw to cut the dadoes and tenons.

Once the shelf system is completely installed, fill all the nail holes with colored wood putty to match the stain. Then apply a final coat of clear finish.

INSTALL THE SHELF SYSTEM

12

SHIM

WAXED PAPER

LEVEL

13

CODE REQUIRES METAL EXTENSION COLLAR

ELECTRICAL BOX IN WALL

90° DUCT ELBOW

Shim and level the system before attaching the backs. Add the fronts to the columns at each end, trimming to fit the walls tightly.

Make cutouts for electrical receptacles and switches. Add metal extension collars for fire protection. Extend floor heating or cooling ducts out through the base.

Adding a Plate Rail and Mantel

If you'd like to add the handsome plate rail or mantel shown in the photo on page 36, refer to the construction plan at right to draw up your own working sketch and list of materials.

Making the Plate Rail

The plate rail is quite simply constructed of 3/4 x 3-1/2-inch oak strips butt-joined and screwed to wall studs. Before joining the strips, rout a plate groove in the top piece to fit what you plan to display there.

Once you have assembled and attached the rail, add the optional corbels below (see Figure 5, page 39). Supply the vertical casing between the plate rail and mantel next, if you choose to add it.

Constructing the Mantel

If you would like an elegant compliment to what you've just completed, construct the mantel shown at right, which is made of the same veneered MDF as the shelf units, cut to the dimensions shown.

First screw a 3/4 x 1-inch cleat firmly to the wall studs, recognizing that it may have to support the weight of an occasional elbow as well as what you'll plan to set there. Then construct the mantel itself, adapting the suggested sizes as needed. Once it has been completed, slide it over the wall cleat. Have a helper hold it securely while you attach it with 6d finish nails.

Finally, set the nailheads, fill the holes, and stain the filler to match. But first experiment with scrap MDF and stain to match the surface as closely as possible. Finish the mantel as you did the shelves.

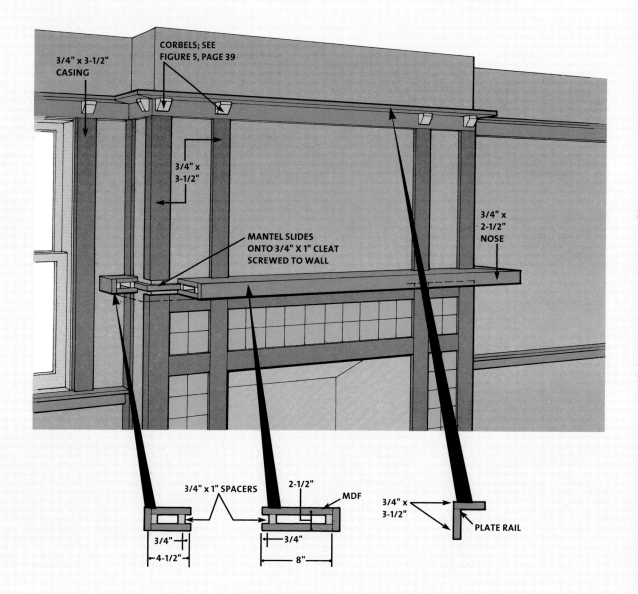

3/4" x 3-1/2" CASING

CORBELS; SEE FIGURE 5, PAGE 39

3/4" x 3-1/2"

MANTEL SLIDES ONTO 3/4" X 1" CLEAT SCREWED TO WALL

3/4" x 2-1/2" NOSE

3/4" x 1" SPACERS

2-1/2"

MDF

3/4" x 3-1/2"

PLATE RAIL

3/4"

4-1/2"

3/4"

8"

Window Seat Cabinets

Add both storage and seating with this easy, inviting window seat and cabinet combination piece.

If you can handle a circular saw and a drill, you can build these cabinets. They're especially easy to construct when you use ready-made doors.

Construction Plan: Storage Cabinets

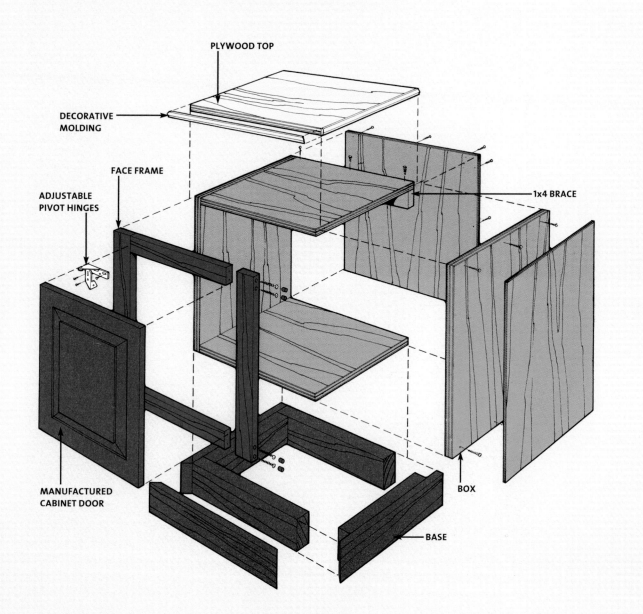

PLYWOOD TOP

DECORATIVE MOLDING

FACE FRAME

ADJUSTABLE PIVOT HINGES

1x4 BRACE

MANUFACTURED CABINET DOOR

BOX

BASE

An Easy, Versatile Design

These storage cabinets require no elaborate tools or advanced woodworking skills. In fact, thanks to their simplified design, an electric drill and a circular saw are the only power tools you'll need.

Here are some of the special features that make this project attractive, strong, and easy to build.

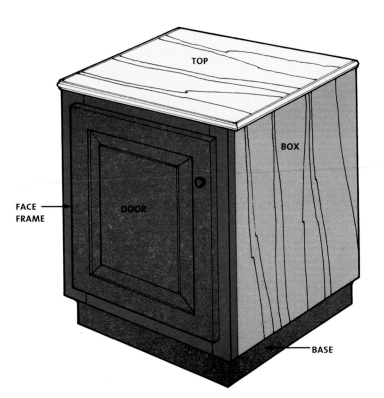

Five Basic Components

These cabinets have a total of just five basic components:

▶ **Doors.** The design shown here uses ready-made frame-and-panel cabinet doors, which are sold at home centers as replacement doors for kitchen cabinets. You'll design your cabinets based on the available door sizes. For a more contemporary look, you could build your own flush-front doors.

▶ **Base.** Each undercabinet base is simply a box made from 2x4's, with a finished plywood face. The cabinet is screwed to the base from the inside. For better mobility, you can add floor glides or casters to the base, or attach the base to the floor permanently.

▶ **Box.** The basic cabinet is just a 3/4-inch plywood box with a 1x4 brace along the top of the back for attaching the cabinet to the wall. Screwheads that are visible on the edges are covered with 1/4-inch plywood panels held with brads and glue.

▶ **Face frame.** The face frame is made of 1x2, 1x3, or 1x4 material attached to the front of the box to cover the plywood's edges.

▶ **Top.** A top of finished plywood or other material with solid-wood edging gives the box a clean, finished look. If the cabinet is to be mounted on a wall so its top will be above eye level, you won't need a finished top.

Simple Screw Joinery

These cabinets are assembled with hardened drywall screws, not glue, so there's no messy glue to clean up.

Using screw joinery means you won't have to make dadoes, rabbets, or bevel cuts, which would require a table saw or a router (Photo 1). If you make a mistake, you can simply unscrew the parts, fix the problem, and reassemble them. And because all the cabinet parts are rectangular, if you cut a piece too large or out of square, you can trim it without ruining an entire joint.

Assembling these cabinets with hardened drywall screws gives them all the strength they need and eliminates messy glue clean-up.

Design Options

Because these cabinets are designed around manufactured doors, the doors largely determine the size of the cabinets. But you can make slight variations in the cabinets' height and width by choosing 1x2's, 1x3's, or 1x4's to make their face frames. For greater height variations, however, you should select taller or shorter doors. To widen the cabinets significantly, use two doors in place of one. These options allow you to adjust the cabinets' size to whatever space is available.

The construction plan (page 47) and the instructions for this project show the cabinets mounted on a simple base. You could also design a different base, stack one cabinet on top of another, or hang individual cabinets on the wall.

You can adapt this basic design to any number of storage situations: a kitchen island, an entertainment center, a bathroom vanity, cabinets for a den or bedroom, or toy storage for a child's room. By adding an appropriate top, you could even design a handsome desk.

Tools and Materials

To build these cabinets, you'll need the basic hand and power tools listed at the right and some specialized items that are shown below (Photo 2).

Choose your wood according to the kind of finish you want. If you plan to paint your cabinets and don't care if the grain is prominent, use inexpensive A-C grade fir plywood. More costly birch plywood is smoother and takes paint better. For a varnish finish, with or without stain, select 3/4-inch hardwood-veneer plywood. Or buy a less-expensive wood and cover it with 1/4-inch hardwood veneer.

For the face frames, it's a good idea to use solid hardwood, which is more attractive and durable than are the softwoods like pine or fir.

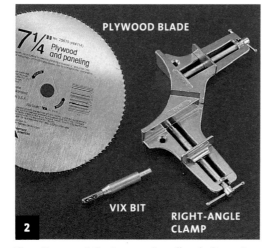

These three specialized accessories will make it easy to achieve clean-edged cuts in plywood, square face-frame joints, and accurately centered hinge holes.

Draw Up Your Plans

Although the construction plans on page 47 show how the cabinet parts fit together, you'll need something more specific to lay out and cut the parts for your own design.

First, draw a rough sketch of the overall installation. For the sake of simplicity, avoid trying to slip the cabinets tightly between two walls, which may require sophisticated fitting techniques. Then draw a plan for each unit, showing the individual parts and their dimensions. Here are some guidelines to consider:

▶ When planning specific cabinet sizes, begin with the doors. Select a size and style that best fits your space.

▶ Plan the face frames from the door sizes. To use the kind of hinges shown for this project, make the frame opening 1-1/2 inches less than the height and width of the door, because the door will overlap the frame by 3/4 inch all around. With surface-mount hinges, a 3/8-inch overlap is standard. Make the frame opening 3/4 inch less than the door dimensions.

▶ The outside dimensions of the face frame will depend on the size of the stock you use. Some hardwoods are supplied in exactly the named size—1x2, 1x3, or 1x4, for example—but the finished sizes of other woods are 1/4 inch thinner and 1/2 inch narrower than the nominal size.

▶ The overall height of a standing cabinet includes the base under it and the thickness of the finished top as well as the dimension for the cabinet itself.

▶ The base under a standing cabinet is usually set back 3 to 4 inches from the front—and sometimes from exposed sides—to provide a toe-kick space for people standing in front of it.

▶ Determine the width of the cabinet box from the dimensions of the face frame. Construction is easier if the box is a bit narrower and shorter than the face frame, letting it overlap the box by 1/8 to 1/4 inch. Be sure to allow for any 1/4-inch finished panels on the outside when figuring out the size of the basic box. Note that the top and bottom pieces fit between the sides, not on top of them. For a face frame that is flush with the box sides, make the box a bit smaller and plane or sand the face frame to size after you assemble the cabinet. This is much easier than trying to arrive at an exact match.

▶ For a standing cabinet, make the box height the same as that of the face frame so the finished top will sit flat across them and the bottom edges of the box sides will be flush with the bottom of the frame. For a hanging cabinet, size the box for the frame so that it overlaps the edges by the same amount all around.

▶ When figuring the dimensions of the various parts, add up all the relevant widths and thicknesses. For instance, to determine the depth of the finished top of a cabinet having sides 12 inches wide, add together 1/4 inch for the back's thickness, 12 inches for the side, 3/4 inch for the face frame's thickness, and 3/4 inch for the door's thickness, for a total of 13-3/4 inches. If the top is to overhang the doors by 1/2 inch, add that too, for a final measurement of 14-1/4 inches.

Finally, draw up on graph paper a plan showing how the cabinet parts can be laid out on sheets of plywood. Make sure the long dimension of each part runs parallel to the face grain of the plywood. Use these graph-paper plans first to determine how many sheets of plywood to buy, then to lay out the parts for cutting.

Build the Base

The base for each cabinet is made of 2x4's, or wider stock if you prefer. For a finished installation, cover the faces with plywood.

Begin by cutting pieces of base stock to length according to your plan. Butt the base sides inside the front and back pieces. Be sure to allow for the thickness of the plywood facing, if you plan to use it, to give the proper 3 to 4 inches of toe-kick space under the cabinet.

Nail the base pieces together using 10d common nails (Photo 3). Make sure the corners are square and the top edges flush so the cabinet will not rock when mounted on the base. The long base shown in the photos below is for two cabinets with a window seat in between.

Now cut plywood to cover each of the exposed faces of the base. You can use 1/4-, 1/2-, or 3/4-inch thick plywood. Miter the corners at the visible joints to conceal the inner plies, then attach the plywood to the base with glue and finish nails. Set the nailheads and fill the holes to finish completing the base.

If you plan to install your cabinets permanently or attach them to the wall, remove any carpeting from where the bases will go. Use shims as necessary to level each base (Photo 4). Toenail the base to the floor, driving the nails into the inside edges of the base, or use metal angle braces and screws. The cabinet box will later be screwed to the base.

BUILD THE BASE

3

Build the base from straight 2x4 pieces attached with 10d common nails. On the exposed sides, make it 3 to 4 in. narrower than the cabinets for toe-kick space.

4

Level the base, front to back and end to end, using shims. Toenail it to the floor on the inside edges, or secure it with metal angle braces and screws.

Build the Boxes

Start by attaching the 1x4 brace to the back edge of the top. Clamp the brace to the cabinet top, then tap it flush with the back edge (Photo 5).

Now drill pilot holes for screws, in the following two stages.

First, use a combination bit to drill clearance holes and countersinks for the screwheads simultaneously (Photo 6).

Second, extend the pilot holes for the screws into the edge of the brace. For No. 6 drywall screws, as in this project, use a 7/64-inch diameter bit (Photo 7). Drive the screws before removing the clamps. It's easiest to use a hardened driver bit and a magnetic bit holder in your drill.

Assemble the rest of the box in the same way. Screw the box's sides to the top and bottom. If you don't plan to add finished side panels, drill pilot holes with a combination bit that also drills holes for 3/8-inch plugs to cover the screwheads.

When you attach the bottom, raise it enough—about 3/4 inch—for its inside face to be flush with the top edge of the face frame at the bottom of the box opening. The frame will be installed later.

Now turn the assembled box face down and attach the back (Photo 8). Space the screws about 4 inches apart.

If your cabinet design calls for finished 1/4-inch thick panels on the sides, glue and nail them on now with finish nails. The cabinet's face frame will hide the front edges of these panels and the finished top will obscure the top edges.

BUILD THE BOXES

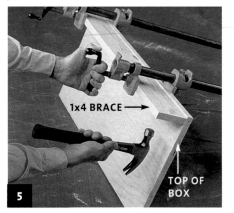

5

1x4 BRACE →

TOP OF BOX

Start with the brace piece and the cabinet box top. Clamp the parts together and adjust their alignment by tapping with a hammer to make the back edges flush.

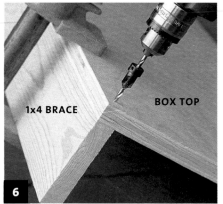

6

1x4 BRACE   BOX TOP

Use a combination bit to countersink clearance holes. Where needed, select a bit that also drills a 3/8-in. hole for a wood plug to hide the screwheads.

7

With the pieces still clamped together, use a straight bit to extend each pilot hole into the brace edge. For No. 6 drywall screws, use a 7/64-in. diameter bit.

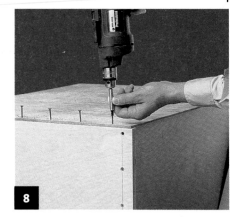

8

Attach the back with screws spaced about 4 in. apart. Be sure to cut it square, so that when you align its edges precisely this will keep the entire box square.

Build the Face Frames

Make the face frames with care, because they and the doors will largely determine the appearance of the finished cabinets. You can make a large face frame to cover all the boxes or construct several smaller ones and screw them together edge to edge. The smaller face frames are easier to handle, which is one reason they were used for these cabinets and window seat.

Cut the pieces of the face frames in a miter box to ensure having perfectly square corners (Photo 9). Make sure your measurements are precise and clearly marked on the wood.

Assemble each frame one corner at a time. Use a right-angle clamp to hold the rail (horizontal) and stile (vertical) pieces together with their ends precisely aligned (Photo 10). Drill pilot holes as you did to build the box. Then drill holes for wood plugs to conceal the screwheads. Drive the screws before removing the clamp.

Now attach the assembled face frame to the cabinet box with glue and 6d finish nails (Photo 11). Run a bead of glue along the box edges, and put the face frame in place. If it overlaps the sides, make sure that it does so uniformly all around. Drill pilot holes and drive the 6d finish nails.

Don't dent the wood: Use a nail set to sink the nailheads 1/16 inch below the surface.

You may find it easier to attach the individual pieces of the face frame to the edges of the box one at a time. If you've cut the pieces carefully, this method can work well, especially if you plan to paint the cabinets. You can fill any small gaps later with spackling compound.

Cut plugs to cover the screwheads and insert them in their holes with glue. When the glue is dry, cut the plugs off as close as possible to the wood's surface with a sharp chisel. Then plane or sand them flush with the face frame.

Assembly Tip

For finish work, drive screws by hand—a slip with a power driver could scar the wood's surface beyond repair.

BUILD THE FACE FRAMES

9

Cut the face-frame pieces in a miter box to ensure making square ends. Care now is essential for establishing square corner joints.

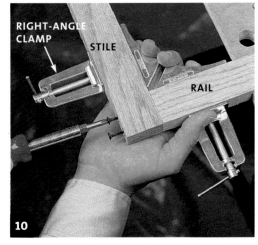

RIGHT-ANGLE CLAMP
STILE
RAIL

10

Assemble the face frames using a right-angle clamp. Drill clearance, pilot, and countersink holes, then drive screws to join the pieces.

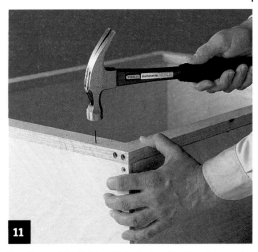

11

Use glue and 6d finish nails to fasten the face frames to the cabinet box fronts. Predrill holes for the nails, then put a line of glue along the plywood edge.

Install Shelf Supports

If you designed your cabinets to have adjustable shelves, install metal standards and support clips now. Screw the standards to the inside walls of the cabinets, two on each side (Photo 12). You can do this either before or after attaching the face frames.

For full-depth shelves, install standards 1-1/2 to 2 inches from the inside back edge and an equal distance from the front edge, including the thickness of the face frame. For partial-depth shelves, mark the front-edge locations, then place the front standards 1 inch behind that line.

Make sure that all four of the standards are plumb vertically and that their slots are aligned correctly.

Attach the Tops

To edge the tops, attach 3/4-inch wide panel-cap molding or other ready-made edging. Miter the corners, then attach the edging with glue and either short finish nails or brads.

Position each finished top on the cabinet with the desired amount of overhang at the sides and front. If the cabinet will be mounted against a wall, set the rear edge of the top flush with the back of the box. Drill one pilot hole at each corner from inside the cabinet up into the bottom surface of the top. Then drive the screws to attach the top.

If it suits your design, add 1/2-inch cove molding under the overhanging edges as a finishing touch.

Install metal standards for adjustable shelves in the cabinets. Make sure all four standards are plumb vertically and their slots aligned horizontally.

Screw the cabinets to the base and the wall, keeping them level as you go. Insert 3-in. drywall screws through the braces and into the studs.

Hang the Doors

The cabinets for this project use full-overlay doors, which are the easiest type to install, because they don't have to fit precisely into the face-frame opening. Instead, they overlap the opening on all four sides.

Pivot hinges like the ones shown below are virtually invisible and give a more finished appearance than other types. They're also adjustable, which makes it easier to establish the doors as plumb.

Use a self-centering Vix bit to drill pilot holes for the hinges.

First, position the hinges on each door and drill pilot holes through the elongated holes in the hinges (Photo 14). Don't drive the screws in yet, however.

Next, remove the hinges. Hold them in place on the face frame, drill pilot holes, and screw the hinges in place. Position the door in the hinges, align the pilot holes with the elongated holes in the hinge leaf, and drive the screws (Photo 15).

Check the swing of the doors and their alignment on the face frame. If an opening has two doors, their tops must align and the gap between their edges must be uniform. Use a level to make sure each vertical edge is plumb. To make adjustments, loosen the hinge screws and shift the door as necessary.

When everything is aligned properly, tighten the adjustment screws. Then drill pilot holes through the round holes in the hinge leaves and drive those screws.

Finish the Cabinets

Before finishing the cabinets, remove the doors and all hardware such as hinges and knobs. Sand all surfaces with fine-grit (120–180) paper. Pick up the sanding dust with a vacuum cleaner and a tack cloth.

For a painted finish, brush on a coat of primer, then fill all the cracks, nail holes, and dings with spackling compound. Sand again, and spot-prime where necessary. Apply two coats of latex enamel, sanding between coats.

For a varnish-only or a stain-and-varnish finish, follow the product instructions carefully. Once the paint or finish is thoroughly dry, rehang the doors and reattach the hardware.

HANG THE DOORS

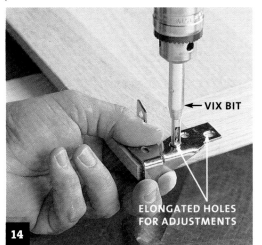

VIX BIT

ELONGATED HOLES FOR ADJUSTMENTS

14

Use a self-centering Vix bit to make pilot holes. Drill only through the elongated adjustment holes in the hinge leaves for the first installation.

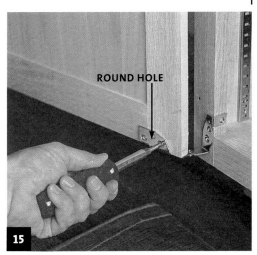

ROUND HOLE

15

Adjust the doors by loosening the screws in the elongated holes. Once the doors are correctly aligned, drive screws through the round holes in the hinges.

Construction Plan: Window Seat

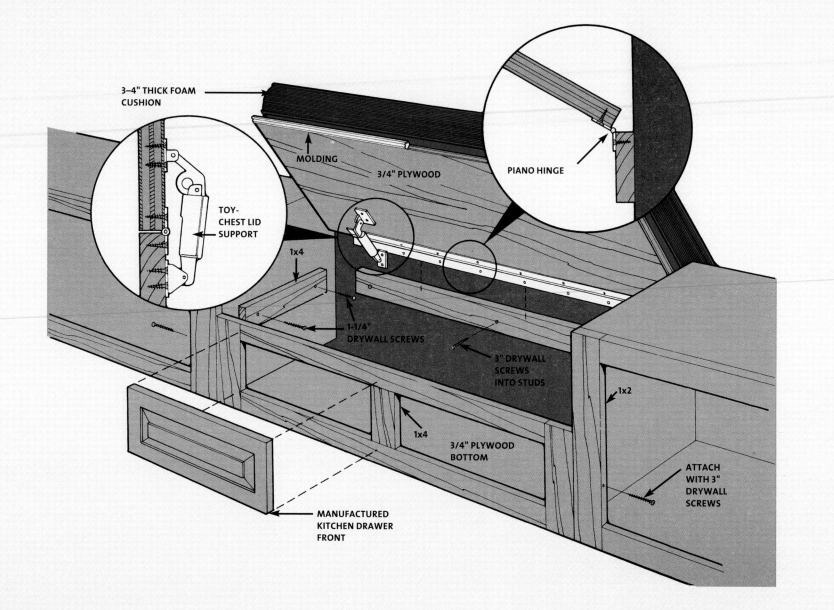

3–4" THICK FOAM CUSHION

MOLDING

3/4" PLYWOOD

PIANO HINGE

TOY-CHEST LID SUPPORT

1x4

1-1/4" DRYWALL SCREWS

3" DRYWALL SCREWS INTO STUDS

1x2

1x4

3/4" PLYWOOD BOTTOM

ATTACH WITH 3" DRYWALL SCREWS

MANUFACTURED KITCHEN DRAWER FRONT

Build the Window Seat

The window seat with its lift-up lid provides additional storage space (see Photo 17, below, and the construction plan on page 56). To begin, build a face frame of 1x4's and 1x2's with openings to be covered by decorative panels. If you bought ready-made cabinet doors at a home center, you can probably find matching drawer fronts to use as panels.

Screw 1x4 braces to the rear wall studs and the adjoining cabinet sides so their top edges will be at the same height as the top of the face frame. The lid rests on these braces and the face frame.

Attach the window seat's face frame flush with the cabinet face frames, with their bottom edges aligned. Clamp it in position, drill pilot holes, and drive 3-inch drywall screws through the cabinet frames into the edges of the window-seat frame (Photo 16).

Make the lid of 3/4-inch plywood with a finished front edge. Attach it to the brace on the wall with a piano hinge (Photo 17). Install a toy-chest lid support to hold the lid safely in an opened position (see the lefthand detail in the construction plan on the opposite page).

Attach the decorative front panels with screws driven through the face frame from behind (Photo 18).

Finally, cut a plywood bottom for the window seat, put it in position, and fasten it with screws driven into the base stringers below, as you did with the cabinets themselves.

Finish the window seat to match the cabinets, following the steps on page 55.

BUILD THE WINDOW SEAT

16

Clamp the window-seat face frame to the adjoining cabinet frames, then screw them together edge to edge. Make sure the front faces remain flush.

PIANO HINGE SUPPORTS WINDOW SEAT

1x4 BRACE

17

Install a piano hinge along the full length of the lid. The lid rests on the back and side braces and the top edge of the face frame. Add a toy-chest lid support (page 56).

18

Fasten drawer fronts or other panels to the face frame with screws driven from behind. To complete the job, screw a plywood bottom to the floor frame.

Dinnerware Rack

Show off your dinnerware. This open rack stows twelve place settings of plates, platters, saucers, bowls, and cups.

What You'll Need

The rack shown in the drawing at right uses 3/4-inch thick soft maple, available in the required widths at many home centers and from most suppliers of hardwood lumber, but almost any hard or medium-hard wood will work well.

To build this rack you'll need a jigsaw, a circular saw, an electric drill, a set of 1/4-inch dowel centers, and a self-centering doweling jig. The jig should be available at most full-service hardware stores, home centers, or mail-order suppliers.

Cut and Drill the Pieces

Using a jigsaw or a circular saw, cut the following pieces:

- ▶ Two 12-inch x 30-inch side pieces
- ▶ One 12-inch x 22-1/2 inch shelf
- ▶ Two 5-inch x 22-1/2 inch back braces
- ▶ Four 2-inch x 22-1/2 inch crosspieces
- ▶ Twenty-two 3/8-inch diameter x 12-1/8 inch dowel-rod plate dividers
- ▶ Twelve 3/8-inch diameter x 1-3/4 inch dowel rod cup pegs.

Begin preparing the pieces by marking and cutting the 4-inch and 4-1/2 inch over-lapping radiuses on both side pieces, as shown in Figure 3 (right).

Mark the placement for the eleven rows of 3/8-inch dowel divider holes on all four crosspieces. Then drill them 9/16 inch deep, using a doweling jig.

Now, center, mark, and drill six 3/8-inch holes 9/16 inch deep in each bottom crosspiece for the cup-peg dowels.

Assemble the Unit

▶ Glue the front and back dowel-rod sections together by rounding the ends of each rod slightly and placing glue into the holes, not on the rods. Use a wooden or rubber mallet to tap the dowels first into the bottom crosspiece, then into the top. If necessary, use bar clamps to pull each crosspiece into alignment both vertically and horizontally.

▶ Now form half-round notches at the ends of the cup pegs by clamping pairs of pegs together in a vise and then drilling between them with a 3/8-inch bit, as shown in Figure 1 (opposite). Then glue the pegs into the two bottom crosspieces.

▶ Cut two 1/4-inch wide plate grooves 1/4 inch deep in the shelf top, using a circular saw or a router.

▶ Locate and drill 1/4-inch dowel holes in the ends of all back braces, the shelf, and all crosspieces, as shown in Figure 2 (opposite).

▶ Using 1/4-inch dowel centers, locate the placement for each corresponding hole on both side pieces.

▶ Next, glue the 1/4-inch dowels into both ends of all the horizontal pieces, then glue and tap these into each side piece. Clamp the assembly if necessary to secure it until the glue sets completely.

▶ Drill two 1/4-inch holes 16 inches apart through the top and bottom back braces to use in mounting the unit to wall studs.

▶ Finally, finish-sand the entire unit, first with 150-grit sandpaper, then 220-grit paper. Apply the finish of your choice.

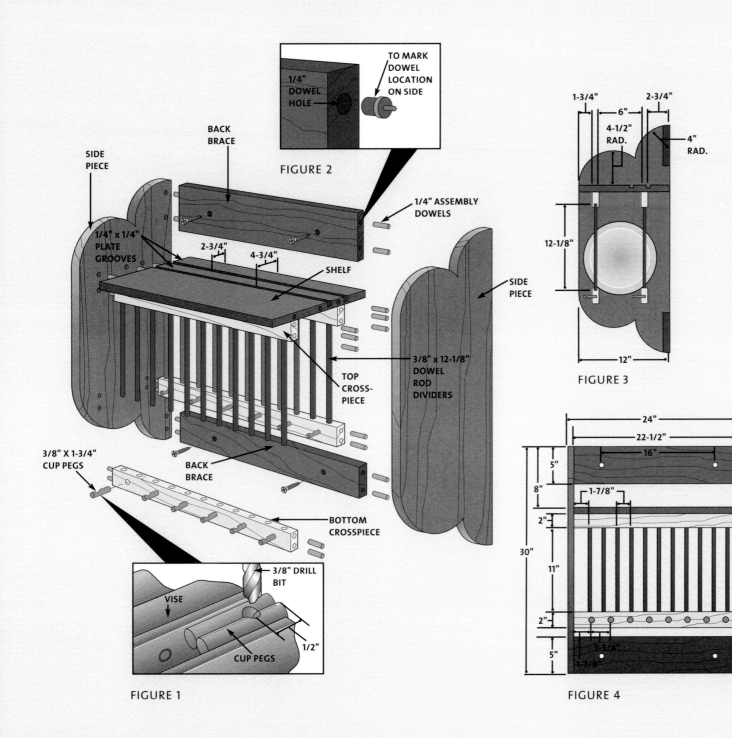

FIGURE 2

1/4" DOWEL HOLE

TO MARK DOWEL LOCATION ON SIDE

BACK BRACE

SIDE PIECE

1/4" ASSEMBLY DOWELS

1/4" x 1/4" PLATE GROOVES

2-3/4"

4-3/4"

SHELF

SIDE PIECE

3/8" x 12-1/8" DOWEL ROD DIVIDERS

TOP CROSS-PIECE

3/8" X 1-3/4" CUP PEGS

BACK BRACE

BOTTOM CROSSPIECE

3/8" DRILL BIT

VISE

CUP PEGS

1/2"

FIGURE 1

1-3/4"

2-3/4"

6"

4-1/2" RAD.

4" RAD.

12-1/8"

12"

FIGURE 3

24"

22-1/2"

16"

5"

8"

1-7/8"

2"

11"

2"

30"

3-3/4"

5"

1-7/8"

FIGURE 4

Family Room & Home Office

Make your recreation area more attractive *and* more functional, or make your workspace more efficient with one of these good-looking, practical, adaptable projects.

Wall-to-Wall Cabinets

Create a peaceful retreat for your family with a shelf-lined room that is much more than just a place to store books.

62

"Antique" Stereo Cabinet

Keep your stereo gear cool—instead of Grandma's pies—in this charming cabinet that looks like an antique pie safe.

High-Tech Entertainment Center

Accommodate components of many sizes with this mobile media center. You can move or add shelves to fit your equipment.

Easy Oak Office Set

Organize your home office with this sleek, matching phone desk and shelf system that are each practical and simple to make.

Computer Workstation

Make the most of your workspace with this eye-catching, well-designed computer desk and printer stand.

Wall-to-Wall Cabinets

Create a peaceful retreat for your family, with a shelf-lined room that is much more than just a place to store books.

These wall-to-wall cabinets turned a spare bedroom into a home library. Even if you don't want to transform a whole room, you can find a place for these built-ins in the kids' playroom, a finished basement, or even a hallway.

Size Up the Project

These plans are for a typical set of home-library cabinets and shelves. The step-by-step photos show you the basic process of how to build and install the cabinetry, pointing out along the way potential problems and highlighting the techniques you can use to ensure doing a top-notch job.

This is a big project, but if you've done basic woodworking and trim carpentry you'll find it's not difficult. The only power tools you'll need are a drill, a router, and a table saw or a radial arm saw. For your investment in time and materials you can save significantly over having a cabinet-maker build these shelves.

Adapting the Design

This spare bedroom was perfectly suited for a library. We installed cabinetry with plenty of adjustable shelving, closed storage below it, built-in lighting, and a cozy window seat with drawers underneath it. (For a window seat with a fixed front, see Window Seat Cabinets, page 46.) The cabinets for this project are built in, but you could also create a set of freestanding bookcases (see Fast, Flexible Bookcases, page 12).

This design is a perfect starting point for your own library cabinets. Your room's dimensions will be different and you may have other needs, such as for a built-in desk or space for a television set and a VCR. Or you might make a tilted display shelf for magazines. (Add a lip to the shelf, then screw it to a shelf-support cleat to prevent sliding.) If you adapt the guidelines here you can be sure of success.

For information about shelf spans and widths on the various items you might put on the shelves, see Standard Shelf Depths on page 14. To accommodate longer spans or heavier loads, beef up your shelves by gluing a brace, 1-1/2 inches wide and as long as the shelf, to the front and/or back edges, or by using a double thickness of material and correspondingly wider edging in front.

These built-in cabinets incorporate open shelving and closed storage, recessed lighting and direct natural illumination over a cozy window seat.

TOOLS

HAND TOOLS

Bar clamps

Compass

Hammer

Handsaw

Level

Nail set

Plane

Screwdriver

Self-centering dowel jig; two drill guides

Staple gun; staples

Tape measure

Tin snips

Wire cutters

POWER TOOLS

Electric drill; brad-point bit

Router

Table saw or radial arm saw

Construction Plan

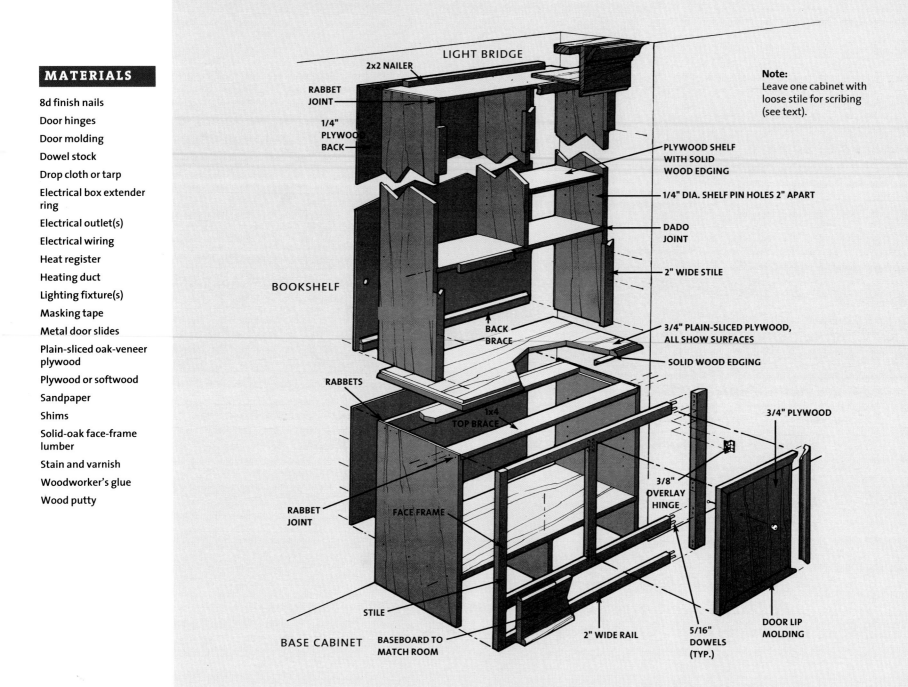

MATERIALS

- 8d finish nails
- Door hinges
- Door molding
- Dowel stock
- Drop cloth or tarp
- Electrical box extender ring
- Electrical outlet(s)
- Electrical wiring
- Heat register
- Heating duct
- Lighting fixture(s)
- Masking tape
- Metal door slides
- Plain-sliced oak-veneer plywood
- Plywood or softwood
- Sandpaper
- Shims
- Solid-oak face-frame lumber
- Stain and varnish
- Woodworker's glue
- Wood putty

Note:
Leave one cabinet with loose stile for scribing (see text).

LIGHT BRIDGE

2x2 NAILER

RABBET JOINT

1/4" PLYWOOD BACK

BOOKSHELF

PLYWOOD SHELF WITH SOLID WOOD EDGING

1/4" DIA. SHELF PIN HOLES 2" APART

DADO JOINT

2" WIDE STILE

BACK BRACE

3/4" PLAIN-SLICED PLYWOOD, ALL SHOW SURFACES

SOLID WOOD EDGING

RABBETS

1x4 TOP BRACE

3/4" PLYWOOD

RABBET JOINT

FACE FRAME

3/8" OVERLAY HINGE

STILE

BASE CABINET

BASEBOARD TO MATCH ROOM

2" WIDE RAIL

5/16" DOWELS (TYP.)

DOOR LIP MOLDING

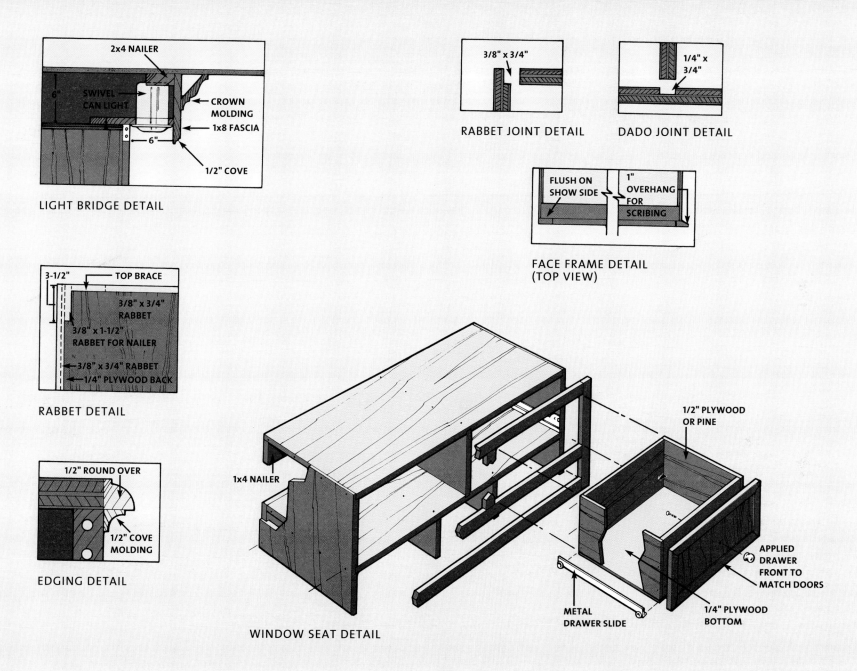

2x4 NAILER

6"

SWIVEL
CAN LIGHT

CROWN
MOLDING

1x8 FASCIA

6"

1/2" COVE

LIGHT BRIDGE DETAIL

3/8" x 3/4"

RABBET JOINT DETAIL

1/4" x
3/4"

DADO JOINT DETAIL

FLUSH ON
SHOW SIDE

1"
OVERHANG
FOR
SCRIBING

**FACE FRAME DETAIL
(TOP VIEW)**

3-1/2"

TOP BRACE

3/8" x 3/4"
RABBET

3/8" x 1-1/2"
RABBET FOR NAILER

3/8" x 3/4" RABBET

1/4" PLYWOOD BACK

RABBET DETAIL

1/2" ROUND OVER

1/2" COVE
MOLDING

EDGING DETAIL

1x4 NAILER

1/2" PLYWOOD
OR PINE

APPLIED
DRAWER
FRONT TO
MATCH DOORS

METAL
DRAWER SLIDE

1/4" PLYWOOD
BOTTOM

WINDOW SEAT DETAIL

Construct the Cases

Use a table saw or a radial arm saw to build the plywood cases. Keep the joints simple, with rabbets and dadoes reinforced by glue and nails (see the Rabbet and Dado Joint details on page 65). Building the cabinets is straightforward, but here are a few helpful suggestions.

▶ For a cleaner appearance that's more like solid lumber, buy plain-sliced veneer plywood, available at larger lumberyards. The cabinets in this project used plain-sliced oak-veneer plywood (Photo 1).

▶ Plywood varies in thickness, sometimes even within a single sheet, so test your dado setup as you cut (Photo 2).

▶ When you drill the holes for the shelf pins, using a hardwood template, be sure to position the template the same way for each set of holes (Photo 3). It's easy to become disoriented, and if the holes for each end of a shelf aren't in the same plane the shelf will wobble. Use a brad-point drill bit and a slow feed for the cleanest holes. If you have shelf pins on both sides of a center partition, such as in the bookshelf units, offset the rows slightly so the holes won't meet. For information about various shelf support techniques see page 21.

Now assemble the cases with glue and 8d finish nails. Attach nailer strips to screw the cabinets to the wall (Photo 4). Before the glue sets, check that the cabinet is square by measuring both diagonals and making sure they're equal (Photo 5). Use bar clamps, offset slightly from square, to make adjustments.

1

Cut the cases' plywood to width and length. This system uses plain-sliced oak-veneer plywood, which has a realistic grain pattern that looks like lumber.

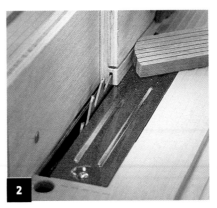

2

Use rabbets and dadoes to connect the case and bookshelf pieces. Cut them with a table saw, a radial arm saw, or a router, being extra careful at the ends of cuts.

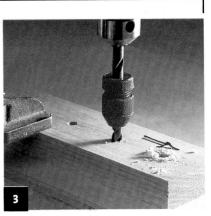

3

Drill shelf-pin holes with a template and a brad-point drill bit. Be sure to orient the template the same way every time for the proper shelf alignment.

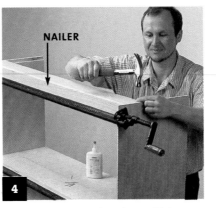

NAILER

4

Assemble the cases, using glue and 8d finish nails. Notice the nailer strip that will be used eventually for screwing the cabinet to the wall.

5

Before the glue sets, check that both diagonals measure the same so the unit will be square. To make adjustments, use bar clamps set at a slight angle.

Freestanding Bookcases

Freestanding bookcases are not only easier to construct than built-in cabinetry but also let you rearrange them as your needs change. For these units you can adapt the same plans shown on pages 64–65 for the large library unit: a plywood case joined with rabbets, dadoes, nails, and glue and a face frame on the front. Here are some specific suggestions to consider in designing your freestanding bookcases.

▶ Build a base or plinth that raises the lowest shelf off the floor, to help keep books cleaner and give the bookshelf a furniturelike appearance. You can use a wide face frame and molding, as shown here, or simply build a box for the case to rest on.

▶ If the bookcase is tall, run an unobtrusive molding around the top as shown at the right. But if the top is low enough to be seen, you'll need to add a separate top like the one on the base cabinets (see the Edging Detail on page 65).

▶ If necessary, you can fit the bookcase tightly to the wall by cutting notches in the sides for the baseboard as shown in the detail below, right. Then you can continue to run baseboard trim around the bookcase's base.

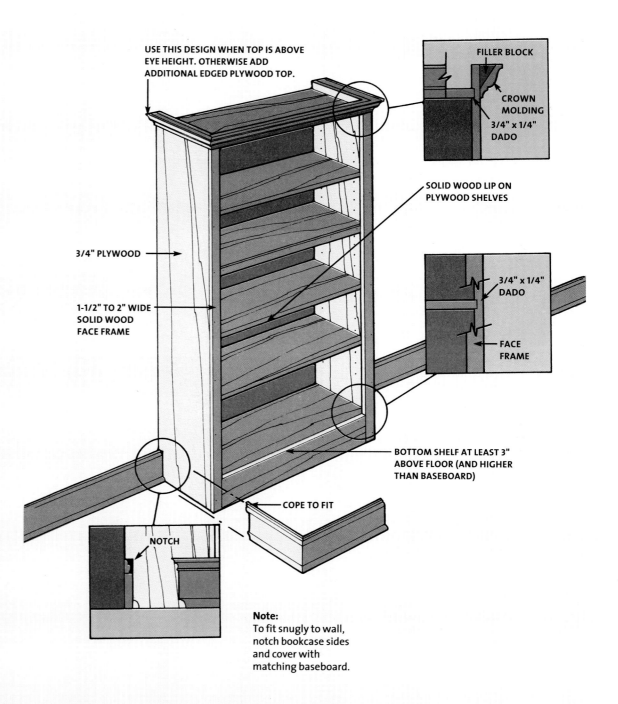

USE THIS DESIGN WHEN TOP IS ABOVE EYE HEIGHT. OTHERWISE ADD ADDITIONAL EDGED PLYWOOD TOP.

FILLER BLOCK

CROWN MOLDING

3/4" x 1/4" DADO

SOLID WOOD LIP ON PLYWOOD SHELVES

3/4" PLYWOOD

1-1/2" TO 2" WIDE SOLID WOOD FACE FRAME

3/4" x 1/4" DADO

FACE FRAME

BOTTOM SHELF AT LEAST 3" ABOVE FLOOR (AND HIGHER THAN BASEBOARD)

COPE TO FIT

NOTCH

Note:
To fit snugly to wall, notch bookcase sides and cover with matching baseboard.

Frame Out the Cases

You can save a lot of time by buying special face-frame lumber, which is available from lumberyards that cater to cabinetmakers. This type of wood is already carefully chosen, ripped to standard face-frame widths, and planed on all four sides when you buy it.

You'll save even more time if you supply yourself with a self-centering doweling jig having double drill guides (Photo 6). It greatly simplifies aligning dowels and is a big help in doweling face frames together.

Building the Face Frames

The face frames for the case are made of solid wood cut to size and joined with dowels. Then they're glued and nailed to the plywood cases. They should overhang the sides enough that they can be trimmed to fit snugly against the wall (Photo 7). One stile (a vertical piece) of one face frame is left separate, not glued to the rest of the frame. This will be the very last piece you'll install. Having it loose makes it possible to achieve a neat, tight, wall-to-wall installation. (See the box Scribe for a Perfect Fit, page 73.)

Building the Tops

Next, make the tops for the cabinets from plywood, then glue and clamp solid wood to the edges. After sanding the edging even with the plywood surface, rout a profile in the edging (Photo 8). Add cove molding underneath for a smooth look and to help cover nail holes (see the Edging Detail on page 65).

Notice that the edging on these tops was routed to create a little step, or rabbet. Rabbets create a shadow line that helps to conceal the change in grain and color where solid wood meets veneered plywood.

FRAME OUT THE CASES

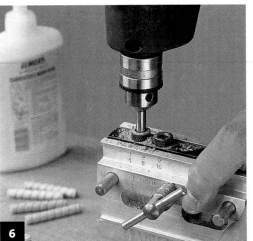

6

Dowel the face frame together. A self-centering jig with two drill guides like the one shown here eliminates dowel-alignment problems.

BEVEL FOR EASIER TRIMMING →

7

Glue and nail the face frame to the cabinet, flush on the visible side and overhanging 1 in. on the wall side for easier trimming to your scribed line.

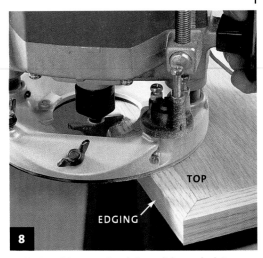

TOP

EDGING

8

Make the cabinet tops by gluing solid-wood edging, mitered at the corners, to the plywood. Sand it flush, then rout a rabbet to hide the change of grain.

Make the Doors and Drawers

These doors and drawers are good looking and simple to build. They rely on a special mitered molding that, when glued to the edge of 3/4-inch plywood, provides a 3/8-inch lip on all sides (Photo 9). This common building technique is easy to carry out and, even better, is especially forgiving of errors.

The drawers are simply boxes of 1/2-inch plywood or softwood with nailed-on bottoms. Metal drawer slides provide smooth operation and also cover the butt-joined edges of the plywood bottom (Photo 10).

Finishing Touches

The last shop chores are to cut the nailers and the light bridge (see the Light Bridge Detail, page 65), finish-sand all of the exposed surfaces, clean them, and prepare to apply your finish.

Although you could begin installing the cabinets now and wait to finish the pieces until later, you will achieve significantly better results—in considerably less time—if you stain and varnish all the cabinetry pieces first.

Don't attempt to fill the nail holes until the first coat of varnish is dry. This way you can see exactly what color the wood has become, then blend together a few shades of soft, tinted wood putty for just the right match. Once it has set, apply the second coat of varnish over this putty. Or, to fill nail holes in regular unknotted wood, you can make your own filler by mixing together sawdust from the wood with white glue.

Design Alert

Most metal drawer slides require 1/2 in. of clearance on both sides. Be sure to check the requirements of your slides and make your drawers narrower than the cabinet's openings by the appropriate amount.

MAKE THE DOORS AND DRAWERS

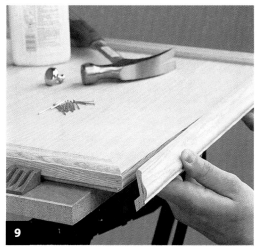

To make the doors, use a special molding, mitered at the corners, to fit around the 3/4-in. plywood and produce a 3/8-in. lip.

Make the drawers as butt-joined boxes with applied fronts. Metal drawer slides cover the bottom edges and ensure smooth operation.

Prepare the Room

Prepare the room for the installation by removing the trim and painting the wall. You might want to extend wiring from an existing wall outlet across the floor so you can install outlets in the base of the cabinets (Photo 11). And you could also add surface-mounted outlets on the ceiling to plug in recessed fixtures in the cabinetry. The installation shown here also required routing a heat duct underneath the new cabinets (Photo 12). To prevent overheating, be sure to leave at least an inch between the electric wiring and the duct when installing.

To protect your floors, tape down a heavy drop cloth or tarp while you install the cabinets.

An outlet inside the cabinets is a must (Photo 13). Having one makes a tidy job of installing a television set, sound system, computer, or lighting.

PREPARE THE ROOM

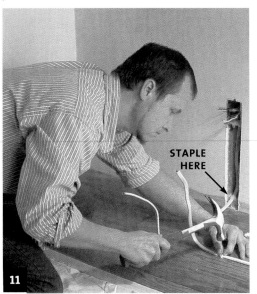

STAPLE HERE

11

Connect new wiring for outlets in the baseboard to the old outlet. Then staple the wire to the wall plate and continue it along the floor.

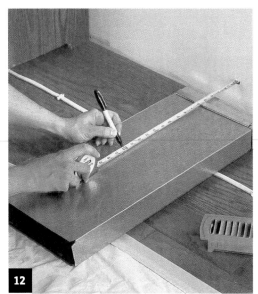

12

Bring heat ducts to the front of the cabinet with 90-degree bends and short lengths of prefabricated duct that are cut to length with tin snips.

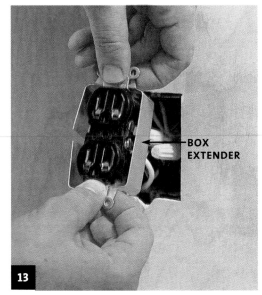

BOX EXTENDER

13

Mount the old outlet into the cabinet back with a box extender ring to keep the wiring away from wood and decrease the possibility of fire.

Install the Completed Components

Level the cabinets with thin shims, and make sure their faces are flush. Then simply nail them to the floor and screw them to the walls (Photo 14). Squeezing an entire system tightly between two walls isn't always easy, especially in an older home, where settling of floors and walls may have occurred. This is where scribing can help (see page 73).

The key to successful scribing of a single cabinet is to position and level the cabinet correctly before you begin scribing. Don't waste time carefully scribing a tight fit, only to have it go askew when you then level the cabinet.

Wall-to-wall cabinets present their own special problem. It can be tricky fitting the last cabinet in place. To do this, the best approach is to leave one stile loose, to scribe to fit the wall. Don't attach this stile to the face frame; scribe it separately and face-nail it in place (Photo 15). Be sure that the width of the stile you leave after scribing equals the space between the end of the rails and the wall, as shown in the bottom left photo on page 73, and check that the stile is square to the rails when you scribe it.

INSTALL THE COMPLETED COMPONENTS

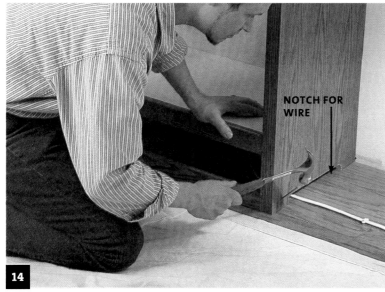

14

After shimming them level, nail the cabinets to the floor and screw through the nailer into the studs.

15

Nail on the loose stile after scribing it to fit the wall. Then screw on the cabinet tops from underneath.

Add the Finishing Touches

Now you are ready to scribe the cabinets, window seat, and bookshelves to fit together snugly. Once that's done, attach them to the wall and floor (Photo 16). Next, add a light bridge to hold the recessed, movable spotlights above the shelving (see the Light Bridge Detail on page 65 and Photo 17). Then fit a fascia board in front of it and install the crown molding and baseboard (Photo 18). Finally, attach the doors and drawers, then covers for the outlets and heat ducts, and your library is ready for you to start stocking it with books.

16

Mount the shelves on top of the cabinets, scribing the shelving to fit the walls. Screw them to the wall on top, and toenail them to the cabinets on the bottom.

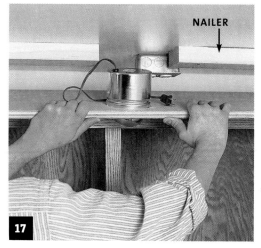

NAILER

17

Attach a light bridge across the top of the bookshelves. Note here one of the 2x4 nailers used for attaching the fascia board across the front.

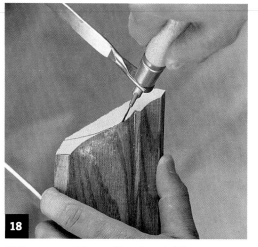

18

Fit the crown molding and baseboard at the corners, using a coping saw; then install the outlet and heating register covers.

Scribe for a Perfect Fit

Scribe the face frames with a compass, following the wall with its fixed point as you trace its contour onto the cabinet as shown (near right). Then sand or plane down the marked area to the line so the cabinet will fit tightly. After checking for fit, nail the cut stile onto the cabinet. Then you are ready to secure the cabinet tops from underneath.

Scribe the end cabinet after leveling it by marking the contour of the wall on the face frame with a compass as shown.

Fit the last cabinet by leaving a stile loose and scribing it separately. The stile must be square to the rail, and the marked distances must be equal.

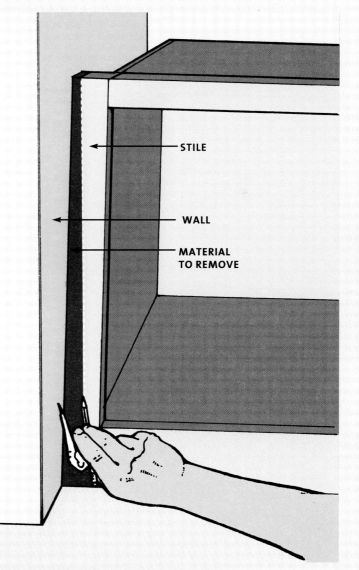

STILE

WALL

MATERIAL TO REMOVE

This schematic view, exaggerated for clarity, shows (in magenta) the strip of excess material that must be planed or sanded down to make the loose stile fit the gap between wall and cabinet.

"Antique" Stereo Cabinet

Keep your stereo gear cool—instead of Grandma's pies—in this charming cabinet that looks like an antique pie safe.

Behind the pierced-metal doors is a versatile entertainment center with three adjustable shelves and holes in the back that provide ventilation and power cord access. The bottom shelf holds dividers to store records, and there's space in the drawers for cassette and CD racks.

This project requires at least moderate woodworking skills and tools, but it's not especially difficult. The fact that it's large and made of solid rather than veneered wood does mean that it involves a lot of work, however, so the best approach is to take your time and set a comfortable pace for yourself.

The decorative pierced-metal panels in the door frames are made of tin that's been treated with vinegar overnight and finished to look aged. You could pierce the tin panels yourself with a hammer and a small punch and a lot of time, but excellent prepunched tin panels are available from a variety of mail-order sources.

Before you start this project, measure each of your electronic components and determine how you'll want to route all the wires and power cords. Then make any necessary adjustments to the Cutting List on page 77. Don't change the dimensions of the tin door-panel openings, however, unless you have decided to buy different-size tin panels.

All the joints in this project are assembled with the contemporary joinery technique known as biscuits. This modern way to make wood joints is faster and much stronger than dowels. You can rent a biscuit joiner machine at many tool-rental outlets or, if you'd rather, simply assemble this cabinet with dowels as usual. (For more on dowels and to see a shelving system that makes particularly good use of dowel joinery using dowels as ends for a unit, see pages 32–33.)

MATERIALS

Qty.	Size and Description
75 board ft.	4/4 cherry
1 sheet	1/4" X 4' X 8' cherry plywood
100	No. 20 biscuits
8	No. 10 x 1-1/4" pan-head screws with flat washers
1	No. 10 x 1-1/4" steel flathead wood screw
6	No. 4 x 5/8" flathead wood screws
14	1-1/4" drywall screws
12	1-1/4" brads
30	1" brads
100	3/4" brads
16	1/4"-dia. brass shelf supports
4	1/4"-dia. wood knobs
3 pairs	2" x 1-9/16" plain steel loose-pin butt hinges
6	Pierced-tin panels*
1 quart	Danish oil finish
	Sandpaper
	Vinegar
	Brass record dividers (as needed)
	CD holders (as needed)
	Audio cassette holders (as needed)
	Woodworker's glue

*Available from Country Accents, P.O. Box 437, Dept. TFH, Montoursville, PA 17754; (717) 478-4127.

Unpierced panels are available from Van Dyke's, P.O. Box 278, Woonsocket, SD 57385; (800) 843-3320.

Construction Plan

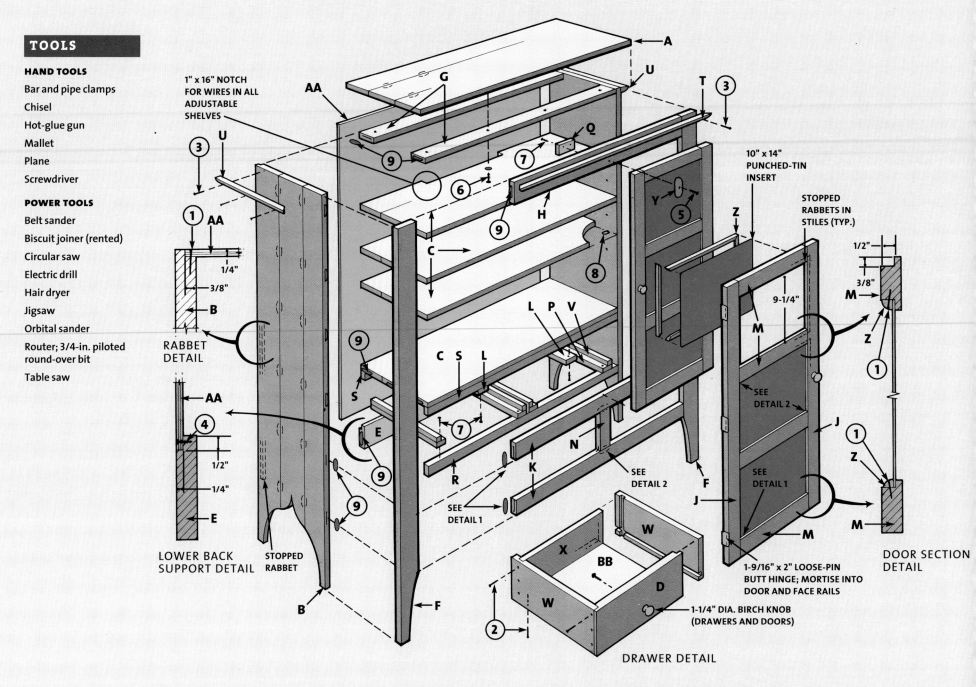

TOOLS

HAND TOOLS

Bar and pipe clamps

Chisel

Hot-glue gun

Mallet

Plane

Screwdriver

POWER TOOLS

Belt sander

Biscuit joiner (rented)

Circular saw

Electric drill

Hair dryer

Jigsaw

Orbital sander

Router; 3/4-in. piloted round-over bit

Table saw

1" x 16" NOTCH FOR WIRES IN ALL ADJUSTABLE SHELVES

RABBET DETAIL

1/4"

3/8"

LOWER BACK SUPPORT DETAIL

STOPPED RABBET

1/2"

1/4"

10" x 14" PUNCHED-TIN INSERT

STOPPED RABBETS IN STILES (TYP.)

1/2"

3/8"

DOOR SECTION DETAIL

9-1/4"

SEE DETAIL 2

SEE DETAIL 1

SEE DETAIL 2

SEE DETAIL 1

1-9/16" x 2" LOOSE-PIN BUTT HINGE; MORTISE INTO DOOR AND FACE RAILS

1-1/4" DIA. BIRCH KNOB (DRAWERS AND DOORS)

DRAWER DETAIL

Fastenings

① 3/4" brad

② 1" brad

③ 1-1/4" brad

④ No. 4 x 5/8" flathead screw

⑤ No. 10 x 1-1/4" steel flathead screw

⑥ No. 10 x 1-1/4" pan-head screw and flat washer

⑦ 1-1/4" drywall screw

⑧ 1/4" dia. brass shelf pin

⑨ No. 20 biscuit

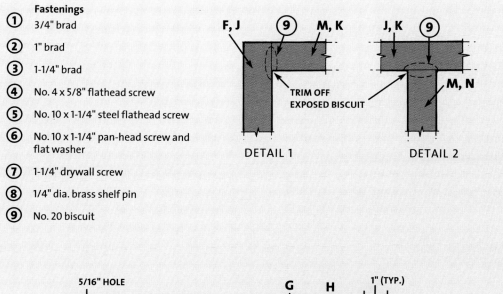

DETAIL 1

DETAIL 2

TRIM OFF EXPOSED BISCUIT

TOP SECTION

DOOR LATCH DETAIL

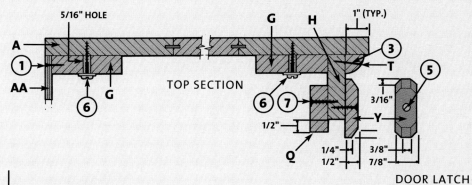

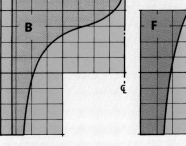

PATTERN DETAILS

EDGE OF REAR LEG

EDGE OF FRONT LEG

EACH SQ. = 1"

CUTTING LIST

Key	Qty.	Size and Description
A	1	3/4" x 17 x 42-1/2" cherry (top)
B	2	3/4" x 15-1/4" x 57" cherry (sides)
C	4	3/4" x 15" x 39" cherry (shelves)
D	2	3/4" x 6-3/8" x 16-1/8" cherry (drawer fronts)
E	1	3/4" x 4" x 39" cherry (lower back support)
F	2	3/4" x 3" x 57" cherry (face stiles)
G	2	3/4" x 3" x 39" cherry (top supports)
H	1	3/4" x 2-3/4" x 34-1/2" cherry (top rail)
J	4	3/4" x 2" x 35-3/4" cherry (door stiles)
K	2	3/4" x 2" x 34-1/2" cherry (face rails)
L	2	3/4" x 2" x 15" cherry (drawer runners)
M	8	3/4" x 2" x 13-1/4" cherry (door rails)
N	1	3/4" x 2" x 6-1/2" cherry (drawer divider stile)
P	4	3/4" x 1-1/2" x 15" cherry (drawer runners)
Q	1	3/4" x 1-1/2" x 3" cherry (doorstop)
R	1	3/4" x 1-5/16" x 39" cherry (drawer-runner cleat)
S	2	3/4" x 1-1/16" x 39" cherry (drawer-runner cleats)
T	1	3/4" x 3/4" x 42" cherry (molding)
U	2	3/4" x 3/4" x 16-3/4" cherry (molding)
V	4	3/4" x 3/4" x 15" cherry (drawer runners)
W	4	1/2" x 6-3/8" x 15-1/2" cherry (drawer sides)
X	2	1/2" x 5-7/8" x 15-5/8" cherry (drawer backs)
Y	1	1/2" x 7/8" x 2-1/2" cherry (door latch)
Z	24	3/8" x 3/8" x 15" cherry (tin-panel stops)
AA	1	1/4" x 39-3/4" x 48-3/16" cherry plywood (back)
BB	1	1/4" x 14-3/4" x 15-5/8" cherry plywood (drawer bottoms)

Prepare the Pieces

Refer to the Tools List on page 76 and the Cutting List on page 77 as you put together what you need for this project.

Assembling Your Tools and Materials

If you decide to use biscuits to assemble this cabinet, you'll need a biscuit joiner, the machine that cuts the grooves for the biscuits (see Joining with Biscuits, facing page). You'll also need a table saw, a router, a jigsaw, an electric drill, a belt sander, an orbital sander, and an assortment of bar and pipe clamps.

With the exceptions of the back and the drawer bottoms, the entire cabinet shown in this project is made of solid cherry. Because the color of raw cherry can vary greatly from piece to piece and even within an individual piece, be especially selective and try to buy color-matched boards when you choose your lumber.

Most cherry boards will contain some sapwood, the almost-white wood from the outer parts of the trunk. Cut your lumber, or have it cut, so that the pieces on the outside of the cabinet are free of sapwood. Use those with sapwood for the inside, where they won't show. This will help you maintain even coloration of the wood on the outside of the cabinet. When you're done, if the wood is still too light, simply apply an oil finish. After a few months, the wood will darken considerably.

Edge-joining Wide Stock

Refer to the Construction Plan (page 76) and the Cutting List (page 77) as you proceed now to prepare the basic components of the cabinet.

Begin by gluing and biscuit-joining three boards to make pieces wide enough for the top (A), sides (B), and shelves (C). Cut the biscuit grooves about 6 inches apart for the best results, making sure there aren't biscuits where you'll be cutting the ends.

Use plenty of clamps, and place wood strips at least 1 inch wide and as long as the boards between the clamps and board edges. This protects the board and helps distribute clamping pressure.

Cut the Pieces

Now cut the rest of the pieces to the dimensions given in your Cutting List, except for the molding pieces (T and U) and the tin-panel stops (Z), which you'll save to cut later.

Draw the contours you want to appear on the bottom ends of the sides (B) and face stiles (F) onto the stock pieces for them (see the Pattern Details, page 77). Then cut out these shapes with a jigsaw.

Use a table saw to cut the rabbet on the top edge of the lower back support (E), referring to the Lower Back Support Detail (page 76). Then rout the stopped rabbets on the back edges of the sides (B) for the back (AA). Take care to stop these rabbets at the point where the lower back support (E) is attached.

Joining with Biscuits

Once you have used a biscuit joiner, or plate joiner, as it's formally called, you may very well want to use one to assemble almost everything you build.

The "biscuits" in question are beech wood compressed and cut into the shape of a thin football (see the dotted outlines in Details 1 and 2 on page 77). The biscuit joiner cuts a semicircular groove that is half the shape of the biscuit into each piece of wood to be joined, as in the shelf shown in Photo B. You then squirt glue into the grooves, insert the biscuit, and briefly clamp the pieces together. The moisture in the glue causes the biscuit to expand, locking it tenaciously within its grooves.

Biscuits make a joint extremely strong, and also make it easy to align and glue the edges of long boards. You don't need to align the pieces manually, since they're clamped together.

There are three common sizes of biscuits: No. 20, which are 1 inch wide x 2-3/8 inches long; No. 10, 3/4 inch x 2-1/8 inches; and No. 0, 5/8 inch x 1-3/4 inches. The No. 20 biscuits have the most surface area and therefore make the strongest joints. Try to use this size whenever possible, filling in with smaller ones only when these are too big.

Some of the typical joints you can assemble with biscuits include edge-to-edge joints (Photo A), corner joints, T joints (Photos B and C), edge miter joints, 45-degree frame joints (as in picture frames), butt joints, and joints to connect boards of uneven thicknesses, whether or not they're flush on one surface.

The particular joining process needed depends of course on which type of joint you are making. Follow the step-by-step instructions with the illustrations here to prepare the common joints referred to. Then refer back to these steps throughout this project.

If this is your first acquaintance with biscuit joinery, practice edge-joining scrap pieces before under-taking the highly visible—and more expensive—solid cherry pieces you'll be making here.

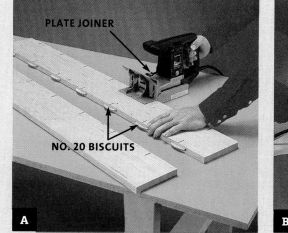

A

To make edge-to-edge joints, align and glue the edges of long boards with biscuit joints. Cut the biscuit grooves about 6 in. apart, making sure not to place biscuits where you cut the ends.

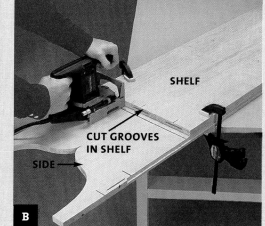

B

To join a shelf and a cabinet side in a T joint, clamp the shelf flat on its side so its end marks the joint's location. Mark the biscuit locations, rest the base of the joiner on the side piece, and cut the grooves.

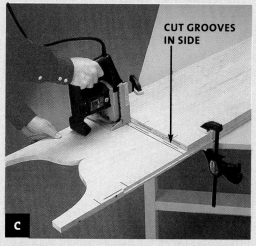

C

To cut grooves in the side flip the joiner upright, with its base against the end of the shelf. Squirt glue in the grooves, insert the biscuits, raise the shelf into position, and clamp the joint.

Assemble the Cabinet

Biscuits are a simple, fast, strong way to join two pieces such as the shelf and cabinet side for this stereo unit.

Biscuit-joining the Shelves and Supports

First lay out and cut the grooves for the No. 20 biscuits used to join the bottom shelf (C), lower back support (E), and top supports (G) to the sides (B).

Clamp the shelf flat on its side so the end of the shelf is where you want the joint (see Photo B on the previous page). Mark the locations of the biscuits 6 inches apart. Then rest the base of the biscuit joiner on the side piece and cut the grooves in the shelf, as in the photo.

After you have cut these grooves, flip the joiner to the upright position shown in Photo C, with its base against the end of the shelf. Cut the grooves in the side. Finally, finish-sand the pieces, insert glue into the grooves, position the biscuits, assemble, and clamp the joint.

When you clamp together a wide joint, it's important to apply pressure to the center of the joint as well as the ends. Do this by inserting a scrap-wood "caul" or spacer block between the clamps and sliding in a thin shim under it, in the middle of the joint. As you tighten the clamp, the joint will be pulled up evenly both in the middle and at the ends (Photo 1). Choose a "caul" stiff enough to be firm but flexible enough to make contact with the cabinet sides when you tighten the clamps. For further information on clamps, see the box on page 81.

Joining the Sides, Shelves, and Supports

Lay out and drill the shelf-support pin holes in the sides and the record-divider holes in the bottom shelf. The diameter of the support-pin holes will depend on the particular type of supports you select. (See page 21 for information on the four main types of support pins available.) Space the record-divider holes to accommodate the single or multiple-record albums in your collection. Drill 5/16-inch holes in the top supports for the No. 10 x 1-1/4 inch screws that you'll use to attach the top.

Now lay out and cut the three sets of hinge mortises on the inside edges of the face stiles (F). Either start your cuts with a router and square the round corners with a chisel or cut the mortises entirely with a chisel and mallet.

Assembling the Face Frame and Doors

Glue, biscuit-join, and clamp together the face stiles and rails (F, H, K, and N) and the door-frame pieces (J and M). To cut circuit grooves in narrow pieces like door rails, improvise a simple scrap-wood jig like that shown in Photo 2. Make sure to offset the centers of the biscuits as shown in Details 1 and 2 on page 77.

Start by joining the drawer divider stile (N) to the face rails (K), then complete the assembly. Notice that the rails are narrower than the biscuits. After the glue has dried, trim off the exposed ends of the biscuits (see Details 1 and 2). The drawer fronts will cover these cuts.

Next, use a table saw to cut the rabbets on the inside edges of the door rails (M);

see the Door Section Detail (page 76). Cut these rabbets deep enough so the biscuits will be completely concealed behind the tin panels. After you assemble the door frames, cut the rabbets on the inside edges of the stiles.

Now glue, biscuit-join, and clamp together the door stiles and rails (J and M). It's essential to build the doors completely flat. To do this, assemble them on a perfectly flat work table and use identical clamps. Set thin pieces of wood the same size under each door to hold them up slightly off the clamps (Photo 3). This will avoid making the black marks that can occur when pipes react with glue. Push the door down hard onto the clamp bars. If the clamps are in fact resting flat on the table, the door will be flat as well.

Once the glue is dry, use a router and a 3/8-inch rabbet bit to cut the rabbets in the door stiles. Then square up the corners of the panel openings with a sharp chisel.

Lay out and cut the biscuit grooves to join the face frame to the sides (B) and front top support (G). Again, try spacing the grooves about 6 inches apart for best results. Then apply glue, insert the biscuits, and clamp the face frame in place. Apply a small amount of glue to the lower front edge of the bottom shelf (C), then clamp it to the face frame.

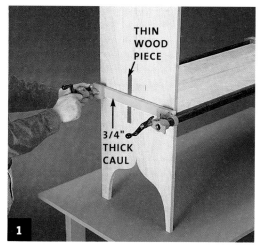

THIN WOOD PIECE

3/4" THICK CAUL

1

Apply pressure to the center of a wide joint as well as the ends. Insert a scrap-wood "caul" between the clamps. Slide a shim under it mid-joint.

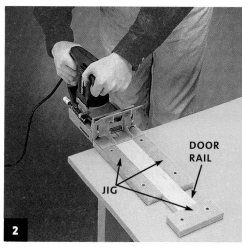

DOOR RAIL

JIG

2

To cut biscuit grooves in narrow pieces like door rails, screw a temporary scrap-wood jig to a utility surface to hold the piece securely while you work.

DOOR FRAME

FLAT ASSEMBLY TABLE

THIN STRIPS OF WOOD

3

Assemble the doors on a perfectly flat surface. Use the same kind and size clamps. Set identical pieces of wood under each door. Push the doors down hard onto the clamps.

Woodworking Clamps

The following clamps are some of the most useful in the sort of cabinetmaking done for all the projects in this book, and you'll find them equally helpful for household repairs.

Light-duty bar clamps are among the most useful for the home shop. The adjustable part of the clamp can be positioned anywhere along the bar. The real pressure is applied with the screw portion.

SPACERS

Pipe clamps can be as long or as short as the pipe the two clamps are secured to. Place pipe clamps on alternate sides of the work-piece to prevent bowing. Use spacer blocks for even pressure.

Hand screws have wide wooden jaws that apply even pressure without marring. They are ideal for holding cabinets together during installation.

Strap or band clamps are ideal for gluing up odd-shaped objects, as here, or large pieces. A small wrench turns a nut to tighten the clamp.

Complete the Cabinet

Refer to the Drawer Detail (page 76), the photos below, and the Drawer and Runner Construction box (opposite) as you assemble and mount the drawers.

Assembling and Mounting the Drawers

Cut the dado and rabbet grooves in the drawer fronts (D) and sides (W). Finish-sand the insides of the drawer pieces, then glue and nail them together with 1-inch brads. Don't install the drawer bottoms (BB) yet, however. Drill pilot holes for the brads to make them easier to drive and to avoid splitting the wood.

There are many different ways to mount drawers, but the system used for this stereo cabinet is one of the simplest and most reliable. As can be seen in the Front View (facing page) and Photo 4, the lower drawer runners capture the sides of the drawers to eliminate their sideways movement, and the upper drawer runners (L) stop the drawers from tipping down when they're pulled out. All the runners are easy to shim or trim for perfect alignment.

Begin by gluing and clamping the drawer-runner cleats (R and S) in place. Drill pilot holes in the drawer runners (L and P) for 1-1/4 inch drywall screws. Glue and clamp together the drawer runners (P and V). Then align and screw the drawer runners in place, using the assembled drawers as guides (Photo 4).

Mounting and Fitting the Parts

Before you attach the doors, cut the wire access notches on the backs of the three adjustable shelves. A slot about 1 inch wide by 12 inches or so long should do it. Then trim the lengths and widths of the shelves for the best fit (Photo 5).

Trim the doors so they fit tightly in the face-frame opening, without gaps. Lay out and cut the hinge mortises on the outside edges of the door frames.

Remove the hinge pins and separate the hinge leaves. Then screw the hinge leaves to the cabinet and the doors. Mount the doors and reinsert the hinge pins. Mark where to trim the edges of the doors, separate the hinge leaves again, and trim the doors to fit.

Cut out the door latch (Y), as in the Door Latch Detail (page 77), and mount it and the doorstop (Q). Lay out and drill the knob screw holes in the drawers and doors. Make as many evenly spaced 1-1/2 inch ventilation holes in the back (AA) as are called for by the equipment that needs to be cooled.

COMPLETE THE CABINET

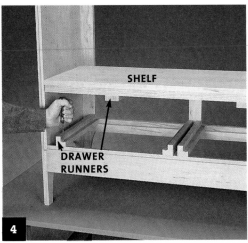

4

The lower drawer runners shown here eliminate sideways movement, and the upper runners keep open drawers from tipping down. These runners are easy to trim and shim for perfect alignment.

5

Cut notches about 1 in. deep x 12 in. long in the backs of the adjustable shelves to simplify the task of routing and connecting the stereo system's cables, power cords, and speaker wires.

Making Moldings and Applying the Finish

Now make the moldings (T and U) and the tin-panel stops (Z). You can buy moldings made of pine, oak, birch, and maybe even mahogany, but if you want moldings made of cherry, you've got to cut them yourself. To make the quarter-round moldings to go around the top of this stereo cabinet, cut a 4-inch wide piece of cherry and round-over the edges with a 3/4-inch piloted round-over bit in your router. Then cut the mold-ing pieces off the edges with a table saw. To make the 3/8-inch tin panel stops, rout the edges of 4/4 cherry with a 3/8-inch round-over bit. Then run the piece through the table saw, first flat and then on edge to create these smaller moldings.

Finish-sand all the pieces now, and slightly round-over all exposed sharp edges. Then apply three coats of Danish oil. To age the hinges a bit so they match the tin panels, submerge them in vinegar overnight, then rinse them off with water and dry them with a hair dryer. Once the finishing is complete, you can assemble the cabinet and install your stereo.

Drawer and Runner Construction

To construct the runners in the drawers, first glue and clamp runner cleats R and S in place. Use light-duty bar clamps like those shown in the box on page 81.

Next, drill pilot holes in drawer runners L and P to take 1-1/4 in. drywall screws. Glue and clamp together runners P and V now. Finally, align the drawer runners and screw them into position with the drawers as guides.

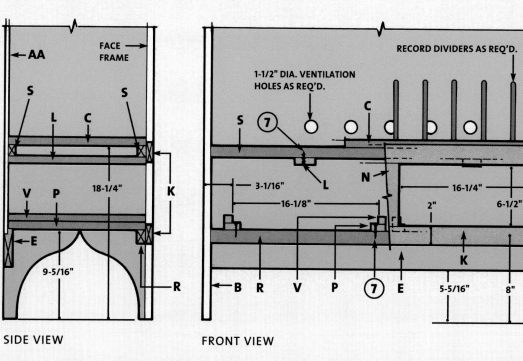

SIDE VIEW

FRONT VIEW

High-Tech Entertainment Center

Accommodate components of many sizes with this mobile media center. You can move or add shelves to fit your equipment.

Cut the Pieces

First cut the large parts to size with a circular saw, or save time by having your lumberyard cut them to size for you. Order the glass or Plexiglas cut to size. The only power tools you'll need besides a circular saw are an electric drill with 1-inch and 15/16-inch hole saws and, optionally, a router with a 3/8-inch round-over bit.

Cut four 18-1/2 inch x 47-1/4 inch uprights from 3/4-inch birch-veneer plywood. Then cut the following pieces from 3/4-inch x 3-inch solid birch:

▶ Four 3-inch x 47-1/4-inch front and back edge pieces.
▶ Two 3 inch x 20-inch tops.

Last, cut these pieces from stock 2x2 fir:

▶ Four 44-1/4 inch front and back inner spacers.
▶ Four 18-1/2 inch top and bottom inner spacers.

Assemble the Parts

▶ Align two 3/4-inch plywood upright panels flat on top of each other. Mark them as shown in the plans at right. Then drill the six 15/16-inch diameter holes through the first upright. Allow the hole saw's drill bit to protrude into the second upright about 1/8 inch to make starter holes.

▶ Now remove the top upright and drill six 1-inch diameter holes through the bottom upright, using the starter holes you just made as guides.

▶ Glue and nail one top and one bottom 2x2 inner spacer to a side of the remaining two 3/4-inch plywood uprights, making it flush with the edges. Use 4d finish nails.

▶ Temporarily nail the two pairs of uprights together top and bottom with rod halves through the holes. Slide the rods together, then stand the assembly on a flat surface and square it up. Adjust the

You can adjust this contemporary-style unit to suit your space and equipment. Telescoping closet rods provide flexible shelf support.

rods so the end bracket of each one presses against the surface of the outside plywood panel. Mark the location of each bracket.

▶ Disassemble the uprights, then drill pilot holes for the six rods on the outside upright panels. Attach the rods with the mounting screws provided.

▶ Glue and nail the last two inner spacers flush to the outside front and back edges.

▶ Fit the uprights together with the rods through their holes. Glue and nail each assembly together, using 4d finish nails.

▶ Now glue and nail the 3/4-inch hardwood front and back edges and tops to the assembly with 6d finish nails. Predrill pilot holes for the nails in the hardwood pieces. Countersink and fill the nail holes and any gaps with a matching wood filler.

▶ Sand the hardwood edges flush with the veneered plywood surfaces and round-over all eight vertical edges of the uprights. Use sandpaper or a 3/8-inch round-over bit.

▶ Set the width of the telescoping rods, drill a 1/8-inch hole in each, and secure with short No. 4 sheet-metal setscrews.

▶ Mount the four casters to the base, following their manufacturer's instructions.

▶ Mask the rods and casters. Spray the uprights with two coats of satin-black paint and a clear satin top coat. Of course, you can also apply your own finish.

▶ Apply adhesive sponge-rubber tape to the top surface of each rod. Set in place the glass or Plexiglas shelves ordered previously and your new media center is done.

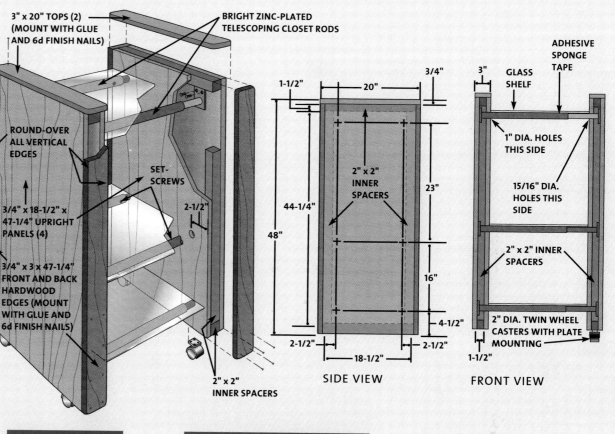

3" x 20" TOPS (2) (MOUNT WITH GLUE AND 6d FINISH NAILS)

BRIGHT ZINC-PLATED TELESCOPING CLOSET RODS

ROUND-OVER ALL VERTICAL EDGES

SET-SCREWS

3/4" x 18-1/2" x 47-1/4" UPRIGHT PANELS (4)

3/4" x 3 x 47-1/4" FRONT AND BACK HARDWOOD EDGES (MOUNT WITH GLUE AND 6d FINISH NAILS)

2" x 2" INNER SPACERS

2-1/2"

ADHESIVE SPONGE TAPE

GLASS SHELF

3"

3/4"

1-1/2"   20"

2" x 2" INNER SPACERS

44-1/4"

48"

23"

16"

4-1/2"

2-1/2"   2-1/2"

18-1/2"

SIDE VIEW

1" DIA. HOLES THIS SIDE

15/16" DIA. HOLES THIS SIDE

2" x 2" INNER SPACERS

2" DIA. TWIN WHEEL CASTERS WITH PLATE MOUNTING

1-1/2"

FRONT VIEW

TOOLS

HAND TOOLS
Hammer
Nail set
Sandpaper
Screwdriver

POWER TOOLS
Circular saw
Drill; 1-in. and 15/16-in. hole saws

OPTIONAL
Router; 3/8-in. round-over bit

MATERIALS

Qty.	Size and Description	Qty.	Size and Description
1 sheet	3/4" x 4' x 8' birch-veneer plywood	3	Plate-glass or Plexiglas shelves 1/4" x 18-1/2" x desired length, with finished edges
3 pieces	2x2, 8' long		4d finish nails
4 strips	Birch hardwood, 3/4" x 3" x 47-1/4"		6d finish nails
2 strips	Birch hardwood, 3/4" x 3" x 20"		Clear satin finish
			Masking tape
6	18–30" or 44–72" telescoping adjustable closet rods, 1" dia. and 15/16" dia.		No. 4 sheet-metal screws
			Sandpaper
			Satin-black paint
	Adhesive sponge-rubber weather-stripping tape 1/4" x 3/8"		Wood putty
			Woodworker's glue
4	Twin-wheel casters, 2" dia., medium weight, plate fastener		

Easy Oak Office Set

Organize your home office with this sleek, matching phone desk and shelf system that are each practical and simple to make.

These sturdy furniture shelves are great for housing books, binders, and supplies in the office, but they're good-looking enough to suit any room in your house.

Be forewarned: Once you build this phone desk for your office and discover all the things it can keep handy—but out of sight—you'll want one for *every* room in the house.

Phone Desk

This attractive desk will keep your telephone and fax machine, as well as notepads and pencils, neat and close at hand. Build it from standard-size oak boards to keep cutting to a minimum.

For the back, use a length of 1x12, (which measures 3/4 inch x 11-1/4 inches), cut to 22 1/2 inches long. For the lid, use the same width stock, but cut it to 24 inches. For the other parts use 1x10's (3/4 inch x 9-1/4 inches). Make the top 24 inches long to run flush with the sides. Cut down 1x10's for the shelf to the dimensions shown at right.

All the joints are butted together, then glued and secured with No. 6 x 1-3/4 inch drywall screws. Measure the diagonal dimensions to make sure the case is exactly square before screwing the top, bottom, and sides together.

Countersink the screwheads about 1/4 inch, glue in oak wood plugs, then trim and sand the plugs smooth. Rout grooved finger pulls in the near outside lid edges.

After assembling the desk, sand all its surfaces smooth with 80-grit sandpaper, rounding the edges and corners slightly; then sand once more with finer sandpaper. Finish the piece with clear polyurethane or a wipe-on oil finish. Attach a brass piano hinge for the lid and brass sliding lid supports to hold the lid flat when open.

Mount the desk to the wall with screws driven into studs. The open desk surface should be 27 to 30 inches above the floor. Now you're ready for your first call.

TOOLS

HAND TOOLS

Plane

Screwdriver

Tape measure

POWER TOOLS

Circular saw

Electric drill; combination bit

Router; cove bit

MATERIALS

Brass lid support

Brass piano hinge

Magnetic catch

No. 6 x 1-3/4"drywall screws

Oak 1x10's and 1x12's

3/8" diameter oak wood plugs

Polyurethane or oil finish

Woodworker's glue

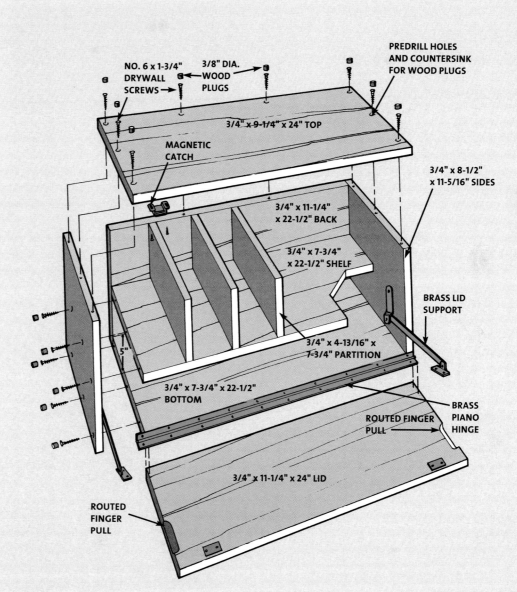

NO. 6 x 1-3/4" DRYWALL SCREWS

3/8" DIA. WOOD PLUGS

PREDRILL HOLES AND COUNTERSINK FOR WOOD PLUGS

3/4" x 9-1/4" x 24" TOP

MAGNETIC CATCH

3/4" x 8-1/2" x 11-5/16" SIDES

3/4" x 11-1/4" x 22-1/2" BACK

3/4" x 7-3/4" x 22-1/2" SHELF

3/4" x 4-13/16" x 7-3/4" PARTITION

BRASS LID SUPPORT

3/4" x 7-3/4" x 22-1/2" BOTTOM

5"

ROUTED FINGER PULL

BRASS PIANO HINGE

3/4" x 11-1/4" x 24" LID

ROUTED FINGER PULL

Furniture Shelves

Nailing Tip

If you nail into the dark part of a wood's grain, the putty you use to fill the holes will be a little less visible.

This oak shelf unit can be built two ways; its shelves can be glued and screwed in place, as shown in the construction plan at right, or they can be made adjustable using simple plug-in supports (see the Shelf Support Detail, opposite). For further suggestions about how to mount adjustable shelves, see the Shelf Support Techniques box on page 21.

Permanently installed shelves give this unit its sturdiness, but they are not as flexible as adjustable shelves when it comes to your storage needs. If you choose to make the shelves adjustable, you will have to provide structural support by adding top and bottom horizontal 1x4 rail fillers and cleats that hold the fillers in place (see the Rail and Cleat Detail, opposite).

In either case, the 1x3 and 1x4 legs for this system are glued together in the L-shaped configurations shown in the construction plan at right. Clamp the two sections for each leg together while the glue dries. The only place nailheads will need to be covered is where you will tack the top and bottom shelves into position.

After you have cut and assembled all the parts, sand the piece smooth and slightly round its corners and edges. Then apply a medium oak stain and an oil finish. Finally, drill holes for the shelf clips, spacing them about 2 inches apart. One way to do this evenly is to clamp a strip of pegboard along the piece and use its holes as a template.

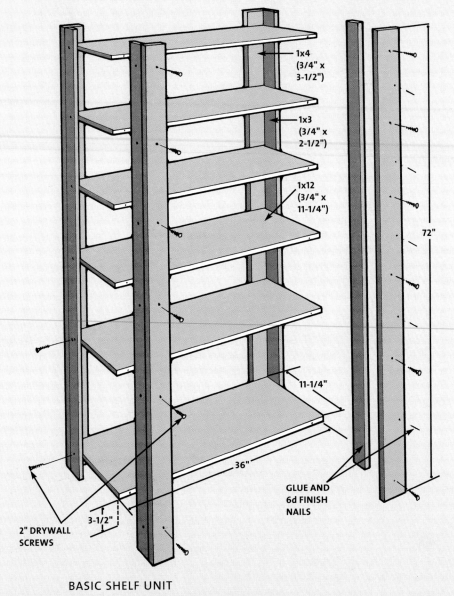

1x4
(3/4" x 3-1/2")

1x3
(3/4" x 2-1/2")

1x12
(3/4" x 11-1/4")

72"

11-1/4"

36"

3-1/2"

2" DRYWALL SCREWS

GLUE AND 6d FINISH NAILS

BASIC SHELF UNIT

(For permanently installed shelves only. See details, opposite, for adjustable shelves.)

Note:
Top shelf (right; not shown) adds rigidity to unit. Attach it to 1x4 support cleats with 1-1/4" drywall screws.

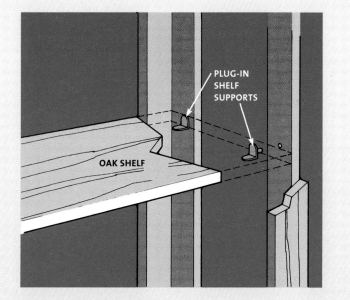

PLUG-IN SHELF SUPPORTS

OAK SHELF

SHELF SUPPORT DETAIL

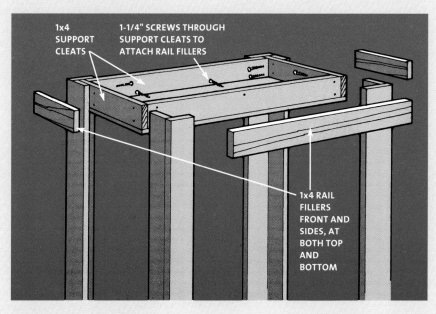

1x4 SUPPORT CLEATS

1-1/4" SCREWS THROUGH SUPPORT CLEATS TO ATTACH RAIL FILLERS

1x4 RAIL FILLERS FRONT AND SIDES, AT BOTH TOP AND BOTTOM

RAIL AND CLEAT DETAIL

Computer
Workstation

Make the most of your workspace with this eye-catching, well-designed computer desk and printer stand.

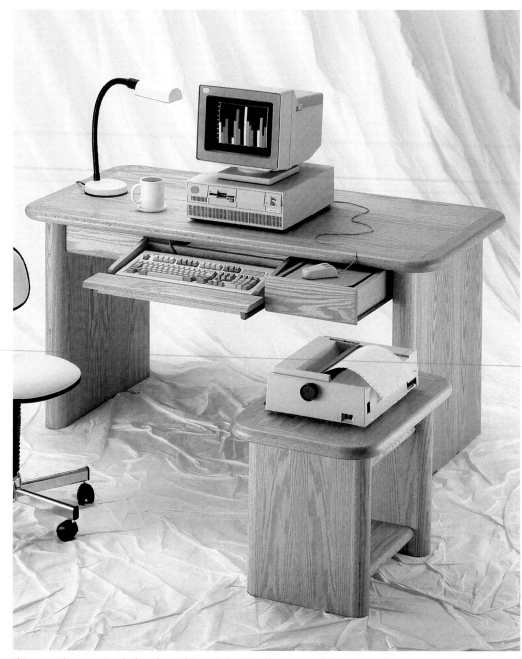

This versatile computer desk and matching printer stand have everything you need in a contemporary home office: a sliding keyboard drawer, a sliding mouse pad, plenty of storage for disks and paper, and a clever way to manage all the wires.

The first thing you may have noticed about this attractive desk is its stylishly large bullnose edges that are just like the ones found on high-end commercial office furniture. In factories these edges are made with elaborate machines, but you can achieve the same effect in your home shop with your table saw, a fine-tooth rasp, and an orbital sander.

To make the desk even easier to build—and easier to maneuver through doorways—it's been designed with knockdown hardware called keyhole fittings. These fixtures are not only strong and inexpensive but easy to install.

Before you start this project, measure your computer equipment to be sure it will fit well on the desk and printer stand, then alter the plans as necessary. The mouse-pad drawer and disk drawer are the same size, so you can swap them from one side to the other for a left-handed person.

Attention to detail pays off even if you don't notice it immediately. Here the drawer faces have been cut from the same piece of wood so that the grain continues from left to right across the front desk.

Depending on whether or not you expect to move these pieces around the room, you might want to consider adding 2-inch diameter metal coasters under the outer corners of each unit.

MATERIALS

Computer Desk

Qty.	Size and Description
2 sheets	3/4" x 48" x 96" oak plywood
1 sheet	1/4" x 24" x 24" oak plywood
20 board ft.	8/4 oak
20 board ft.	4/4 oak
3 pairs	20" drawer runners*
1	1-1/2" x 36" brass piano hinge*
4	Keyhole fittings, single-slot**
1	3" wire grommet*
1	48"-long J-shaped wire manager
4	No. 10 x 1" pan-head screws with washers
32	No. 6 x 2" drywall screws
48	No. 6 x 1-1/4" drywall screws
4	No. 6 x 1" drywall screws
4	No. 6 x 1/2" pan-head screws
1 qt.	Danish oil finish
	Sandpaper
	Woodworker's glue

*Available from The Woodworkers' Store, Dept. TFH, 4365 Willow Dr., Medina, MN 55340; (800) 279-4441. In Canada, available from Lee Valley Tools Ltd., 1080 Morrison Drive, Ottawa, ONT K2H 8K7; (800) 267-8767

**Available from Doug Mockett & Co., Inc., Dept, TFH, Box 3333, Manhattan Beach, CA 90266; (800) 523-1269.

Printer Stand

Qty.	Size and Description
Desk leftovers	3/4" x 48" x 96" oak plywood
15 board ft.	8/4 oak
2 board ft.	4/4 oak
8	Keyhole fittings, single-slot*
1	12" paper-slot grommet**
8	No. 6 x 2" drywall screws
12	No. 6 x 1-1/4" drywall screws
8	No. 6 x 1" drywall screws

Construction Plan

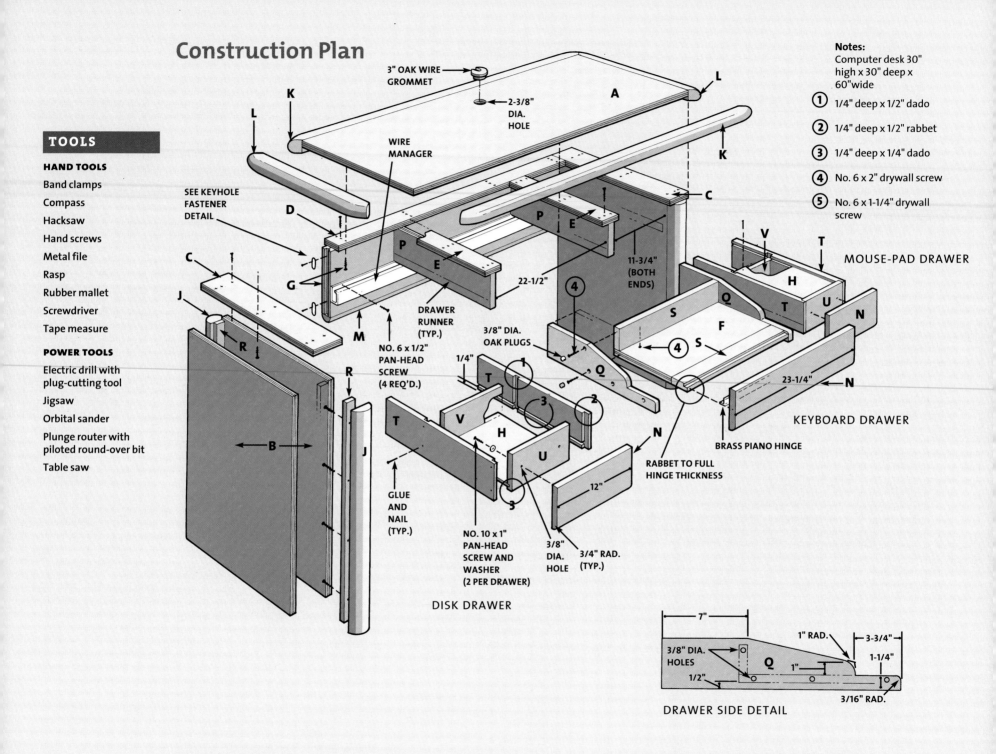

3" OAK WIRE GROMMET

2-3/8" DIA. HOLE

K

L

L

A

K

C

Notes:
Computer desk 30" high x 30" deep x 60"wide

1. 1/4" deep x 1/2" dado
2. 1/4" deep x 1/2" rabbet
3. 1/4" deep x 1/4" dado
4. No. 6 x 2" drywall screw
5. No. 6 x 1-1/4" drywall screw

WIRE MANAGER

D

SEE KEYHOLE FASTENER DETAIL

P

E

P

E

C

11-3/4" (BOTH ENDS)

22-1/2"

V

T

MOUSE-PAD DRAWER

H

G

E

C

R

J

M

DRAWER RUNNER (TYP.)

NO. 6 x 1/2" PAN-HEAD SCREW (4 REQ'D.)

3/8" DIA. OAK PLUGS

4

Q

S

S

F

S

4

Q

U

N

H

T

U

N

23-1/4"

N

KEYBOARD DRAWER

B

R

J

1/4"

T

1

3

2

Q

N

BRASS PIANO HINGE

T

V

H

U

N

3

12"

RABBET TO FULL HINGE THICKNESS

GLUE AND NAIL (TYP.)

NO. 10 x 1" PAN-HEAD SCREW AND WASHER (2 PER DRAWER)

3/8" DIA. HOLE

3/4" RAD. (TYP.)

DISK DRAWER

7"

1" RAD.

3-3/4"

3/8" DIA. HOLES

Q

1"

1-1/4"

1/2"

3/16" RAD.

DRAWER SIDE DETAIL

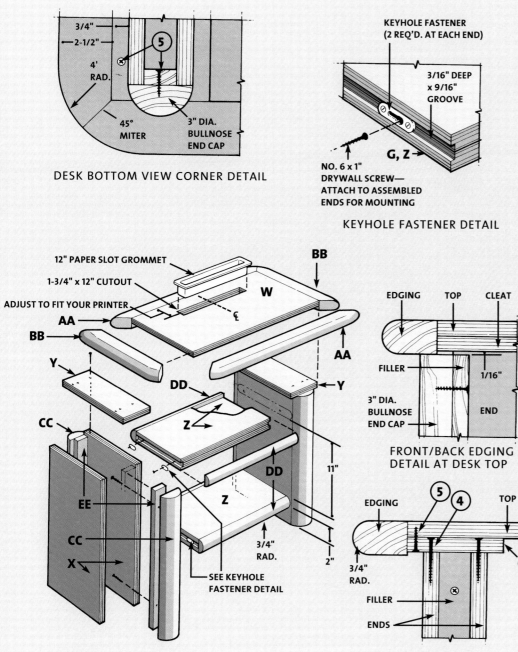

DESK BOTTOM VIEW CORNER DETAIL

3/4"
2-1/2"
4' RAD.
⑤
45° MITER
3" DIA. BULLNOSE END CAP

KEYHOLE FASTENER (2 REQ'D. AT EACH END)

3/16" DEEP x 9/16" GROOVE

G, Z

NO. 6 x 1" DRYWALL SCREW— ATTACH TO ASSEMBLED ENDS FOR MOUNTING

KEYHOLE FASTENER DETAIL

12" PAPER SLOT GROMMET
1-3/4" x 12" CUTOUT
ADJUST TO FIT YOUR PRINTER
AA
BB
BB
W
AA
Y
Y
DD
Z
CC
Z
DD
EE
CC
X
11"
3/4" RAD.
2"
SEE KEYHOLE FASTENER DETAIL

Note:
Printer stand 20" deep x 20" high x 28" wide.

FRONT/BACK EDGING DETAIL AT DESK TOP

EDGING TOP CLEAT
FILLER
1/16"
END
3" DIA. BULLNOSE END CAP

END EDGING DETAIL AT DESK TOP

EDGING ⑤ ④ TOP
3/4" RAD.
CLEAT
FILLER
ENDS

CUTTING LISTS

Computer Desk

Key	Qty.	Size and Description
A	1	3/4" x 25" x 55" oak plywood (top)
B	4	3/4" x 23-1/2" x 28-9/16" oak plywood (ends)
C	2	3/4" x 4-1/2" x 25" oak plywood (end cleats)
D	1	3/4" x 3" x 46" oak plywood (panel cleat)
E	2	3/4" x 3" x 20-1/2" oak plywood (support cleats)
F	1	3/4" x 11" x 20" oak plywood (keyboard drawer bottom)
G	2	3/4" x 10-1/4" x 47-1/2" oak plywood (panel)
H	2	1/4" x 13" x 10-1/4" oak plywood (drawer bottoms)
J	4	1-1/2" x 3" x 28-1/2" oak (end caps)
K	2	1-1/2" x 2-1/2" x 61" oak (top edging)
L	2	1-1/2" x 2-1/2" x 31" oak (top edging)
M	1	3/4" x 1-1/2" x 47-1/2" oak (panel edge)
N	1	3/4" x 4-3/4" x 49" oak (drawer faces)
P	2	3/4" x 5" x 21-1/4" oak (drawer supports)
Q	2	3/4" x 4-1/4" x 19-3/4" oak (keyboard drawer sides)
R	4	3/4" x 1-1/2" x 28-1/2" oak (end fillers)
S	2	3/4" x 2-1/2" x 20" oak (keyboard drawer front, back)
T	4	1/2" x 4-1/4" x 19-3/4" oak (drawer sides)
U	2	1/2" x 4-1/4" x 10-1/4" oak (drawer fronts)
V	2	1/2" x 3-3/4" x 10-1/4" oak (drawer backs)

Printer Stand

Key	Qty.	Size and Description
W	1	3/4" x 15" x 23" oak plywood (top)
X	4	3/4" x 13-1/2" x 18-9/16" oak plywood (ends)
Y	2	3/4" x 4-1/2" x 15" oak plywood (end cleats)
Z	4	3/4" x 12" x 15-1/2" oak plywood (shelves)
AA	2	1-1/2" x 2-1/2" x 29" oak (top edging)
BB	2	1-1/2" x 2-1/2" x 21" oak (top edging)
CC	4	1-1/2" x 3" x 18-1/2" oak (end caps)
DD	4	3/4" x 1-1/2" x 15-1/2" oak (shelf edging)
EE	4	3/4" x 1-1/2" x 18-1/2" oak (end fillers)

Make the End Pieces

If you plan carefully, you'll be able to cut all the plywood pieces for the desk and printer stand from two 4 x 8-foot sheets. It will help if you draw your cutting diagrams on paper first, not just to maximize the number of pieces you can cut from each sheet but also to make sure the grain runs in the correct direction on each piece. As you work up your sketch, refer to the Construction Plan on the previous two pages. Try working out the cuts so that you rip one sheet of plywood to 25 inches wide for top pieces A and W, then crosscut the second sheet 58 inches long for the four end (B) pieces.

Cutting the Pieces to Size

When you've determined where you want to make the cuts, saw out pieces A, B, and W to the dimensions in the Cutting Lists on page 93 or to your own specifications.

Cut panel and shelf pieces G and Z slightly oversize, then glue them together and cut them to their finished dimensions. Next, trim the remaining plywood pieces C, D, E, and F, X and Y, and the 1/4-inch thick drawer bottoms (H) to their finished dimensions.

Now cut the solid-oak desk pieces J through V and printer-stand pieces AA through EE to size. Make one extra end cap (CC) as a test piece for shaping the bullnose edge.

Rough-sawing the End Caps

Shape the 3-inch diameter bullnose end caps (J and CC) by first cutting away most of the waste with a table saw (Photo 1). After that, attach the caps to the end panels and finish contouring the pieces with a fine-tooth rasp and an orbital sander, as described on the next page.

Begin shaping the end caps by drawing a 3-inch diameter half-circle on both ends of your test piece (CC). Use this guide to align the saw blade before making the final cuts. Following the steps shown in the Cutting End Caps box (below left), cut away the waste from the end caps.

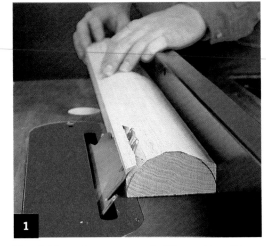

Use a table saw to remove most of the waste on the bullnose end caps. The saw's guard has been removed in this photo for clarity; always use your own guard.

Cutting End Caps

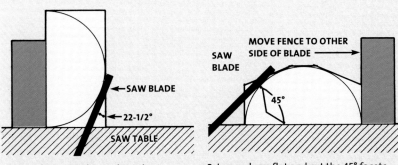

1. Lay end cap on edge and cut the 22-1/2° facets.

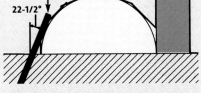

2. Lay end cap flat and cut the 45° facets.

3. Lay end cap flat and cut the remaining 22-1/2° facets.

Assemble the End Panels

Screw the end fillers (R and EE) to the end caps (J and CC) to create the equal-sized rabbets for the plywood ends (B and X) that are shown in the Construction Plan on pages 92–93. After you've determined that the end fillers are centered on the inside faces of the end caps, attach them with No. 6 x 1-1/4 inch drywall screws.

The end caps (J and CC) are intentionally cut 1/16 inch shorter than the plywood ends, to compensate for the plywood tops being thinner than 3/4 inch. This ensures that when the assembled ends are screwed to the undersides of the tops, the end caps won't bind against the top edgings (K and AA), which are thicker than the plywood.

Assemble the ends so the plywood end pieces (B and X) are flush with the bottoms of the end caps and extend above the tops of those caps by 1/16 inch. Glue and clamp the plywood end pieces to their end caps and end fillers (Photo 2).

Complete the rough shaping of the end caps on the assembled ends with a fine-tooth rasp (Photo 3). Finish shaping the end caps with an orbital sander. Start with coarse-grit paper and move through progressively finer grits (Photo 4).

ASSEMBLE THE END PANELS

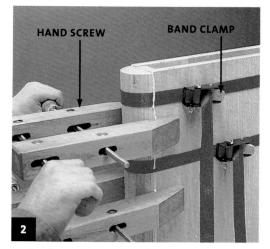

Use hand screws to compress the plywood end pieces firmly as you pull up the end cap tight using band clamps as shown.

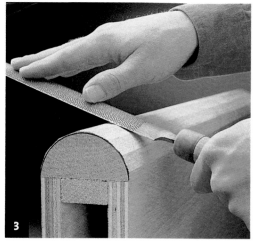

Rough-shape the end caps with a fine-tooth rasp. This will quickly remove the high points remaining from the table-saw cuts.

Finish-shape the end caps with an orbital sander. Start with coarse-grit sandpaper and move through successively finer grades of paper.

Assemble the Desk and Printer Stand

Begin making the units' shelves by gluing the panel edge (M) to the panel (G) and the shelf edgings (DD) to the shelves (Z). Sand the overhanging edging sides flush with the faces of the plywood. Rout the bullnose profiles on the panel and shelf edgings with a piloted round-over bit.

Next, rout the grooves for the keyhole hardware in the ends of the panel and shelves (Photo 5). Then align and screw the keyhole fittings into their grooves. If you've never used this type of fitting, make a test setup to see how they work.

Assembling the Tops

Drill the hole for the 3-inch oak wire grommet in the desk top (A). If your printer uses fan-fold, tractor-feed paper rather than single sheets, cut the hole for the paper-slot grommet in the printer-stand top (W). Then miter and fit top side edging pieces K and AA to their own tops, and glue and clamp them in place one at a time (Photo 6).

Miter and fit the remaining edging pieces (L and BB), then glue and clamp them in place (Photos 7 and 8). Cut the 4-inch radius top corners (see the Desk Bottom View Corner Detail on page 93), then rout the bullnoses on the edging.

5

GROOVE

EDGE GUIDE

Rout the grooves for the keyhole fittings using a plunge router with an edge guide. Be careful not to cut into the solid-wood edgings.

6

Glue and clamp one edging piece at a time. This gives you time to align each one flush with the plywood before the glue sets.

7

Cut the last edging piece a little bit long so you can trim it to fit snugly between the mitered ends of the other two edging pieces.

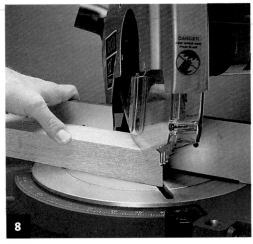

8

Trim the last piece by nibbling away at it with a saw or sanding it to fit. Glue it on, let the glue dry, then round all four corners.

Completing the Units

Lay out and install the end-panel screws that fit into the keyhole hardware. Using a rubber mallet, lightly tap the panel onto the desk ends and the shelves to the printer-stand ends. (Later, when you disassemble the units for the individual pieces' final sanding and finishing, you can separate the panels simply by tapping them out in the other direction.) Tighten or loosen the screws slightly to adjust the tension of the joints uniformly. Locate and drill pilot holes in all the cleats (C, D, E, and Y). Screw the end cleats (C and Y) to the ends and the panel cleat (D) to the panel, then attach the cleats to the undersides of the tops.

Screw the support cleats (E) to the drawer runners (P), and then align and screw the support cleats to the underside of the desk top.

Make the Drawers

Build the keyboard drawer first, by gluing the keyboard-drawer front (S) to the front edge of the keyboard-drawer bottom (F). On the drawer front, cut a rabbet the full depth of the piano hinge. Drill 3/8-inch plug and screw holes in the keyboard drawer sides (Q), then cut the shapes of the keyboard-drawer sides (see the Drawer Side Detail in the Construction Plans, page 92). Finish-sand the drawer components, glue and screw them together, then cut and insert the plugs.

To make the mouse-pad and disk drawers, cut the rabbets and dadoes in the drawer sides and fronts (T and U). Drill 3/8-inch holes in the drawer fronts for the screws to attach the drawer faces (N).

Finish-sand the drawer pieces (T, U, V, and H), then assemble the drawers.

Screw the drawer runners to the drawers, desk ends, and drawer supports, using the slotted adjustment holes first. Set the drawers in their runners, check for a good fit, and make any necessary adjustments.

Cut the drawer faces (N) from one long piece of wood so that the grain in the drawer fronts will be continuous when you close the drawers.

Rout the 3/4-inch radius round-over profiles on the bottom edges of the face pieces (N), as shown in Photo 9. Then cut the drawer faces to length. Align and screw the faces of the mouse-pad and disk drawers to their drawer fronts. Cut the piano hinge to length, then file the sawed ends smooth. Align and screw the hinge to the keyboard drawer front and face.

9
DRAWER FRONT
STRAIGHTEDGE

Clamp a straight-edged board flush with the bottom edge of the drawer face piece to guide the ball-bearing pilot of the router bit.

Apply the Finish

For a professional finish, disassemble the two units. Finish-sand all their components, and slightly round any sharp edges. Apply the finish of your choice. The desk and stand shown in this project received three coats of Danish oil, with sandings between coats with 600-grit wet-or-dry carbide paper lubricated with a little Danish oil.

When the finishing work is complete, reassemble the desk and printer stand. Glue the paper-slot grommet in place. Cut the plastic wire manager to length, screw it to the inside of the panel, and you are ready to "plug and play" with your computer in its new home.

Bedroom & Closet

Maximize space in cluttered bedrooms and cramped closets—or just update your surroundings—with any of these versatile units.

Traditional Wardrobe

Expand your storage capacity with this handsome piece. It has plenty of hanging room and spacious shelves.

Neat Bedroom Storage Options

Organize and store bedroom clutter with one of these good-looking, versatile projects.

108

Streamlined Closets

Organize chaotic closets with this simple system. A combination of clothes rods, shelves, and drawers puts everything at your fingertips.

116

Closet-Door Shelving

Make use of all the space in your walk-in closet with this shelving for clothes and accessories.

124

Traditional Wardrobe

Expand your storage capacity
with this handsome piece.
It has plenty of hanging room
and spacious shelves.

Gracefully arched doors give this roomy Craftsman-style
wardrobe its classic good looks.

Frame-and-Panel Construction

This project is a fairly complex one that requires above-average woodworking skills. The sides and doors of the wardrobe are made using frame-and-panel construction—the frames of solid oak, the panels of 1/4-inch thick oak-veneer plywood. This type of construction demands patience and precise joinery. Take your time, and test your tool setups on scrap wood before you cut the finished pieces.

Frame-and-panel construction rewards your efforts with one distinct advantage. Wood naturally expands and contracts in width whenever the relative humidity changes. This can be a potential problem in cabinetmaking, as it stresses the joints. But because each panel floats freely within its frame, it can grow and shrink with only minimal effect upon the frame joints. The wood panels in this wardrobe are sized to allow space for the panels to expand and shrink as necessary.

Another benefit of frame-and-panel construction is that you can use materials other than solid wood for your panels. The 1/4-inch oak-veneer plywood used here is more stable than many materials.

TOOLS

HAND TOOLS

Carpenter's square

Clamps: one 6-ft. pipe clamp; four 36-in. pipe clamps; four 24-in. bar clamps; six 6-in. bar clamps

Framing square

Hammer

Sawhorses

Screwdrivers

Tape measure

Wood file

POWER TOOLS

Belt sander

Cordless or electric drill; countersink bit and dowel-hole jig

Miter saw

Orbital sander

Router; 1/2-in. deep x 1/8 in. thick three-wing slot-cutting assembly; 1/4-in. round-over bit; 1-in. long x 1/2 in. diameter two-flute straight bit; 1/2-in. cove bit; router edge guide; router pad for small pieces

Saber saw or band saw

Table saw with miter gauge, dado blade

OPTIONAL

Drill press

Jointer

Thickness planer

MATERIALS

Qty.	Size and Description
45 board ft.	4/4 red oak
1 sheet	3/4" x 4' x 8' red oak plywood
2 sheets	1/4" x 4' x 8' red oak plywood
20	No. 6 x 1-5/8" drywall screws
24	No. 6 x 1-1/4" drywall screws
42	No. 8 x 1-1/4" wood screws
36	No. 4 x 3/4" wood screws
25	1" brads
8	3/8" dia. x 2" spiral dowel pins
3 pairs	Polished brass spring overlay hinges
1 pair	1-1/4" dia. oak knobs
1	1-3/8" dia. x 29" closet rod
1 set	Closet rod end holders
1 quart	Danish oil finish
	Sandpaper
	Woodworker's glue

Construction Plan

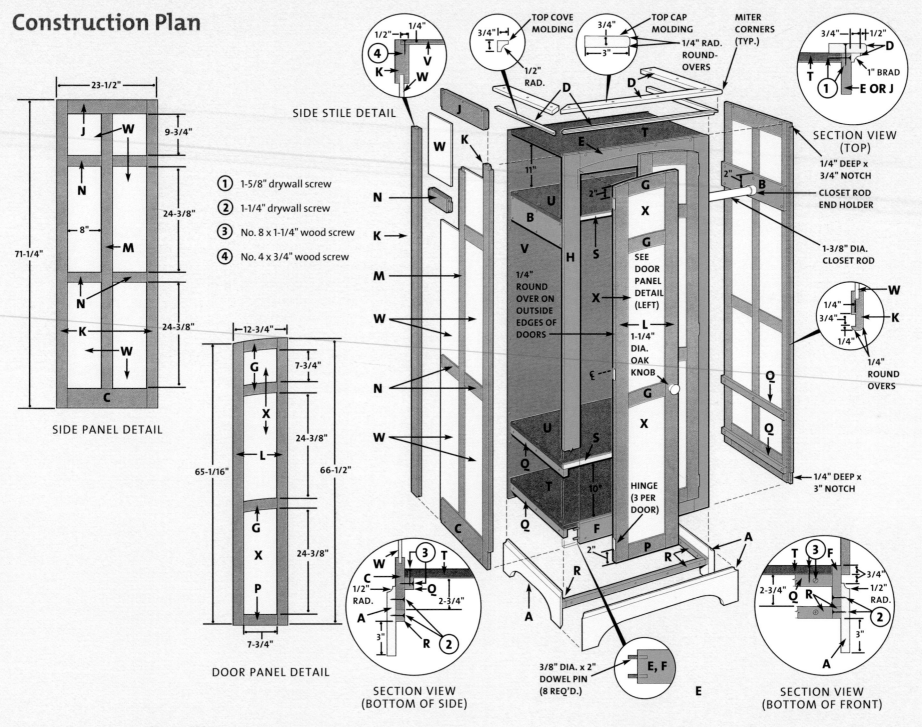

SIDE STILE DETAIL

SIDE PANEL DETAIL

23-1/2"

71-1/4"

9-3/4"

24-3/8"

24-3/8"

J W

N

8"

M

N

K

W

C

① 1-5/8" drywall screw

② 1-1/4" drywall screw

③ No. 8 x 1-1/4" wood screw

④ No. 4 x 3/4" wood screw

DOOR PANEL DETAIL

12-3/4"

65-1/16"

66-1/2"

7-3/4"

24-3/8"

24-3/8"

G

X

L

G

X

P

7-3/4"

1/2" 1/4"

1/4"

④ K V W

11"

N

K

M

W

N

W

C

TOP COVE MOLDING

3/4"

1/2" RAD.

TOP CAP MOLDING

3/4"

3"

1/4" RAD. ROUND-OVERS

MITER CORNERS (TYP.)

D

J

W

K

D

E

U

B

V

H

S

X

X

L

1-1/4" DIA. OAK KNOB

1/4" ROUND OVER ON OUTSIDE EDGES OF DOORS

SEE DOOR PANEL DETAIL (LEFT)

G

X

G

G

S

U

Q

T

10°

Q

F

HINGE (3 PER DOOR)

2"

P

R

A

R

R

A

A

T

D

3/4" 1/2"

T

1" BRAD

① E OR J

SECTION VIEW (TOP)

1/4" DEEP x 3/4" NOTCH

2"

B

CLOSET ROD END HOLDER

1-3/8" DIA. CLOSET ROD

W

1/4"

3/4"

1/4"

K

1/4" ROUND OVERS

Q

Q

1/4" DEEP x 3" NOTCH

3/8" DIA. x 2" DOWEL PIN (8 REQ'D.)

E, F

E

W

③ T

C

1/2" RAD.

A

3"

Q

R ②

2-3/4"

SECTION VIEW (BOTTOM OF SIDE)

T ③ F

2-3/4"

Q R

3/4"

1/2" RAD.

②

3"

A

SECTION VIEW (BOTTOM OF FRONT)

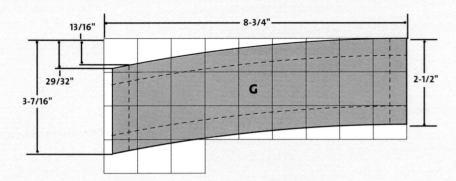

ARCHED DOOR RAIL TEMPLATE DETAIL

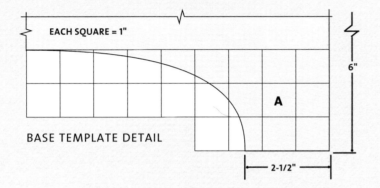

EACH SQUARE = 1"

BASE TEMPLATE DETAIL

CUTTING LIST

Key	Qty.	Size and Description
A	1	3/4" x 6" x 84" oak (base)*
B	2	3/4" x 4-1/2" x 22-1/4" oak (upper shelf supports)
C	2	3/4" x 4-1/2" x 19-1/2" oak (side bottom rails)
D	1	3/4" x 3-7/8" x 90" oak (top molding)*
E	1	3/4" x 3-3/4" x 24-1/2" oak (face top rail)
F	1	3/4" x 3-1/2" x 24-1/2" oak (face bottom rail)
G	6	3/4" x 3-7/16" x 8-3/4" oak (curved door rails)
H	2	3/4" x 3-1/4" x 71-1/4" oak (face stiles)
J	2	3/4" x 3-1/4" x 19-1/2" oak (side top rails)
K	4	3/4" x 2-1/2" x 71-1/4" oak (side stiles)
L	4	3/4" x 2-1/2" x 66-1/2" oak (door stiles)
M	2	3/4" x 2-1/2" x 64-1/2" oak (side center stiles)
N	8	3/4" x 2-1/2" x 9" oak (side rails)
P	2	3/4" x 2-1/2" x 8-3/4" oak (door bottom rails)
Q	4	3/4" x 1-1/4" x 22-1/4" oak (shelf supports)
R	1	3/4" x 1" x 78" oak (base cleats)*
S	2	1/4" x 3/4" x 30-1/2" oak (shelf edging)
T	2	3/4" x 22-1/4" x 30-1/2" oak plywood (top and bottom)
U	2	3/4" x 22" x 30-1/2" oak plywood (shelves)
V	1	1/4" x 31-1/2" x 68-1/2" oak plywood (back)
W	4	1/4" x 8-15/16" x 63" oak plywood (side panels)*
X	2	1/4" x 8-11/16" x 63" oak plywood (door panels)*

* Cut to finished length during assembly.

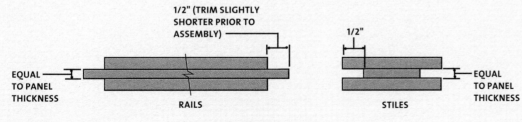

1/2" (TRIM SLIGHTLY
SHORTER PRIOR TO
ASSEMBLY)

1/2"

EQUAL
TO PANEL
THICKNESS

RAILS

STILES

EQUAL
TO PANEL
THICKNESS

TONGUE AND GROOVE DETAILS

Cut the Pieces

For successful frame-and-panel construction, all the oak boards must be exactly the same thickness so that you can accurately cut the panel grooves and tenons. The best way to ensure uniform thickness is to plane the boards yourself, using a thickness planer, or ask your lumberyard to do it for you.

Carefully lay out cutting diagrams for all the pieces before you start to cut them. Reserve your straightest boards for the door stiles. Also try to match the grain of pieces that will be next to each other. To do this, cut adjoining pieces from the same board whenever you can.

For example, the Cutting List on page 103 shows that the plywood side and door panels are 63 inches long. First cut these pieces to width, then cut individual panels from the long pieces so the grain will match from top to bottom.

Only one section of panel is cut from the second 4x8 sheet of 1/4-inch oak-veneer plywood, so you can use the rest of this sheet for the wardrobe's back. For even better panel matching, try to choose two sequentially matched sheets; that is, sheets on which the veneer has been cut from the same tree.

Begin by cutting all the wardrobe pieces (A–X) to the dimensions given in the Cutting List on the previous page. You will be cutting some pieces to their final size now, but others will be trimmed to size during assembly, using templates.

Make the Frames and Panels

Make templates for the shapes of the curved door rails (G) and base pieces (A). To do this, enlarge the grids shown in the details on the preceding page to their full size on scrap plywood or particleboard. Cut out the templates, then sand their edges smooth.

Routing the Panel Grooves

First use a router to cut the panel grooves (Photo 1). Fit your router with a 1/2-inch deep x 1/8-inch thick three-wing slot-cutting bit. Center the finished grooves on the edges of the stiles and rails. Set your router so the distance from the top edge of the cutter to the base of the router is slightly greater than 1/4 inch.

Test your router setup on scrap wood before making the grooves in the final oak pieces. Make one cut, then flip the wood over and rout a second one to center the groove on the edge. Now test the fit of the panels (W and X) in the groove. If the fit isn't perfect yet, adjust the router base and make another test cut. Once the groove is just slightly wider than the thickness of the plywood panels, the fit is now correct.

When your router setup is right, cut all the panel grooves in pieces C, J, K, L, M, N, and P. Use a router pad (see Photo 1) to hold short pieces in place as you work. Don't change the router setup, because you'll need it later to cut grooves in the curved door rails (G).

Cutting the Frame Tenons

Now cut the frame tenons with a dado blade (Photo 2). First trace the shapes of the curved door rails from your full-size template onto the oak rail pieces (G). Mount a 9/16-inch wide dado blade in your table saw, setting the blade slightly higher than 1/4 inch. Attach a stop block to the saw's fence, with the fence set so that the dado blade will cut 1/2-inch long tenons when you push the pieces through with the saw's miter gauge. Attach another fence to the miter gauge to help support the pieces as you make the cuts.

Again using scrap wood to test your setup, make one cut on one side, flip the wood over, and cut the other side. Check that the length of the tenon is exactly 1/2 inch long, as it should be. Then check the fit of the tenon in the panel grooves; it ought to be neither tight nor loose. When you have the setup right, cut the tenons on the ends of the rails and side center stiles (C, G, J, M, N, and P). Check the fit of each tenon as you cut it. If one is too tight, shape it to the correct size with a wood file or sandpaper.

Cutting Out and Shaping the Curved Pieces

Using a jigsaw or band saw and the appropriate template, cut the arched door rails (G) and sand the sawn edges smooth (Photo 3). If you use a saber saw, clamp the pieces to your worktable. Then, using the same groove-cutting router setup as before, cut the panel grooves on the edges of the curved door rails. Don't cut grooves in the top edges of the top curved rails.

Cutting the Panels to Size

Cut the panels to their finished lengths as given in the Cutting List on page 103. Label the edges of the panels as you cut them so that you can easily set them in the frames with their grain running consecutively. First cut the door panels (X). Align the high side of the curved door-rail template 25-5/16 inches up on the inside edge of one panel. Then line up the low side of this template to the other edge of the panel so it's 29/32 inch lower than the high side. Mark and cut the curve. Now you have the bottom panel as well as the bottom curve of the center panel.

Add 15/16 inch to the door-frame opening dimensions shown in the Door Panel Detail (page 102). Lay out and cut the center and top door panels (Photo 4). Cut panels for the opposite door, then the side panels (W).

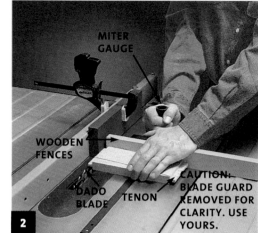

1

Use a router and a three-wing slot-cutting bit to cut the panel grooves in the rails. Hold the shorter pieces in place firmly with a router pad while you work.

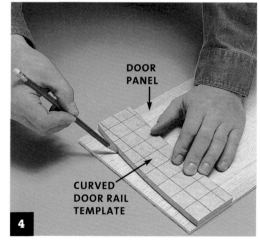

2

Cut the tenons with a dado blade. Set the length of the tenon with a wood fence clamped to the saw's fence. Hold the pieces tight to the miter gauge.

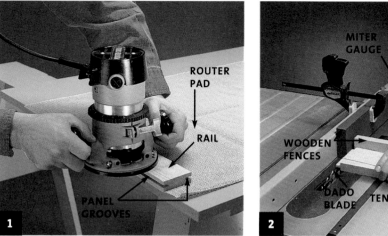

3

Cut the shapes of the curved door rails after you've made their tenons. Clamp the pieces to your work-table as shown here to cut them with a saber saw.

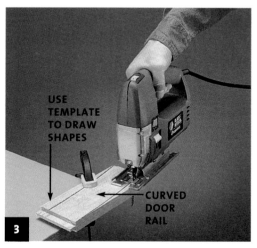

4

Draw the shapes of the curved door panels, using the template as a guide. Cut all the panels 15/16 in. longer than the dimensions of the frame's openings.

Assemble the Doors, Sides, and Face Frame

Assemble the wardrobe beginning with the doors and sides, then going on to the face frame. Once these parts are done, you can assemble the cabinet, or main case.

Slightly trim the lengths of the tenons so they'll fit all the way into their grooves. Lay out and dry-assemble (without glue) the doors and sides. When everything fits correctly, disassemble the parts, finish-sand the panels and inside edges of the frames, and glue and clamp them back together (Photo 5). Don't glue the panels into their grooves; just apply glue to the tenons and their mortise grooves. Apply the glue sparingly to minimize glue squeeze-out and extra cleanup later.

With the curved door-rail template, mark the curves on the tops of the outer door stiles (L). Set the doors aside to cut the shapes later.

Lay out and drill the dowel holes in face-frame pieces E, F, and H, then dowel, glue, and clamp these pieces together. Also glue and clamp the shelf-edging pieces (S) to the shelves (U).

Now use a router to cut rabbets on the inside back edges of the sides (see Side Stile Detail, page 102). Then rout 1/4-inch round overs on the front edges, as shown in the detail two to the right side of the Stile Detail.

Use a 1/2-inch diameter two-flute straight router bit to cut 1/4-inch deep dado grooves in the sides for the face frame (Photo 6). Cut these grooves with two passes of the router, using different settings for the fence. Make the cut closest to the edge first, move the fence away from the bit, then make the second cut.

Lay out and drill all the screw holes in the sides, face frame, shelves (U), bottom (T), upper shelf supports (B), and shelf supports (Q).

Finish-sand the remaining parts made up to this point. Smooth the inside frame edges of the sides and doors with 180-grit sandpaper. Place pieces of cardboard on top of the panels to keep from scratching them as you sand.

ASSEMBLE THE DOORS, SIDES, AND FACE FRAME

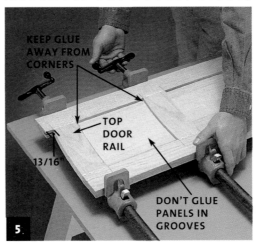

KEEP GLUE AWAY FROM CORNERS

TOP DOOR RAIL

13/16"

DON'T GLUE PANELS IN GROOVES

5

Glue and clamp the door pieces together, working on a perfectly flat surface. Apply glue only to the tenons and the panel grooves where the tenons mate.

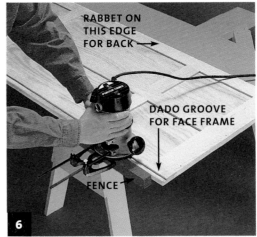

RABBET ON THIS EDGE FOR BACK

DADO GROOVE FOR FACE FRAME

FENCE

6

Use a router with a fence and a straight bit to cut face-frame dadoes in each side panel. It's easiest to use a 1/2-in. diameter bit and make two cuts.

Assemble the Main Case

Set one side assembly on a pair of sawhorses (Photo 7). Glue and clamp the face frame into that side's dado groove. Screw the top (T) to the side and face frame. Screw the shelf supports (Q) to the bottom (T). Glue and clamp the front edge of the bottom to the inside of the face frame, then screw the bottom shelf support to the side. Attach the other side in the same way.

Rout the rounded-over edges of one side of the top cap moldings (D). Next, rout the cove shape on the other edge of those pieces, then rout the top edge of the base pieces (A). Cut the top cap molding to a 3-inch width and the top cove molding to a 3/4-inch width.

Miter the ends of the top moldings and base pieces so they fit neatly on the assembled case. Lay out and drill the screw holes in the top cap molding pieces. Then use your base template to trace the curved cutouts on the base pieces. Cut the shapes using a band saw or saber saw, and sand the sawn edges smooth.

Cut the notches at the top and bottom of the main case where the base and cove molding pieces go (see the plans on page 102 and Photo 8). Cut the top notches so the cove molding will fit snugly. After you attach the cap molding, use a file as needed to fit the cove molding in place.

Attach the top and base moldings, gluing the mitered corners as you position each piece. Drill pilot holes for 1-inch

brads and cross-pin the mitered joints with these brads. Cut the base cleats (R) to length. Glue and screw them in place.

Screw the hinges to the doors and then to the face frame. Fit the doors, then remove them and drill the knob holes. Rout the rounded-over edges of the doors. Finish-sand any remaining parts, and lightly sand off any sharp edges.

Finish the Piece

Apply three coats of Danish oil to the wood. Wipe the oil off once an hour until it stops bleeding from the wood's pores.

When the finish is dry, screw the shelf supports (B and Q) in place on the inner surfaces of the sides. Attach the shelves, the back, and the hanging rod. Once you remount the doors, your classic wardrobe unit is ready to start using.

One final word of advice: Be careful in moving this piece into position where you want to use it. Don't tilt it over on its side, which could put too much pressure on the base pieces and snap them off.

ASSEMBLE THE MAIN CASE

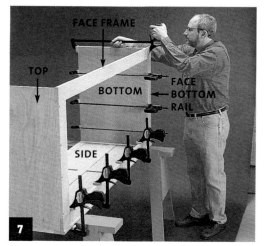

Glue and clamp the front edges of the sides, top, and bottom to the inside of the face frame. Be sure to align the parts carefully.

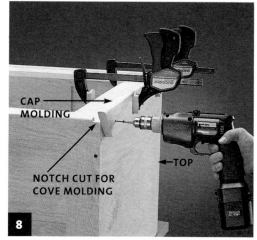

Position the top cap moldings to overhang the face frame and sides by 1-1/4 in. Align and clamp them, then screw them in place.

Neat Bedroom Storage Options

Organize and store bedroom clutter with one of these good-looking, versatile projects.

Take your pick of these four weekend storage projects:

- **Ladder Shelving System**
- **Children's Shelving Unit**
- **Multiple-Use Cubes**
- **Stacking Totes**

All four projects in this section can be built with basic hand and power tools, moderate skills, and a bit of patience. In fact, you can put the finishing touches on any one of them in a single weekend. The unit you build can be finished as shown in the pictures at the right, or painted or stained to match your decor.

You can easily adapt any of these storage solutions shown at the right to the space you have available and the time you've got to build them. The Ladder Shelving System (pages 110–111) gives you four large and four small shelf units in a flexible piece that could either be modified to fit a particular space or left freestanding. The Children's Shelving Unit (pages 112–113) is a stand-alone storage or display unit that will work in a variety of spaces. And the last two projects (pages 114–115) are nesting or stacking units that make the most of your materials. They are also expandable enough to solve your needs for flexible bedroom storage.

Because you'll need to cut a lot of plywood to very precise dimensions and with smooth edges, a table saw or radial arm saw will greatly simplify your work. But with care you can cut plywood accurately using a circular saw and a clamped-in-place straightedge as a guide. (For more information on cutting plywood, see the box on page 19.)

Ladder Shelving System

Children's Shelving Unit

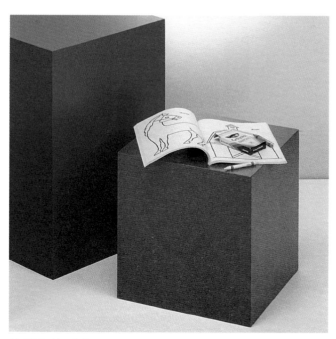

Multiple-Use Cubes

Stacking Totes

Ladder Shelving System

The supporting ladders for this shelving system are constructed of ordinary 2x4s and 1-1/4 inch dowels, usually called closet rods. The adjustable shelf units are made from 3/4-inch birch plywood joined with simple nailed and glued butt joints.

▶ Begin building the ladders by drilling all the dowel holes in the 2x4s; make them exactly 3/4-inch deep with a 1-1/4 inch spade bit. You can mark the correct depth on the bit by placing a strip of masking tape around it at the right point. Space the holes exactly 7-5/8 inches apart from center to center, as shown in the plans at right.

▶ Cut the dowels to length, then glue the ladder assembly together on a flat floor or other large, level work area. Apply a bar clamp at each dowel in sequence and secure the dowels with 6d finish nails. After the glue dries, drill and countersink holes as shown in the Mounting Detail at bottom right to mount the ladder securely to the wall.

▶ Next, cut all the parts for the shelf units to the dimensions shown in the plans on the facing page. Make your cuts smooth and straight so the glued edges will adhere well. Lay out and cut the rounded notches and corners with a saber saw.

The 1/4-inch thick hardwood edging glued onto the shelf fronts is not essential, but it will provide a more durable edge, especially on shelf units you'll be using as work surfaces. Cut and glue on the edging before you assemble the units.

▶ Assemble the shelf units with glue and 6d finish nails. Set the nailheads and fill the nail holes with wood filler. Position the backs of the shelving units carefully, because the backs hang from the dowels.

▶ If necessary, fill any voids in the plywood edges with wood filler. Sand all the assembled parts smooth, especially the edges and corners. Apply an oil-base primer, sand lightly once dry, and finish with a durable enamel paint.

▶ Drill and countersink mounting holes in the 2x4 uprights, then attach the ladders to the wall with expansion anchors or toggle bolts as shown, and that's all there is to it. For more information about other fasteners to use with different wall surfaces, see pages 186–189.

TOOLS

HAND TOOLS

Bar clamps

Carpenter's square

Hammer

Nail set

Screwdrivers

Tape measure

POWER TOOLS

Circular saw

Drill; 1-1/4" spade bit

Saber saw

OPTIONAL

Table saw or radial arm saw

MATERIALS

(For two ladders, four large shelf units, and four small shelf units)

Qty.	Size and Description
4	Straight 8' 2x4s
72 ft.	1-1/4" closet rod dowel
2 sheets	3/4" birch plywood
21 ft.	1/4" x 3/4" hardwood edging
	6d finish nails
16	Expansion anchors or toggle bolts
	Sandpaper
	Woodworker's glue
	Wood filler
	Oil-base primer
	Enamel paint

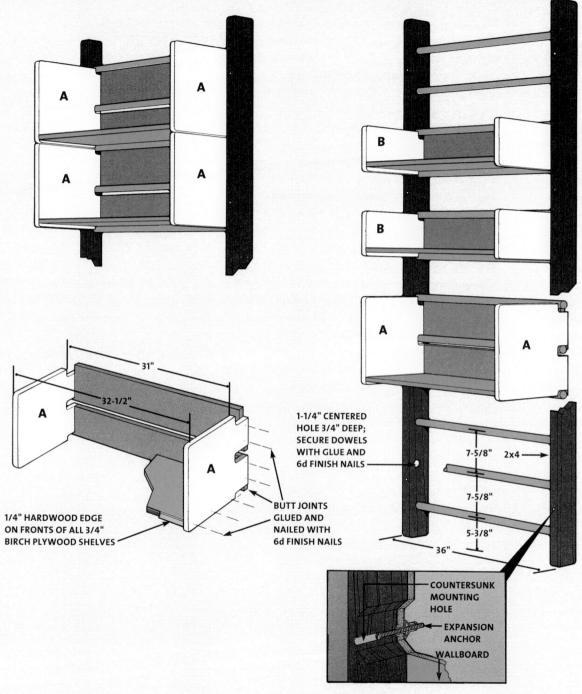

A

A

A

A

A

A

31"

32-1/2"

A

A

1/4" HARDWOOD EDGE
ON FRONTS OF ALL 3/4"
BIRCH PLYWOOD SHELVES

B

B

A

A

1-1/4" CENTERED
HOLE 3/4" DEEP;
SECURE DOWELS
WITH GLUE AND
6d FINISH NAILS

7-5/8"

2x4

7-5/8"

5-3/8"

36"

BUTT JOINTS
GLUED AND
NAILED WITH
6d FINISH NAILS

COUNTERSUNK
MOUNTING
HOLE

EXPANSION
ANCHOR

WALLBOARD

MOUNTING DETAIL

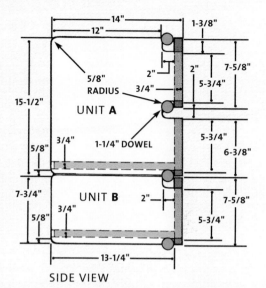

14"
12"
1-3/8"

5/8"
RADIUS

2"

3/4"

2"

7-5/8"

5-3/4"

UNIT **A**

1-1/4" DOWEL

15-1/2"

5-3/4"

6-3/8"

5/8"

3/4"

5-3/4"

7-3/4"

UNIT **B**

2"

7-5/8"

5/8"

3/4"

5-3/4"

13-1/4"

SIDE VIEW

This multipurpose ladder wall system can be
rearranged in any number of configurations.

Children's Shelving Unit

The spacious plywood shelves of this children's storage unit slide into slots cut into PVC plastic plumbing-pipe legs. The whole structure is ingeniously held together by apron blocks nailed and glued to the shelf edges. You can either paint the shelves to match the white plastic legs or use a contrasting color.

You'll need only a minimum of skill and time to build this project, and just the most basic power tools: a circular saw or table saw, and a saber saw to cut the curved shelf ends and leg caps. A router with a 1-inch round-over bit would be helpful for shaping the leg caps and the apron blocks, but a rasp and sandpaper will also work. Cut the leg slots with a handsaw, then use a coping saw or saber saw to finish making the notches.

▶ Cut four 3/4-inch birch plywood shelves to 13-1/2 inches x 60 inches with a circular saw or a table saw. Then lay out the 6-3/4 inch radius ends and carefully cut them with a saber saw, following the plans shown at the right.

▶ Now locate and mark the locations of the slots for the shelves in all four legs. Draw a pencil line down the length of each leg and make another one exactly opposite it. Mark the slots perpendicular to these lines, laying out identical 3/4-inch wide slots on each leg, following the spacing intervals shown in the plans (opposite).

▶ Cut the top and bottom of each slot with a handsaw, stopping exactly on the pencil lines. Finish cutting out the slots with a coping saw or a saber saw, and file the corners square.

▶ Make the top cap for each leg from two discs cut from 3/4-inch plywood and screwed together with three 1-1/4 inch drywall screws as follows: Cut the bottom disc slightly smaller than the inside diameter of the PVC pipe. Trim the top disc to the outside diameter of the pipe. Then either rout the discs' top edges with a 1-inch round-over bit or use a wood rasp and sandpaper.

▶ Cut eight shelf-apron blocks to 33 inches in length and sixteen end blocks to 3-5/8 inches in length. Cut 9-degree bevels on all edges that adjoin the legs, as shown in the detailed plan (center right). Rout 1-inch round-overs on the lower outside corners of the end blocks, or use a rasp and sandpaper.

▶ Now prime and paint the leg top caps, the shelves, and the apron blocks.

▶ Assemble the unit flat on its back on the floor. First lay down the rear legs and slip the shelves into their slots to hold them in position, then fit the front legs over the opposite shelf edges. Position the legs so that they're equidistant from the ends when an apron block is placed between them. Attach the front apron blocks with glue and 6d finish nails so that they're tight against the legs and flush with the shelf tops. Then set the nailheads just below the surface.

▶ Stand the unit upright and glue on the top caps with construction adhesive.

TOOLS

HAND TOOLS
Carpenter's square
Compass
Coping saw
File
Hammer
Handsaw
Nail set
Rasp
Screwdrivers
Tape measure

POWER TOOLS
Circular saw
Saber saw

OPTIONAL
Router; 1" round-over bit
Table saw

MATERIALS

Qty.	Size and Description
1-1/2 sheets	3/4" birch plywood
28 ft.	3/4" x 2" clear pine
4 lengths	3" PVC pipe 54" long
	6d finish nails
	1-1/4" drywall screws
	Wood glue
	Construction adhesive
	Primer and paint

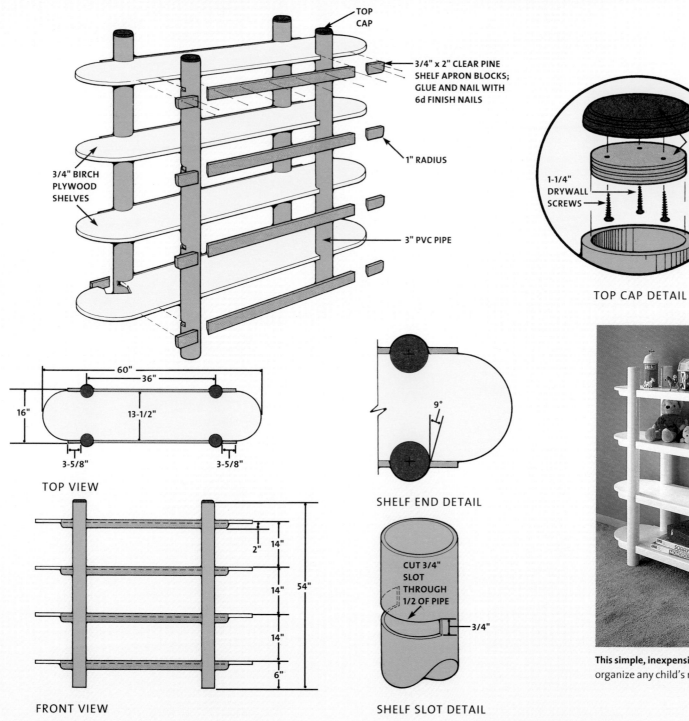

TOP CAP

3/4" x 2" CLEAR PINE SHELF APRON BLOCKS; GLUE AND NAIL WITH 6d FINISH NAILS

1" RADIUS

3/4" BIRCH PLYWOOD SHELVES

3" PVC PIPE

TOP CAP DETAIL

3/4" PLYWOOD

1-1/4" DRYWALL SCREWS

GLUE

60"

36"

16"

13-1/2"

3-5/8"

3-5/8"

TOP VIEW

9°

SHELF END DETAIL

2"

14"

14"

14"

6"

54"

FRONT VIEW

CUT 3/4" SLOT THROUGH 1/2 OF PIPE

3/4"

SHELF SLOT DETAIL

This simple, inexpensive shelving unit can help organize any child's room.

Multiple-Use Cubes

These highly adaptable nesting cubes make efficient use of materials: You can cut everything for all three units from one sheet of 1/2-inch birch-veneer plywood. Turned bottom-up, these make handy stools or pedestals. Or fill them with rarely needed items, cover them with a board top, and use them as side tables.

▶ Cut all the parts to the sizes shown on the plans at right, then sand the edges.

▶ Now assemble the parts with glue and 4d finish nails. Butt-join the sides, then attach the cube bottoms, to square up the assemblies. Set the nailheads slightly below the surface and fill their holes with wood filler or spackling compound.

▶ Finish-sand all the edges, slightly rounding the corners, then apply stain or paint. If you paint the cubes, use a durable oil-base primer before applying an enamel topcoat.

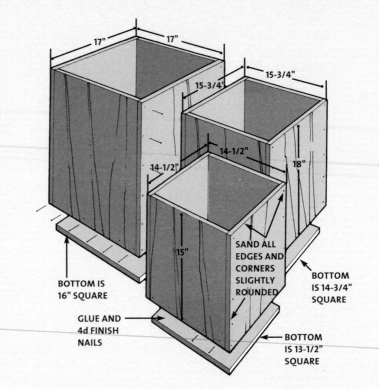

17" 17"
15-3/4"
15-3/4"
15-3/4'
14-1/2"
14-1/2"
18"
14-1/2"
15"

SAND ALL EDGES AND CORNERS SLIGHTLY ROUNDED

BOTTOM IS 14-3/4" SQUARE

BOTTOM IS 16" SQUARE

GLUE AND 4d FINISH NAILS

BOTTOM IS 13-1/2" SQUARE

TOOLS

HAND TOOLS

Bar clamps

Framing or carpenter's square

Hammer

Nail set

Tape measure

POWER TOOLS

Circular saw

Drill

MATERIALS

(For five cubes)

Qty.	Size and Description
1 sheet	1/2" birch-veneer plywood
	4d finish nails
	Sandpaper
	Woodworker's glue
	Wood filler or spackling compound
	Wood stain or paint

These versatile cubes have a multitude of bedroom uses: as storage bins, side tables, decorative pedestals, and work and play tables for children.

Stacking Totes

Make these mobile stacking totes from 1/2-inch birch-veneer plywood. The dimensions shown at right allow each tote to interlock snugly with those above and below. They also let you cut all five totes from just one sheet of plywood.

▶ First cut all the plywood parts to size. Then cut out the handholds and sand all the edges smooth.

▶ Glue and assemble the totes with 4d finish nails. Butt-join the sides, leaving equal portions of the larger pieces extending above and below the smaller ones. Then attach a bottom to each box. Set the nailheads slightly below the surface, then fill the nail holes with wood filler or spackling compound.

▶ Either leave the totes unfinished or apply a wood stain or paint. If you paint the pieces, use an oil-base primer and an enamel top coat for maximum durability.

▶ Finally, mount 2-inch casters on the bottom tote to make the stack mobile.

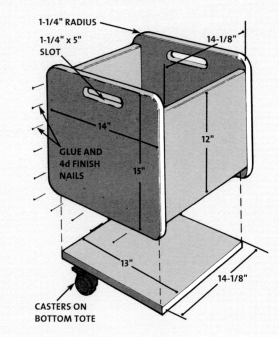

These five mobile interlocking totes can all be cut from one panel of birch-veneer plywood.

TOOLS

HAND TOOLS
Bar clamps
Carpenter's square
Compass
Screwdrivers
Tape measure

POWER TOOLS
Circular saw
Drill
Saber saw

MATERIALS

(For five totes)

Qty.	Size and Description
1 sheet	1/2" birch-veneer plywood
4	2" casters
	Sandpaper
	Woodworker's glue
	Wood filler or spackling compound
	Wood stain or oil-base primer and paint

Streamlined Closets

Organize chaotic closets with this simple system. Clothes rods, shelves, and drawers put everything at your fingertips.

A well-designed organizing system can almost double a closet's storage capacity. This system is easy to adapt to any size closet.

Construction Plan

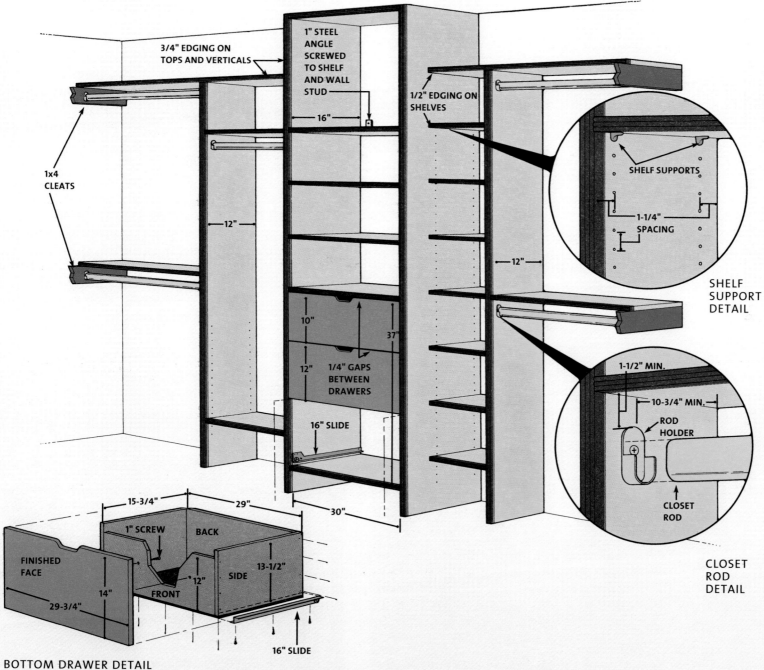

3/4" EDGING ON TOPS AND VERTICALS

1" STEEL ANGLE SCREWED TO SHELF AND WALL STUD

16"

1/2" EDGING ON SHELVES

1x4 CLEATS

12"

12"

10"

37"

12"

1/4" GAPS BETWEEN DRAWERS

16" SLIDE

30"

SHELF SUPPORTS

1-1/4" SPACING

SHELF SUPPORT DETAIL

1-1/2" MIN.

10-3/4" MIN.

ROD HOLDER

CLOSET ROD

CLOSET ROD DETAIL

BOTTOM DRAWER DETAIL

15-3/4"

29"

1" SCREW

BACK

FINISHED FACE

SIDE

13-1/2"

12"

FRONT

14"

29-3/4"

16" SLIDE

TOOLS

HAND TOOLS

Backsaw and miter box

Framing square

Hammer

Handsaw

Level

Nail set

Screwdrivers

Spring clamps

Stud finder

Torpedo Level

Utility knife

POWER TOOLS

Circular saw; plywood-cutting blade

Drill; 1/4" brad-point bit

OPTIONAL

Commercial metal straightedge

Plane

Router; router table, fence, bead-forming bit

Table saw

Plan Your Closet Layout

This project is suitable for all levels of do-it-yourselfer: It doesn't require advanced woodworking tools or expensive materials. Although the system shown here was designed for a 12-foot walk-in closet, it adapts easily to the space you have available. Use the Construction Plan on page 117 for ideas.

Long-Garment Rods and Drawers

Plan your closet storage around two key elements: a rod for long hanging garments, and a set of drawers.

▶ Long garments need plenty of access room; they won't fit into the double clothes rod system used for shorter clothes. To plan rod space, count your long garments and allow about 1-1/2 inches of rod length for each one. The rod will be mounted at about shoulder height.

▶ Drawers should be at or below eye level so you can easily see their contents. Make the drawers spacious—at least 16 inches front to back, 24 to 30 inches wide, and 10 to 14 inches deep. These drawers, with the shelves above, make up the center tower supporting other system components.

With these key dimensions in mind, measure your closet walls and draw a rough sketch to determine the best positions for the drawers and long clothes. Now you can plan the rest of your closet around these elements.

Short-Garment Rods and Shelves

Divide the remaining space between double rods for short clothes and shelves.

▶ Jackets, skirts, blouses, shirts, slacks, and suits will hang less than 40 inches long, so you can place one clothes rod at waist height and another 42 inches above that to save space. Allow 1 inch of rod space for thin blouses and skirts, a generous 1-1/2 inches for jackets.

▶ In addition to the permanent shelves in the center tower, you will probably want one or two permanent shelves above the garment rods, and perhaps shelves near the floor to hold shoes. Adjustable shelves will fit above the drawers in the center tower—between the permanent shelves—and in any remaining space.

Depth

Establish the depth of each section. The tower can be deeper than the adjacent rod and shelf spaces. This minimizes the amount of material required to build the units and makes it easier to remove items from the rods and shelves.

Height

You can extend the center tower all the way to the ceiling, although that isn't necessary. In this installation (see page 116), the tower stops just below the cornice molding. However, the system is still stable, because several components are anchored directly to the back wall and the floor.

Draw a Plan

When your plans are complete, draw them on graph paper to determine the exact dimensions of the various parts. The components that you will need to take into account are:

▶ The central tower (two sides, permanent and adjustable shelves, drawers)
▶ Vertical dividers
▶ Permanent shelves
▶ Edging
▶ Adjustable shelves
▶ Cleats (to hold permanent shelves and closet rods)
▶ Closet rods.

Use your plan to make a shopping list for the materials you'll need and a cutting list for assembling the parts.

MATERIALS

3/4" plywood
1/2" plywood
1/4" plywood
1x4 stock
8d finish nails
6d finish nails
4d finish nails
1" brads
Drawer glides
1" steel angle brace and attachment screws
Wood filler
Woodworker's glue
Paint or stain

Select Your Materials

This closet system is built from 3/4-inch birch plywood, but you can use any other wood that fits your taste and budget. Plywood is flat, straight, and easy to nail. Shelves of 3/4-inch plywood can span about 3 feet without sagging. Birch-veneer plywood has a smooth surface for painting.

You can also use rough but functional unpainted No. 2 pine boards or sanded fir plywood (grade A-B or the coarser grade C-D). If you use fir plywood, remember that the coarse grain pattern will show through even a careful paint job.

If you decide on plywood, cover the exposed edges, both for appearance and to avoid snagging clothes on unfinished edges. Solid-wood edging is a better choice than iron-on or self-adhesive veneer. You can buy 3/4-inch wide edge molding or make your own, as shown at right.

Working with Plywood

Cutting Plywood

Plywood must be cut cleanly, without splintering or tearing the face veneers. Edging, too, requires clean cuts.

To cut plywood, use a sharp plywood-cutting blade in a circular saw and turn the workpiece with its best face down. Make sure the panel is adequately supported on saw-horses, or place it on the floor with a scrap panel or long boards underneath to support it off the floor.

To cut shelves and uprights, clamp on a piece of plywood with a factory-cut edge to use as a guide strip, or use a commercial metal straight-edge to guide the side of the saw base. One model has two sections that can be joined with a collar and setscrews for a total length of a bit more than 8 feet. This allows you to clamp it on a full-length panel with enough overhang at each end to guide the saw before the blade enters and exits the wood.

Splintering usually isn't a problem when you are cutting along the length of a panel—if it's done in the same direction as the grain on the face veneer. Cutting across the grain can be a problem, however. To avoid tearing the veneer, score the cut line deeply with a utility knife. Do this on both faces, then cut just to the outside—the waste side—of the visible cut line.

For cuts across pieces up to about 20 inches wide, hold the short tongue of a carpenter's square against the far edge of the workpiece and use the long tongue of the square to guide the saw (see photo). Make sure that the cut starts at the front edge of the piece and exits at the back, so if there is any corner tear-out it will be concealed after you have completed the assembly. For more on making clean crosscuts, see the box on page 19.

Making Solid-Wood Edging

If you use plywood for this project, you'll want to add edging. If you prefer not to purchase edging, here's how you can make your own.

Rout an edging profile on both long edges of a 1x6 or wider board. Use a router table and fence to guide the boards past the bit, then use a table saw to cut off the edges as 1/2- or 3/4-inch molding and repeat the process. Once the board is reduced to about 4 inches wide, you can use it for shelf cleats in the closet (see illustration).

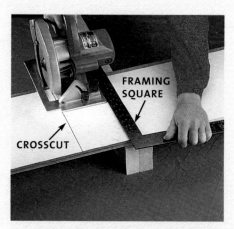

Use a framing square or other straightedge as a guide for making straight cuts. Score the cut line with a utility knife (see page 19) to avoid tearing the face veneer in cross-grain cuts.

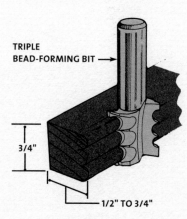

Cutting triple-bead edging puts strain on a bit and router, so use a bit with a shank no smaller than 1/2 in. Make sure your router is rated at 1-1/4 horsepower or greater.

Cut the Framework Pieces

Cutting plywood can be tricky. For some helpful working techniques, refer to the box on page 119.

Cut all of the tower parts to size using your plan and cutting list as guides. Cut at least three permanent shelves to fit between the sides of the tower: one at the bottom, one directly above the top drawer, and one that will be the highest shelf. If you put a top on the unit, cut it to be butt-joined between the sides of the tower also, as shown in the plans. If you place it across the tower's top edges, its untrimmed ends will show at the sides.

Cut the remaining permanent shelves: long ones to run between the center tower and the walls, and shorter ones to go between the vertical dividers and the end walls or the tower, as shown in your layout. You don't need to cut dadoes in the sides for the ends of the permanently attached shelves; just cut the pieces to length for butt joints.

Cut vertical dividers and cleats according to your plan. If you make your own edging, you can fashion cleats at the same time, using the same material.

Cut the Drawers

Building the drawers requires more accuracy than any other part of this closet system. The drawers must be square, which means that you must be sure to cut the sides and bottom perfectly square. Though not essential, a table saw will make this job easier.

Even though the drawers may have different heights, they are all constructed the same way (see the Bottom Drawer detail, page 117). Each drawer is simply a box with a finished face. The sides and back are 3/4-inch shorter than the finished face, the front of the box 1-1/2 inches shorter than the back and sides.

The dimensions shown on page 117 for the Bottom Drawer Detail can be adapted to your space, as can the other drawer sizes suggested there.

Cut the drawer sides, backs, and fronts from 1/2-inch plywood and the bottoms out of 1/4-inch plywood. Trim the drawer faces from higher-grade 3/4-inch plywood.

Cut the Edging

You may want to attach the edging strips to some scrap pieces to hold them firmly before cutting them to length. In other cases, cut the edging separately with a fine-tooth handsaw. For clean, square cuts, use a backsaw in a miter box.

Stain the Pieces

Stain or paint all the pieces before you begin assembly. You'll still need to do a bit of touching up later, but prefinishing the pieces will save a great deal of time.

Attach the Edging

Attach the edging pieces with glue and nails (Photo 1). Use 4d finish nails with edging that is 3/4 or 1/2 inch thick, and 1-inch brads with thinner edging. Test your assembly with a piece of scrap edging; if the piece shows any tendency to split, drill tiny pilot holes in the edging (none are needed in the plywood edges). Wipe off any glue squeeze-out with a damp rag immediately after nailing.

4d FINISH NAIL

Glue and nail trim to the unfinished plywood edges. Paint or stain the edging and the boards before assembly. Fill nail holes and touch up the finish later.

Construct the Center Tower

The fundamental section of this closet system is the center tower, which contains permanent shelves, adjustable shelves, and drawers to support the components on each side. Depending on your design, the tower may also have a top. You'll build the basic components of this unit first; these are the sides and permanent shelves. It's important that you make the permanent shelves square.

Assemble the tower on the floor, with the finished (front) edges facing up. Nail through the sides into the ends of the permanent shelves (Photo 2). Use 8d finish nails spaced no more than 3 inches apart, because veneers don't have as much gripping power as the end grain of a solid-wood board. Locate the bottom shelf about 4 inches above the floor, or higher if there is a baseboard on the back wall that it must clear. You also may have to notch the rear corners of the side pieces to fit around the baseboard so their back edges will be against the wall. Check frequently, using a carpenter's square, to make sure that the assembled pieces are square with one another.

Make sure the shelves are level and that the sides are plumb both side to side and front to back. Otherwise, when you install the drawers they won't fit squarely. If your floor isn't flat and level, plane or sand the bottom edges of the side pieces until the unit stands both level and plumb when you put it in place.

Mark a layout line on the wall for one side of the tower. Move the tower into position and use a level to make sure the sides are plumb (Photo 3).

Anchor the tower to the floor with two 6d finish nails in each side. Toenail the sides near the front and rear corners. Check again for plumb near the top. Fasten a steel angle brace to the top permanent shelf and screw it to a stud in the back wall (Photo 4). If you attach the angle brace to the top of the shelf as shown, it will not be visible. If you secure it to the underside of the shelf, it will not interfere with items you push all the way to the rear. The angle brace will keep the unit plumb until you add the other components of the system. More importantly, it's a safety measure that will prevent the tall unit from tipping forward.

CONSTRUCT THE CENTER TOWER

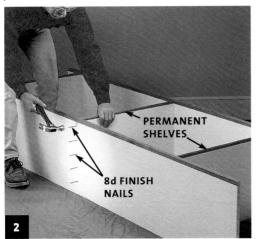

Nail the permanent shelves in place in the center tower with 8d finish nails. Make sure they are at a right angle to the sides. Space the nails about 3 in. apart.

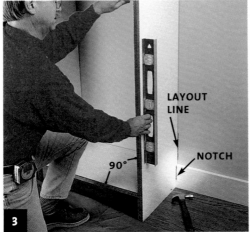

Make sure the sides are plumb. Notch the lower rear corners for the baseboard, if necessary. Toenail each side to the floor with a 6d finish nail front and rear.

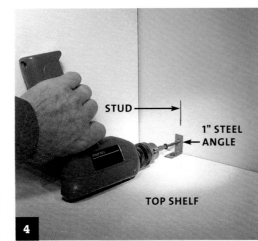

Screw a 1-in. steel angle brace to a permanent shelf and a wall stud to hold the tower plumb and secure. The brace can fit on either the top or bottom shelf.

Complete the Framework

Now that you have built and erected the primary tower structure, you can install the secondary pieces that will make the system rigid and strong.

Installing Cleats

On the end walls of the closet, install 1x4 cleats to support each permanent shelf and closet rod. Nail each cleat to the wall studs under each end and in the middle, using three nails at each point (Photo 5).

Installing the Permanent Shelves and Vertical Dividers

Draw a level line from the top of the upper cleat to the side of the center tower. Then install a shelf along that line; it will be the top of the compartments on that side of the tower (Photo 6). Nail through the side of the tower into the end of the shelf, and then through the shelf into the top edge of the wall cleat.

Space the vertical dividers as shown in your plans. Nail through the top shelf into the top edge of each divider, check the dividers for plumb, then toenail each one to the floor with 6d nails at front and back as you did for the center tower.

Install the tower top, if your design calls for one, and the shorter permanent shelves between the dividers, just as you installed the permanent shelves in the center tower.

Installing the Closet Rods

Clothes hangers have become fairly standardized, so you can center your closet-rod brackets 10-3/4 inches or more from the back wall. Attach them as recommended in their installation instructions. Be sure that a rod is at least 1-1/2 inches below any shelf above so you can easily slip the hangers up over the rod (see the Closet Rod Detail on page 117 and Photo 7). Oval metal rods like the one shown are more expensive than other types but won't bend under the weight of clothes that would cause a lightweight round metal or wooden rod to sag.

Install the Adjustable Shelves

The adjustable shelves rest on four shelf supports that you insert into holes drilled in the vertical sides of the closet system (see the Shelf Support Detail on page 117). For more information on shelf support options, see the "Shelf Support Techniques" box on page 21.

The more holes you drill, the more flexibility you will have to change your shelf position and spacing. But don't get carried away. At first, drill equally spaced holes in the most likely areas of adjustment. You can always drill additional holes later if you need them.

Use a template to make hole-drilling easier and more accurate (Photo 8). Cut a piece of 1/4-inch stock the same width as the vertical sides and about 14 inches long. Lay out and drill two lines of holes directly opposite one another and set back an equal amount from the edges of the template. The spacing shown in the photo was designed to support shelves that are 12 inches deep.

Clamp the template in place flush with the rear edge of a vertical divider or a side of the center tower. Drill the holes with a 1/4-inch brad-point bit to avoid chipping the plywood veneer. To keep from drilling

COMPLETE THE FRAMEWORK

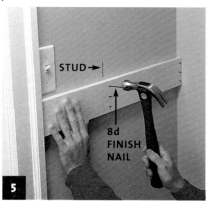

Nail a 1x4 cleat to at least two studs in the walls to support each shelf and closet rod. Make sure all the cleats are level so the shelves won't tip or rock.

Assemble the permanent shelves and vertical dividers to section off the closet system. Drive 8d finish nails through the upright members into the shelf ends.

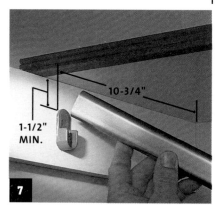

Position and screw closet-rod brackets to the cleats and vertical dividers. Cut the rods to length and drop them in place. Oval metal rods are stronger than round metal or wood.

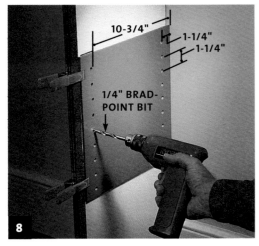

Drill 1/4-in. holes for the adjustable shelf supports using a template and a sharp brad-point drill bit. For consistent spacing, overlap the holes when you reposition the template.

all the way through the vertical supports, mark the drill bit with a felt-tip pen or wrap a strip of masking tape around it as a depth gauge.

Before moving the template out of its first position, use a level to extend a line to the opposite divider or tower side. Mark a reference line to help you position the template accurately when you drill the opposite holes.

When you move the template down to continue the lines of holes on the same vertical support, put a nail or short piece of 1/4-inch dowel through the top hole of each line in the template. Insert these in the bottom holes that you just drilled so the spacing between groups of holes will be consistent.

After you have drilled the holes, install the shelf supports and adjustable shelves.

Build and Install the Drawers

Assemble the drawers with glue and 4d finish nails. Nail through the drawer sides into the edges of the front and back. Then turn the box upside down, apply a bead of glue to the edges, and nail the bottom in place (Photo 9). If you've cut the bottom piece perfectly square, attaching it will square up the box.

Turn the drawer right side up and attach the finished face with two screws. Drill pilot holes for the screws through the box front and into the back of the finished face. Set the bottom edge of the finished front flush with the drawer bottom. Do not use glue; you might want to make adjustments later.

The drawers are supported on two-piece glides. Screw one half of the drawer glides to the drawer, along the sides (Photo 10).

Attach the other half of the glides to the sides of the center tower (Photo 11). This requires careful work. First, measure and mark their positions carefully so there is a consistent 1/4-inch gap between adjacent drawer faces (see the plans). Use a torpedo level to make sure that opposite pairs of channels are aligned at the same height. Then mark and drill pilot holes through the oblong holes in the channels, and drive screws only through these holes.

Now you can install the drawers. If they don't fit precisely, loosen the screws and adjust the channels as necessary. After all the drawers are aligned, remove them and drill pilot holes through the round mounting holes. Drive screws through them to lock the channels in position.

Leveling Tip

A torpedo level—short, with tapered ends—will fit into small spaces a full-size carpenter's level won't. Torpedo levels are available with horizontal, vertical, and 45° vials for checking different angles.

BUILD AND INSTALL THE DRAWERS

Glue and nail the edges of the drawers together with 4d finish nails. Take care to cut the pieces square so the drawer will be self-squaring when assembled.

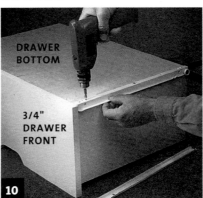

Screw on the finished drawer front from the inside so it's flush with the bottom of the drawer. Then attach one half of the drawer glides to the bottom edges.

Screw the fixed channels of the drawer glides to the tower sides. Make sure they are level and equally spaced. The slotted mounting holes permit adjustments.

Closet-Door Shelving

Make use of all the space in your walk-in closet with this shelving for clothes and accessories.

This simple closet-door unit is easy to build from 1/4-inch and 1/2-inch oak-veneer plywood. What's more, it's lightweight, so you can mount it even on a hollow-core closet door. Select the wood and finish to match your existing door. The only power tool you'll need is a saber saw.

Cut the Pieces

Cut the following pieces from 1/4-inch oak-veneer plywood:

- One 24-inch x 80-inch back
- One 23-inch x 72-inch front.

Now cut these pieces from 1/2-inch oak-veneer plywood:

- One 10-inch x 22-1/2 inch top
- One 10-inch x 22-1/2 inch bottom
- One 10-inch x 72-inch end
- Three 10-inch x 22-1/2 inch shelves.

Assemble and Mount the Unit

- Following the construction diagram at the right, glue and nail the front to the end piece, using 3d finish nails. Keep the pieces flush at the top and bottom.
- Next, glue and nail the top and bottom pieces to the front and end sections you just assembled. Take special care to align these parts correctly to square up the unit.
- Mark the placement of all three shelves, adapting the suggestions in the plans to your needs. Glue and nail each one to the assembled front and end pieces.
- Position the back on the partially assembled unit. Make sure to place the end piece 3/4 inch from the rear edge, and place the top and bottom pieces 4 inches in from the top and bottom edges, as shown in the plans. When the pieces are aligned correctly, glue and nail the back to the unit.
- Cut the L-shaped trim pieces to length from 3/4 x 3/4-inch oak corner guard strips. Saw to measure the pieces for each shelf front edge, the top and bottom front edges, and the two front-piece vertical edges.
- Glue and nail on all the trim pieces, set the nailheads slightly below the surface of the wood, and apply wood filler.

- Finish-sand the unit using 150-grit sandpaper. Apply a paint or stain finish to match that of the closet door.
- Mount the unit to the back of the closet door using No. 10 x 1-1/4 inch flathead brass screws at the top and bottom and along the rear edge of the back. If you're attaching the unit to a hollow-core door, make sure to drive the screws only into the door's solid structural members.

You may want to replace the original hinge screws in the closet door jamb with sturdier 2-inch drywall screws so that the door won't sag under the extra weight of stored items.

This clever design needs just 24 in. or less of clearance behind a closet door, and the side opening makes everything quickly accessible.

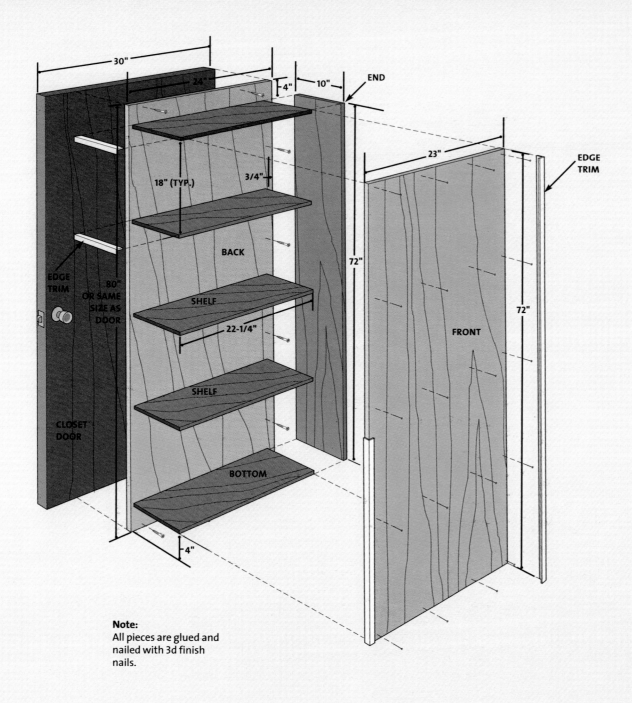

30"

24"

4"   10"   END

18" (TYP.)   3/4"

BACK

72"

EDGE TRIM

SHELF   22-1/4"

EDGE TRIM

80" OR SAME SIZE AS DOOR

SHELF

CLOSET DOOR

BOTTOM

4"

23"

FRONT

72"

EDGE TRIM

Note:
All pieces are glued and nailed with 3d finish nails.

HAND TOOLS

Framing square

Hammer

Nail set

Screwdriver

Tape measure

POWER TOOLS

Saber saw

OPTIONAL

Circular saw or table saw; plywood-cutting blade

MATERIALS

Qty.	Size and Description
1 sheet	4' x 8' x 1/4" oak-veneer plywood
1 sheet	4' x 8' x 1/2" oak-veneer plywood
3	3/4" x 3/4" x 96" oak corner-guard trim strips
1 box	3d finish nails
	No. 10 x 1-1/4" brass flathead screws
	150-grit sandpaper
	Woodworker's glue
	Wood filler
	Paint or stain
	2" drywall screws (optional)

Kitchen & Bathroom

Find creative ways to use existing kitchen and bathroom space, or expand it by building a new, sleek cabinet or divider.

Multipurpose Room Divider

Stretch the work space in your kitchen *and* the storage in your living area with this double-duty room divider.

128

Multipurpose Room Divider

Who says you can't have it all? With this multipurpose room divider you can have a convenient kitchen workspace as well as a small office, library, or media center.

This project requires somewhat advanced woodworking skills in cutting and joining which are not covered here, but if you are comfortable working with detailed construction plans and cutting lists, you should have no difficulty making this attractive, efficient divider.

Stretch the work space in your kitchen *and* the storage in your living area with this double-duty room divider.

In the kitchen (above), the island appliance center opposite the sink carves out an efficient work triangle. On the other side (right) a counter, shelving, cabinets, and drawers serve as a home office or buffet.

CUTTING LISTS

Key*	Qty.	Size and Description
Plywood construction		
A	2	1" x 2' 4-1/2" x 6' 3/4"
B	1	1" x 2' 4" x 6' 3-3/4"
C	3	3/4" x 16" x 2' 3"
D	1	3/4" x 2' 4-1/2" x 2' 3"
E	4	3/4" x 2' 2-1/2" x 2' 5-1/4"
	2	3/4" x 2' 1/4" x 2' 7" (base cabinet doors)
	1	3/4" x 1' 8" x 1' 9-9/16" (door next to microwave)
	2	3/4" x 1' 1-7/8" x 1' 5-1/4" (doors above desk)
	1	3/4" x 2' 1" x 1'6" ± (closure above ovens)
	2	3/4" x 1' 8" x 4' 9/16" (shelf supporting microwave; also floor for adjoining cabinet; see Section B-B, page 132)
	1	3/4" x 3' 4-1/2" x 6' 4-9/16" (island top)
	1	3/4" x 1' 11-1/4" x 4' 9/16" (base cabinet top)
	1	3/4" x 2' x 6' 4-9/16" (desk top)
	4	3/4" x 1' 11-1/4" x 2' 7" (base cabinet dividers)
	1	3/4" x 1' 11-1/4" x 4' 9/16" (base cabinet floor)
	1	3/4" x 12" x 6' 2-9/16" (book cabinet bottom)
	2	3/4" x 12" 1' 6-1/2" (book cabinet speaker bottom)
	1	3/4" x 11-1/4" x 2' 10-9/16" (glued, doweled; book cabinet, upper cabinet bottom)

2x4's (fir)

	1	6' 2-9/16" (sole plate)
	1	6' 2-9/16" (top)
	8	6' 3/4" (studs)
	4	1' 3-1/2" (blocking)
	2	2' 1-9/16" (blocking)
	2	4' 9/16" (base cabinet base, front and back)
	2	1' 5-1/2" (base cabinet, base sides)
	2	1' 8" (base desk cabinet, front)
	4	1' 10-1/4" (base desk cabinet, sides)
	1	2' 1" (base oven cabinet, front)
	2	1' 11" (base oven cabinet, sides)

* See Construction Plan on pages 130–131.

Qty.	Size and Description
Hardwood (around island top)	
1	3/4" x 1-1/2" x 2' 4-1/2"
2	3/4" x 1-1/2" x 3' 6"
1	3/4" x 1-1/2" x 12"
1	1-1/2" x 2-1/2" x 12"
1	1-1/2" x 1-1/2" x 6' 6-1/16"
	1/8" hardwood edging for all visible 3/4" and 1" plywood, as required

Gypsum board

1	4' 9/16" x 6' 3-3/4" (back of base cabinet)
1	2' 10-9/16" x 2' 5-1/4" (back of center of desk)
1	6' 2-9/16" x 3' 10-1/2" (wall above desk)
	Omit gypsum board in speaker areas. Place insulation between speaker and oven.

Radio speaker frames (pine)

4	1 x 2 x 1' 1-1/8"
4	1 x 2 x 1' 6-1/2"
2	1' 1-1/8' x 1' 6-1/2" (wire cloth)
	Glued and nailed mitered frame

Desk top braces (fir)

2	1 x 4 x 6' 2-9/16"

Cleats (pine)

2	1 x 2 x 4' 9/16" (below microwave and cabinet)
2	1 x 2 x 10-1/2" (below microwave and cabinet)
2	3/4" x 3/4" x 1' 6" ± (oven cabinet)
8	3/4" x 3/4" x 11" (speaker cabinet)
16	3/4" x 3/4" x 1' 11-1/2" (base cabinet)
1	3/4" x 1-1/2" x 4' 9/16" (base cabinet)

Plywood drawers

		Fronts (3/4" plywood):
	2	1' 8" x 3-1/2"
	2	1' 8" x 5-9/16"
	3	1' 8" x 11-1/8"
	1	2' 10-9/16" x 3-1/2"

Qty.	Size and Description
	Backup fronts (1/2" plywood):
2	1' 4-1/2" x 2-3/8"
2	1' 4-1/2" x 4-7/16"
3	1' 4-1/2" x 10"
1	2' 8-9/16" x 2-3/8"
	Sides (1/2" plywood):
4	2-3/8" x 21"
4	4-7/16" x 21"
6	10" x 21"
2	2-3/8" x 21"
	Backs (1/2" plywood):
2	1' 5" x 2-3/8"
2	1' 5" x 4-7/16"
3	1' 5" x 10"
1	2' 9-1/16" x 2-3/8"
	Bottoms (1/4" plywood):
7	1' 5" x 20-1/4"
1	2' 9-1/16" x 20-1/4"

Oven tray (plywood)

1	3/4" x 12-1/2" x 2' 1" (front)
1	1/2" x 4-1/2" x 1' 11" (backup front)
1	1/2" x 4-1/2" x 1' 11-1/2" (back)
2	1/2" x 4-1/2" x 21" (sides)
1	1/4" x 1' 11-1/2" x 20-1/4" (bottom)

Base cabinet trays (plywood)

2	1/2" x 4-1/2" x 1' 7" (front)
2	1/2" x 4-1/2" x 1' 6-1/4" (back)
4	1/2" x 4-1/2" x 21" (sides)
1	1/4" x 1' 6-1/2" x 20-3/4" (bottom)

Laminate

1	2' x 6' 4-9/16" (desk top)
1	3/4" x 10' 4-11/16" (desk edges)
1	2' x 4' 9/16" (base cabinet)
1	1-1/2" x 4' 9/16" (base cabinet edges)

Construction Plan

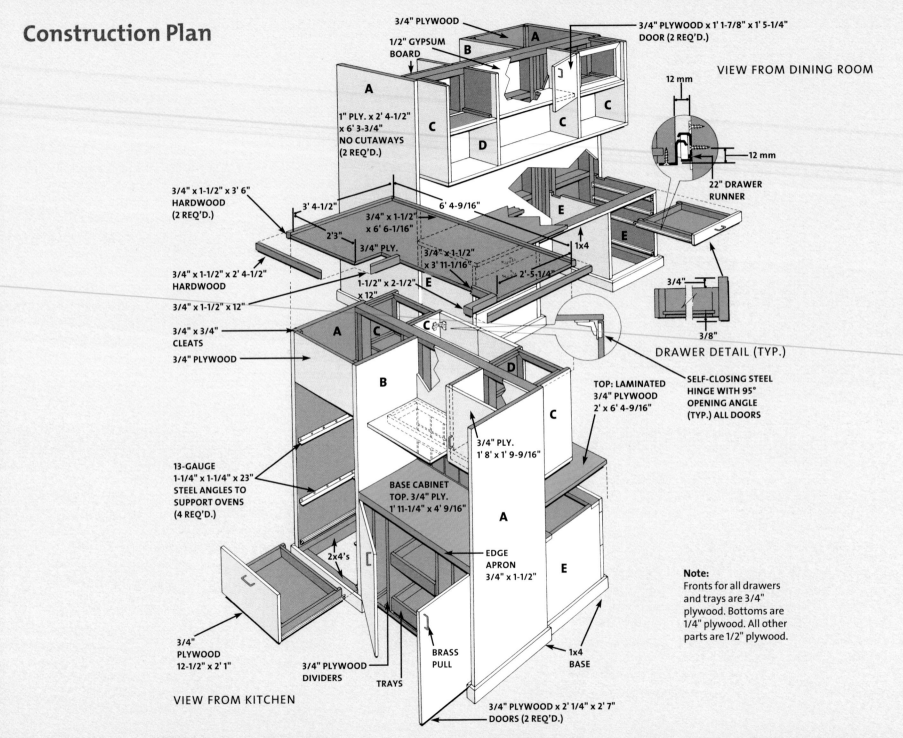

3/4" PLYWOOD

1/2" GYPSUM BOARD

3/4" PLYWOOD x 1' 1-7/8" x 1' 5-1/4" DOOR (2 REQ'D.)

A

B

A

A

C

C

C

C

C

D

D

VIEW FROM DINING ROOM

12 mm

12 mm

22" DRAWER RUNNER

1" PLY. x 2' 4-1/2" x 6' 3-3/4" NO CUTAWAYS (2 REQ'D.)

3/4" x 1-1/2" x 3' 6" HARDWOOD (2 REQ'D.)

3' 4-1/2"

6' 4-9/16"

3/4" x 1-1/2" x 6' 6-1/16"

2'3"

3/4" PLY.

3/4" x 1-1/2" x 3' 11-1/16"

1x4

E

E

E

3/4" x 1-1/2" x 2' 4-1/2" HARDWOOD

1-1/2" x 2-1/2" x 12"

2'-5-1/4"

E

3/4" x 1-1/2" x 12"

3/4"

3/8"

3/4" x 3/4" CLEATS

3/4" PLYWOOD

A

C

C

DRAWER DETAIL (TYP.)

B

D

SELF-CLOSING STEEL HINGE WITH 95° OPENING ANGLE (TYP.) ALL DOORS

C

TOP: LAMINATED 3/4" PLYWOOD 2' x 6' 4-9/16"

3/4" PLY. 1' 8' x 1' 9-9/16"

13-GAUGE 1-1/4" x 1-1/4" x 23" STEEL ANGLES TO SUPPORT OVENS (4 REQ'D.)

BASE CABINET TOP. 3/4" PLY. 1' 11-1/4" x 4' 9/16"

A

E

EDGE APRON 3/4" x 1-1/2"

2x4's

3/4" PLYWOOD 12-1/2" x 2' 1"

3/4" PLYWOOD DIVIDERS

TRAYS

BRASS PULL

1x4 BASE

Note:
Fronts for all drawers and trays are 3/4" plywood. Bottoms are 1/4" plywood. All other parts are 1/2" plywood.

VIEW FROM KITCHEN

3/4" PLYWOOD x 2' 1/4" x 2' 7" DOORS (2 REQ'D.)

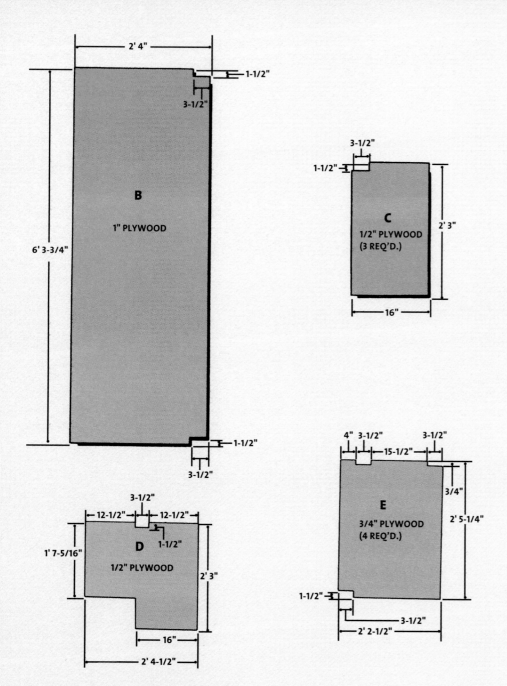

B
1" PLYWOOD

2' 4"

1-1/2"

3-1/2"

6' 3-3/4"

1-1/2"

3-1/2"

C
1/2" PLYWOOD
(3 REQ'D.)

3-1/2"

1-1/2"

2' 3"

16"

D
1/2" PLYWOOD

3-1/2"

12-1/2"   12-1/2"

1-1/2"

1' 7-5/16"

2' 3"

16"

2' 4-1/2"

E
3/4" PLYWOOD
(4 REQ'D.)

4"   3-1/2"   3-1/2"

15-1/2"

3/4"

2' 5-1/4"

1-1/2"

3-1/2"

2' 2-1/2"

KITCHEN ISLAND FRAMING DETAILS

MATERIALS

Qty.	Size and Description
24	6 x 6 ceramic tiles
11	22" drawer runners
5	Steel hinges (self-closing with mounting plates having 95° opening)
4	Steel angles (to support wall ovens, 1-1/4" x 1-1/4" x 23" x 13-gauge: approx. 3/32")
13	Brass cabinet door pulls
	Wire mold
1	Fluorescent fixture (for below microwave and adjoining cabinet)
	Plastic laminate
	1x4 fir
	2x4 fir
	1/4" plywood
	1/2" plywood
	3/4" plywood
	1" plywood
	1x2 hardwood stock
	2x4 hardwood stock
	1/8" hardwood edging
	Gypsum board
	Screws as needed
	Finish nails as needed
	Insulation
	Woodworker's glue
	Stain or varnish

Useful Features

This versatile divider design incorporates a number of useful features on both sides. The kitchen area has the double wall ovens and microwave oven seen in the photo on page 128. Below the microwave is a work counter and an electrical-outlet strip for countertop appliances. And under the ovens you can easily store oversized oven cookware in a large pull-out tray.

This room divider screens out mealtime clutter from the rest of the living space without closing off the kitchen entirely, so that the cooks aren't isolated. And the counter makes a handy staging area to prepare dishes using a food processor or other countertop appliances. The room divider can carve out a long, galley-type kitchen with a highly efficient work area. And the arrangement of the wall cabinets and divider here makes it possible for guests to help with meal preparation without crowding the kitchen. You can even use the counter on the desk side of the divider for extra kitchen workspace or as a serving buffet.

Plan Your Own Divider

The divider shown here incorporates design features you can adapt to just about any kitchen. Use this project as a guide to help design your own room divider, altering the plans to fit your space and needs. For example, although the desk shown on page 128 has a marble top, the plans call for a plastic-laminate top as a cost-saving alternative.

If space is at a premium, one option would be to build a partial wall approximately 6 feet high, place the oven and work center on the kitchen side, and eliminate the desk on the family-room side. Or you might reconfigure the shelves above the desk to house media equipment.

If you decide to choose materials such as cabinet-grade oak, birch, or pine plywood to match your existing kitchen cabinets, buy lumber for the cabinet sides to match your plywood. Then stain or varnish the room divider to match your cabinets.

For a project this size, you may want to ask your lumberyard to help you estimate the cost of materials, based on your final plans. When you have the lumber and hardware quotes in hand, you'll be better able to decide which materials and finishes will keep you within your budget.

Details

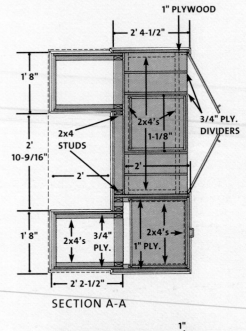

SECTION A-A

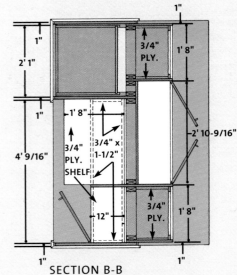

SECTION B-B

Note:
All visible edges to be finished with 1/8" hardwood edging, included in dimensioning.

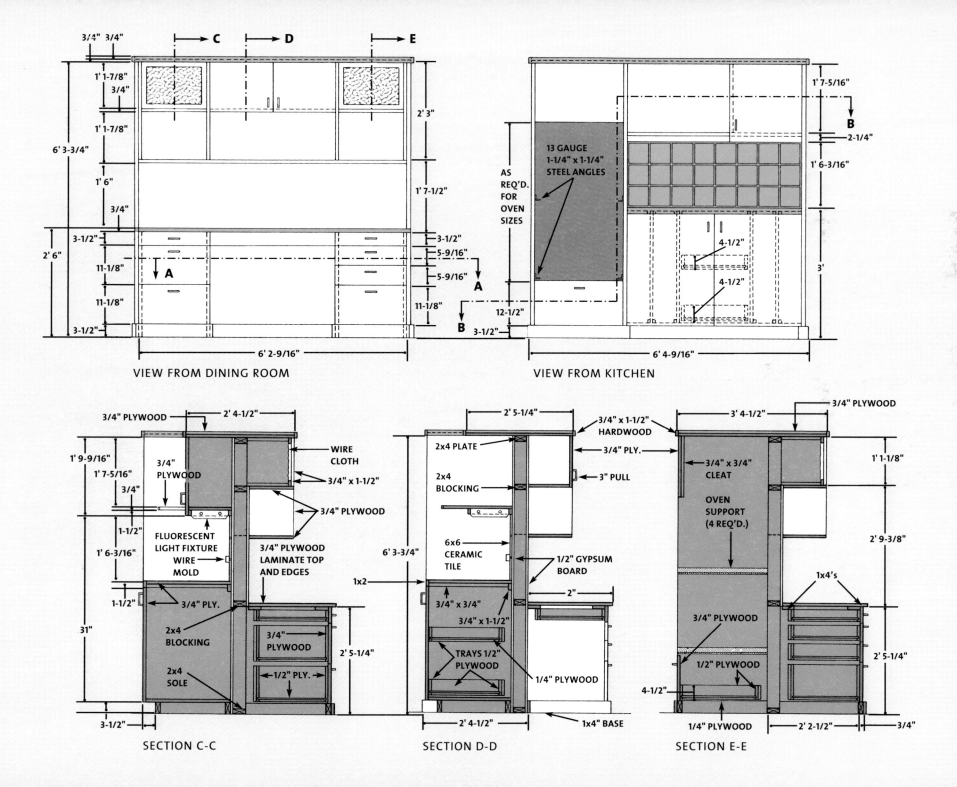

VIEW FROM DINING ROOM

3/4" 3/4"
1' 1-7/8"
3/4"
1' 1-7/8"
6' 3-3/4"
1' 6"
3/4"
2' 6"
3-1/2"
11-1/8"
11-1/8"
3-1/2"

C   D   E

2' 3"

1' 7-1/2"

3-1/2"
5-9/16"
5-9/16"
11-1/8"

A   A

6' 2-9/16"

VIEW FROM KITCHEN

13 GAUGE
1-1/4" x 1-1/4"
STEEL ANGLES

AS REQ'D. FOR OVEN SIZES

B

1' 7-5/16"
2-1/4"
1' 6-3/16"
3'

4-1/2"
4-1/2"

B

12-1/2"
3-1/2"

6' 4-9/16"

SECTION C-C

3/4" PLYWOOD
2' 4-1/2"

1' 9-9/16"
1' 7-5/16"
3/4"

3/4" PLYWOOD

WIRE CLOTH
3/4" x 1-1/2"

3/4" PLYWOOD

1-1/2"
1' 6-3/16"

FLUORESCENT LIGHT FIXTURE
WIRE MOLD

3/4" PLYWOOD
LAMINATE TOP AND EDGES

1-1/2"
3/4" PLY.

31"

2x4 BLOCKING

2x4 SOLE

3/4" PLYWOOD

1/2" PLY.

2' 5-1/4"

3-1/2"

SECTION D-D

2' 5-1/4"

3/4" x 1-1/2"
HARDWOOD

2x4 PLATE

3/4" PLY.

2x4 BLOCKING

3" PULL

6' 3-3/4"

6x6 CERAMIC TILE

1/2" GYPSUM BOARD

1x2

2"

3/4" x 3/4"

3/4" x 1-1/2"

TRAYS 1/2" PLYWOOD

1/4" PLYWOOD

2' 4-1/2"

1x4" BASE

SECTION E-E

3/4" PLYWOOD
3' 4-1/2"
3/4" PLYWOOD

3/4" x 3/4" CLEAT

1' 1-1/8"

OVEN SUPPORT (4 REQ'D.)

2' 9-3/8"

1x4's

3/4" PLYWOOD

1/2" PLYWOOD

4-1/2"

1/4" PLYWOOD

2' 5-1/4"

2' 2-1/2"
3/4"

Kitchen Storage Stretchers

Increase the capacity and efficiency of your kitchen storage space with any or all of these four projects.

Improve undersink storage with tilt-down sink fronts, a slide-out tray, perhaps a roll-out basket for trash, and a glide-out towel rack.

Make the most of unused cabinet space with swing-out spice racks.

Reclaim wasted corner space with half-moon-shaped pivot-and-glide shelves.

Step-by-Step Instructions for:

▶ **Tilt-down Sink Front**

▶ **Slide-out Tray**

▶ **Swing-out Spice Racks**

▶ **Pivot-and-Glide Corner Shelves**

Modern kitchens require better storage space than ever. Today we expect our cabinets to accommodate the pots, pans, and utensils they always have—plus small appliances, recycling bins, a variety of cleaning materials, and cartloads of prepackaged supermarket foods. In most cases, your existing cabinets can handle the load if they can be better organized and the space within them made more accessible.

With the help of a few specialty items and kits, you can increase the efficiency of your kitchen storage space for just a small investment of time and money. Best of all, the job requires no complex construction or unusual power tools.

Plan Your Projects

There are four storage projects in this chapter, as well as suggestions for additional storage improvements you can make. Each project requires some woodworking skills, but using ready-made hardware makes installation easy. You'll need basic tools and skills, and a router for two of the projects. A power miter saw will also be helpful, but it is not essential. Look at all the projects and consider the following information before deciding which ones to do.

Frameless Euro-style cabinets, built-in custom cabinets, and modular, stock-size cabinets like those shown on these pages differ considerably in their construction.

Before going too far into a project having specialty hardware or fittings, determine if you need to modify either the product instructions or the directions given here to suit your situation.

These projects will make your cabinets more accessible and better organized, but not all of them create more space. For instance, the pivot-and-glide shelves (left, bottom) provide excellent access to the far reaches of corner cabinets, but you may actually wind up with less total shelf space. So weigh the increase in convenience and efficiency against other factors before deciding to do a project.

Be sure not to overload the cabinets. You can modify the spice rack to hold soup cans (left, top), but hanging an extra 20 pounds from the outer frame of an upper cabinet may cause it to sag.

You can find the special hardware described here at home centers, full-service hardware stores, or through the mail-order source listed at the right. When shopping, keep your eye out for other organizing products that are easy to install. Examples are a glide-out towel rack and a roll-out basket (see the photo at the top left). Each is self-contained and is installed simply by driving screws in the mounting flanges.

TOOLS

HAND TOOLS

Framing square

Hacksaw

Hammer

Handsaw

Miter box

Nail set

Tape measure

Standard and offset screwdrivers

Tape measure

POWER TOOLS

Circular saw

Drill

Router; 3/8-in. rabbet bit

OPTIONAL

Power miter saw (rented)

Table saw

MATERIALS

1x3 pine

3/8" plywood

1/4" plywood

1/4" perforated hardboard

8d box or common nails

6d finish nails

1" brads

Pivot-and-glide kits*

Glide-out towel rack*

Roll-out basket*

4 " fall front" spring-loaded hinges*

36" plastic tray and end caps

Cabinet handles

Drawer glides*

Piano hinge*

Pivot-and-glide or pivot-only shelf kit*

Woodworker's glue

* Available from The Woodworkers' Store, Dept TFH, 4365 Willow Drive, Medina, MN 55340, (800) 279-4441.

In Canada, available from Lee Valley Tools Ltd., 1080 Morrison Drive, Ottawa, ONT K2H 8K7; (800) 267-8767

Tilt-down Sink Front

Most kitchen sink base cabinets have a fixed false front with a few precious inches of empty space between it and the sink. Altering the false front so that it tilts out will give you convenient storage space for pot scrubbers, soap pads, rubber gloves, and other small items that you'd like to have right at hand.

You can make the conversion with four "fall front" spring-loaded hinges, a 36-inch cut-to-length plastic tray, and end caps for the tray. You can either find kits that contain these components or purchase the parts separately. Either way, here's how to install the tray.

▶ First, determine whether or not your sink front has room for a tilt-down tray. Some sinks are too large or are mounted too close to the front of the counter to accommodate one. Remove the false front panels carefully (Photo 1). They are usually held by clips or screw blocks attached to the back side that you can reach from underneath.

Measure the distance between the front of the sink basin and the outer surface of the cabinet face frame. If this space is at least as deep as the accessories tray you'll be installing there, proceed; if not, replace the panels and choose another project.

▶ If you can proceed, drill holes for mounting a handle on each panel. Use the same-style handles as on your other drawers, and position the handles to match.

▶ Predrill holes for the hinges concealed inside the cabinet, and screw the hinges in place (Photo 2).

▶ Hold each panel in position, and mark the locations of the hinge holes on its back. Then remove the panels and predrill the hinge holes.

▶ Cut the trays to the required length, fit on the end caps, and hold each section in position against the back of its panel to mark holes for the mounting screws. Then drill the holes for those screws.

▶ Attach the handles to the panels. Then screw each front panel to the hinges in the cabinet (Photo 3). Finally, mount the accessories tray. You'll need to use an offset screwdriver when working in the awkward space between the panel and the cabinet frame.

MAKE THE TILT-DOWN SINK FRONT

FALSE FRONT PANEL (IN PLACE)
FALSE FRONT PANEL (REMOVED)
CABINET FACE FRAME

1

Measure the space between the sink and the front of the face frame. To remove a false front panel, twist its brackets or loosen the screws on the back of the panel.

CONCEALED HINGE

2

Install hinges on the edges of the cabinet opening. Temporarily reposition the false front panel, then mark and drill holes for the hinge and tray screws.

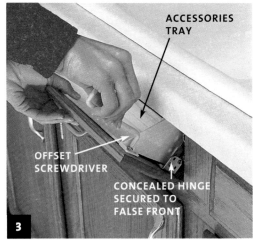

ACCESSORIES TRAY
OFFSET SCREWDRIVER
CONCEALED HINGE SECURED TO FALSE FRONT

3

Attach the handle to the front panel, then mount the panel on the hinge and add the accessories tray. Use an offset screwdriver in the tight spaces.

Slide-out Tray

A slide-out tray brings its contents out of the cabinet, so you don't have to stoop and search inside. It can be a simple box frame, or you can add bins, dividers, or racks to customize it.

▶ Measure the cabinet space, then cut pieces of 1x3 pine for a tray frame that is 1 inch narrower than the cabinet opening and 1 inch shallower than its depth.

▶ Miter the corners of the frame using a miter box and a handsaw (Photo 4). If you're planning to make the spice racks (page 138), consider cutting those pieces at the same time. If you are renting a power miter saw for this project you'll get the most use for your money.

▶ Assemble the frame with woodworker's glue and 4d finish nails (Photo 5). Drive the lower nails 1/2 inch from the bottom edge to stay clear of the bottom of the tray.

▶ Turn the assembled frame face down, and rout a 3/8 x 3/8-inch rabbet all around the inside bottom edge to receive the bottom drawer panel (Photo 6).

▶ Cut the bottom panel from 3/8-inch plywood. If the cabinet has moisture or ventilation problems, use perforated hardboard and paint it. Angle-cut the corners of the bottom panel to fit the rounded corners of the rabbet in the frame.

▶ Glue and nail the bottom in place, then attach a metal glide (Photo 7). A single, center-mounted glide is sufficient for most installations, but for heavy loads use two glides, one at each side. If the tray must be lifted to pass over the lip of the cabinet face frame, raise the fixed channel of the metal glide by mounting it on a strip of plywood on the cabinet bottom.

MAKE THE SLIDE-OUT TRAY

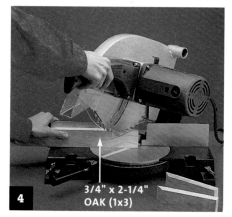

3/4" x 2-1/4" OAK (1x3)

4

Cut the corners of the 1x3 frame pieces to make mitered joints for strength and rigidity. Use a miter box or power miter saw, available for rent at most home centers.

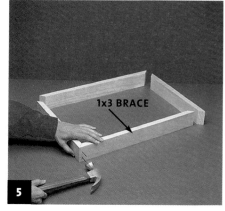

1x3 BRACE

5

Assemble the frame with woodworker's glue and 4d nails. Keep the lower nail 1/2 in. above the bottom. Check with a framing square to make sure that the corners are true.

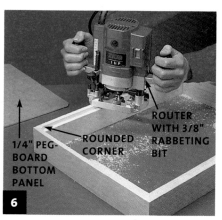

1/4" PEG-BOARD BOTTOM PANEL — ROUNDED CORNER — ROUTER WITH 3/8" RABBETING BIT

6

Rout a 3/8 x 3/8-in. rabbet around the inside of the back edges of the frame. Cut, fit, glue, and nail the bottom panel into the rabbet. Trim the bottom corners to fit the rabbet.

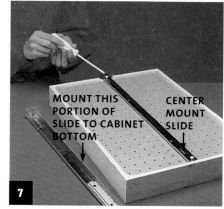

MOUNT THIS PORTION OF SLIDE TO CABINET BOTTOM — CENTER MOUNT SLIDE

7

Screw the movable runner of the glide to the tray bottom, and the fixed runners to the bottom of the cabinet. Use two glides if the tray will need to support heavy loads.

Swing-out Spice Racks

In cabinets that hold packaged foods, air often takes up more space than food. That's because a 2-inch high jar of paprika takes up as much shelf space as an 8-inch tall jar of olives. The result is a lot of wasted space. A good solution to this problem is swing-out racks that let you organize and store short boxes and jars.

Swing-out racks can be used in any type of cabinet—base or upper, short or tall. You can tailor them to hold everything from spices to cleaning supplies. Just don't overload the cabinet so the racks won't swing freely.

You may need to cut 2 inches or so off the depth of the existing shelves so the cabinet can accommodate the racks. In that case, you'll probably have to drill new holes for the clips or pegs that support the front edges of the shelves.

▶ Build a frame for each rack from 1x3 stock, with glued and nailed miter joints at the corners, as described for the slide-out tray frame (page 137, Photo 5).

▶ Rout a rabbet in the back edge of the frame 3/8 inch wide by 1/4 inch deep. Cut a back from 1/4-inch plywood (Photo 8). Angle-cut the corners to fit the rabbeted corners, then fasten the back in place with 4d finish nails.

▶ The shelves must be narrower than the frame because the back is inset 1/4 inch. Rip 1x3 stock to width on a table saw, or use 1x8 stock and a circular saw with a rip guide. The wider stock will support the circular saw better for making rip cuts.

▶ Use the thin strips left over from ripping the shelves for guard slats (Photo 9). Or use 1/4-inch lattice or similar stock. Cut the guard rails so that they reach across the full width of the frame, and nail them to the rack's face with 1-inch brads.

▶ Use a hacksaw to cut a strip of piano hinge to fit between the existing cabinet door hinges. Drill pilot holes and screw the hinge to the rack. Then locate and drill the holes and screw the hinge to the cabinet frame (Photo 10). Set the piano hinge far enough back on the edge of the cabinet frame so the new spice rack doesn't interfere with the swing of the cabinet door.

MAKE THE SWING-OUT SPICE RACKS

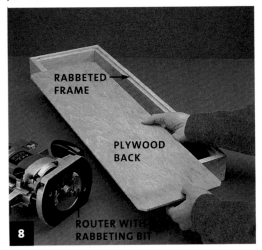

Cut a plywood back for each spice rack. Construct the frame of 1x3's with mitered corners. Glue and nail the back into a rabbet that is routed in the frame.

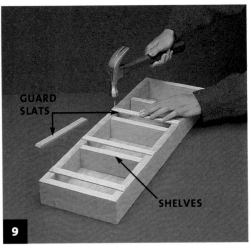

Determine shelf spacing by measuring the items you'll keep on the rack. Fasten the shelves with finish nails; use 1-in. brads for the guard slats on the front.

Mount the spice rack on piano hinges. You may have to reduce the depth of the existing shelves by 2 in. or so to make space for the rack.

Pivot-and-Glide Shelves

For the dark, inaccessible areas where cabinets meet at a corner—and where even a contortionist would have a hard time reaching—install pivot-and-glide shelves to bring stored items to you.

You have two choices for pivoted shelves: pivot-only, which allows you to swing the shelf halfway out of the cabinet, and pivot-and-glide, like the installation shown here. Pivot-and-glide construction allows you to swing the shelf out of the cabinet, then glide it another 10 to 12 inches toward you for even greater acces-

sibility. Both kinds are available in kits that include half-moon-shaped tray-shelves, a post, pivots, and shelf-support assemblies. Installation is not complex.

▶ Measure the cabinet-door opening carefully before buying a kit to determine the minimum door width required for the shelves. Consult the kit's specifications for size requirements. Most kits can be adapted to right- or left-hand blind corners.

▶ Unpack the parts, then rough-assemble them to get an idea of how the components fit together and how the unit operates.

▶ Drill mounting holes for the lower and upper post pivots on the back of the cabinet face frame using the kit template as a guide (Photo 11). Check and adjust the height of the upper pivot so the swinging

shelf doesn't interfere with the existing cabinet shelf.

▶ Screw the pivots in position on the cabinet frame (Photo 12). Put the lower pivot-and-glide assembly in place and install the metal post. It sits on the bottom pivot and extends through the upper one. Tighten the screws in both pivots.

▶ Place the upper pivot-and-glide assembly over the top of the post; it rests on the upper post pivot (Photo 13).

▶ Finally, screw the plastic tray-shelves to the pivot-and-glide assemblies (Photo 14).

MAKE THE PIVOT-AND-GLIDE SHELVES

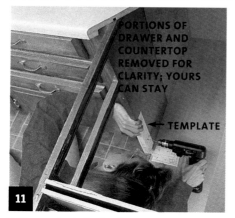

11 Drill mounting holes for the post pivots using the kit template. The upper pivot position sets the height of the upper, movable shelf.

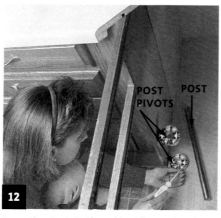

12 Screw the pivots to the cabinet frame. Put the lower pivot-and-glide assembly in place, then insert the post and tighten the setscrews.

13 Place the upper pivot-and-glide assembly over the end of the post that extends up through the pivot. The assembly rests on the pivot.

14 Screw the half-moon tray-shelves to the top and bottom pivot-and-guide assemblies. Plug holes with the plastic screw covers provided.

Spacious Pantry Cabinet

Keep food organized
and easily accessible with this
builder-friendly pantry.

While it's not a project for beginners, this cabinet goes together quickly and
relatively easily. And the final product is immensely practical.

Convenient Design Features

This versatile design, which is practical and relatively easy to build, can be adapted to fit almost any kitchen. In customizing your pantry cabinet, you can take advantage of all or just some of the design features described here.

Roll-out Trays

Roll-out trays are the best possible storage arrangement for a pantry (Photo 1). They use room efficiently, especially if you adjust the spacing of the trays to suit your food-buying habits. Roll-out trays give you instant access to items, since everything is visible and easy to reach.

And because they spread the weight of everything you store over many separate trays, overloading is seldom a problem.

Melamine Interior

This pantry uses special melamine-coated particleboard for interior surfaces (Photo 2). Melamine is a hard plastic that's much thinner than plastic laminate. It's glued to the particleboard at the factory, on one or both sides of the panels, so all you have to do is cut the panels to size. Melamine is durable, and it makes the cabinet interior bright and easy to clean. Because it's so thin, the dimensions of the melamine won't affect your construction calculations.

European-style Hardware

European or Euro-style drawer glides and door hinges are expensive, but worth every penny (Photo 3). These drawer glides are easy to install, and they cover the exposed edges of the plywood tray bottoms. They roll smoothly and extend to almost their full length, making it easy to retrieve items at the back of each tray.

Euro-style hinges adjust in three dimensions by as much as 1/8 inch, making it easy to align the doors for uniform spacing all around. These hinges are also much easier to install than butt hinges.

CONVENIENT DESIGN FEATURES

1

Roll-out trays provide efficient storage. They move easily, even with a full load, and let you reach everything without difficulty.

2

White melamine plastic on the inside makes the pantry bright and easy to clean. It comes already attached to the particleboard, so there's no extra work.

3

Euro-style hinges look good and are practical because they're adjustable in every direction, which greatly simplifies hanging cabinet doors.

Construction Plan

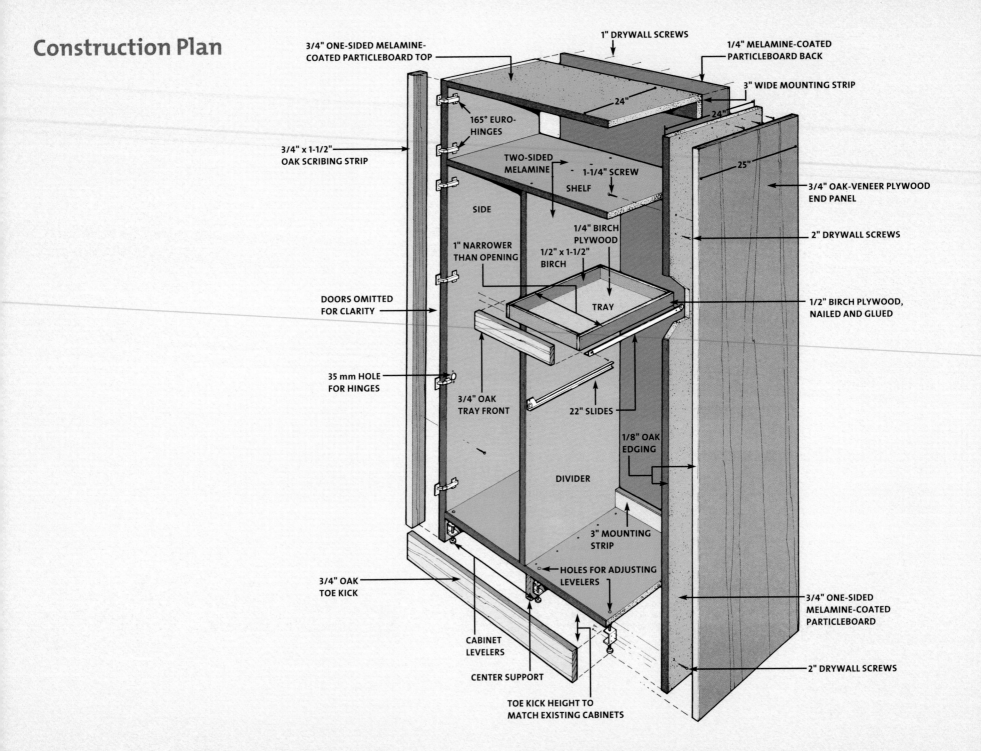

3/4" ONE-SIDED MELAMINE-COATED PARTICLEBOARD TOP

1" DRYWALL SCREWS

1/4" MELAMINE-COATED PARTICLEBOARD BACK

3" WIDE MOUNTING STRIP

24"

24"

165° EURO-HINGES

3/4" x 1-1/2" OAK SCRIBING STRIP

TWO-SIDED MELAMINE

1-1/4" SCREW

SHELF

SIDE

25"

3/4" OAK-VENEER PLYWOOD END PANEL

1/4" BIRCH PLYWOOD

2" DRYWALL SCREWS

1" NARROWER THAN OPENING

1/2" x 1-1/2" BIRCH

TRAY

DOORS OMITTED FOR CLARITY

1/2" BIRCH PLYWOOD, NAILED AND GLUED

35 mm HOLE FOR HINGES

3/4" OAK TRAY FRONT

22" SLIDES

1/8" OAK EDGING

DIVIDER

3" MOUNTING STRIP

3/4" OAK TOE KICK

HOLES FOR ADJUSTING LEVELERS

3/4" ONE-SIDED MELAMINE-COATED PARTICLEBOARD

CABINET LEVELERS

CENTER SUPPORT

TOE KICK HEIGHT TO MATCH EXISTING CABINETS

2" DRYWALL SCREWS

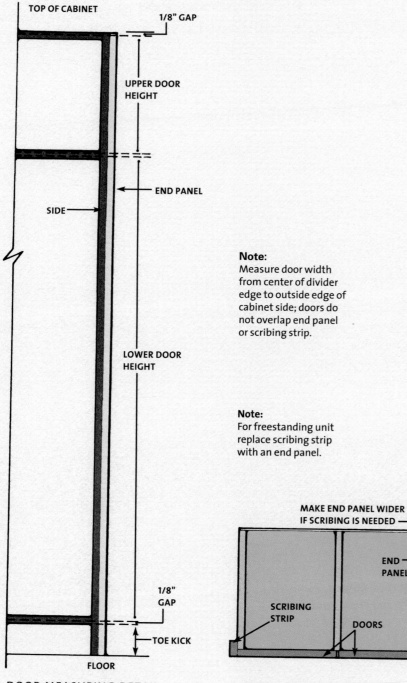

Note:
Measure door width from center of divider edge to outside edge of cabinet side; doors do not overlap end panel or scribing strip.

Note:
For freestanding unit replace scribing strip with an end panel.

DOOR MEASURING DETAIL

Labels (left diagram):
TOP OF CABINET
1/8" GAP
UPPER DOOR HEIGHT
END PANEL
SIDE
LOWER DOOR HEIGHT
1/8" GAP
TOE KICK
FLOOR

CROSS-SECTION DETAIL

Labels (cross-section diagram):
MAKE END PANEL WIDER IF SCRIBING IS NEEDED
END PANEL
SCRIBING STRIP
DOORS

TOOLS

HAND TOOLS
Block plane
Compass
Framing square
Hammer
Level
Nail set
Pipe clamps
Screwdrivers
Straightedge
Stud finder
Tape measure

POWER TOOLS
Drill; twist bits, drill guide
Table saw or radial arm saw with fine-tooth carbide-tip blade

OPTIONAL
Drill press
Router; flush-trimming bit; straight carbide-tip bit
Sander
Self-centering Vix bit; 35 mm Forstner bit

MATERIALS

Qty.	Size and Description
2 sheets	4' x 8' 3/4" particleboard, melamine-coated on one side (frame sides, top, bottom)
1 sheet	4' x 8' x 3/4" particleboard, melamine-coated both sides (shelf, center divider)
1 sheet	4' x 8' x 1/4" particleboard, melamine-coated one side (back)
1 sheet	4' x 8' x 3/4" oak-veneer plywood (end panel or panels)
1 sheet	4' x 8' x 1/4" birch plywood (tray bottoms)
1 sheet	4' x 8' x 1/2" birch plywood (tray frames)
61 linear ft.	3/4" x 3" oak (tray fronts, toe kick, scribing strip, door frames)
1 sheet	4' x 8' x 1/4" oak-veneer plywood (door panels), or purchase doors*
14 pairs	22" drawer glides**
12	Euro-style hinges, 165° **
6	Cabinet levelers**
As needed	Wood dowels (for door-frame construction)
	1/8" oak edging
	1", 2", and 3" drywall screws
	1-1/4" wood screws
	4d finish nails
	Wood putty
	Stain
	Varnish

* Available from Porto Doors Co., Dept TFH, 65 Cogwheel Lane, Seymour, CT 06483, (203) 888-6191; or Quality Doors, Dept. TFH, 603 Big Stone Gap, Duncanville, TX 75137; (800) 950-3667.

** Available from Woodworkers' Supply, Dept. TFH, 5604 Alameda Pl., Albuquerque, NM 87113; (800) 645-9292.

Locate the Pantry

In most kitchens there are a number of possible places to put a pantry cabinet. If you don't have the room to install one as a freestanding unit, you can remove a section of your existing countertop, base, and upper cabinets as we did here. This is bound to reduce your counter space, however.

If you have a closet that backs up to a kitchen wall, you can appropriate some of the closet's space and build the pantry into the wall. Many older kitchens have broom closets, which are prime candidates for outfitting with roll-out trays of the kind shown here. If you really can't fit this cabinet into your kitchen, try implementing some of the kitchen improvement ideas shown in "Kitchen Storage Stretchers" (pages 134–139) instead.

Modify the Design

The cabinet shown is simply a box made from melamine-coated particleboard. The exposed edges are covered with oak trim, and the exposed side is covered with a finished end panel of 3/4-inch oak veneer plywood. The doors can either be purchased or else made of solid oak that is doweled together around panels of 1/4-inch oak-veneer plywood.

The cabinet interior features a center panel to divide the space in half vertically. This avoids having to make roll-out trays so wide that they become overloaded. You can space the trays however you like; you don't need to align them on each side of the vertical divider. And at the bottom,

you may prefer to install a roll-out basket or a tip-out bin for bulky items instead of providing shelves as shown here.

You can make the upper section (with the small doors) just about any height you like, and even add more roll-out trays if you wish. Even though they'll be high, the space will be more accessible than it would be without them.

Match the finished end panel (or both finished end panels if you're building a freestanding pantry) and the doors—if you make them—to your existing cabinet doors. Test your stain and varnish carefully to achieve a good color match.

If you choose to purchase new doors for the pantry cabinet (see the Materials List, page 143), you can reface all of your other cabinet doors to match; many home centers and kitchen design centers offer refacing services. For more money, you can hire a local cabinetmaker to custom-build your doors.

A potential problem with buying custom-made doors is ordering the wrong size. Don't order doors for your pantry until it's completed and you know exactly what size you'll need. The doors will cover the edges of the particleboard frame, but not the end panel or panels. They also must meet over the center divider.

The doors for this pantry are relatively easy to build. The frames are made of white oak joined with dowels, with a panel of 1/4-inch plywood set into the grooves in the frame members. Edged plywood doors would be even easier to make.

Draw a Plan

This cabinet is 32 inches wide and just under 7 feet tall. It's 1 inch deeper than the adjacent countertop, so the doors will clear the dishwasher and the cabinet will conceal the cut edge of the countertop.

You probably will have to alter the pantry's height, width, and depth to conform to the dimensions of your kitchen. Measure the space where the pantry will stand. Then determine the sizes of all of the parts and how many of each you'll need. Don't forget to allow for the 1/8-inch edging on the front edges of the center divider, the cabinet sides, and the end panel or panels.

There are no critical dimensions for the cabinet parts except that the roll-out trays must be 1 inch narrower than their openings to accommodate the glides. Let the vertical spacing of the trays be determined by the room needed for the groceries you typically buy; it can be anywhere from 15 inches for the lower trays to 6 inches for the upper ones. To save on material, keep your cabinet parts no more than 24 inches wide—in other words, half the width of a 4x8-foot sheet of particleboard or plywood.

Make Cutting and Materials Lists

Referring to the plan you have drawn, make a cutting list that indicates the number of pieces in your cabinet and the exact measurements of each. Double-check all of the dimensions to make sure your cutting list is completely correct before you order any materials.

Use the cutting list sizes to determine how much material you need. Remember what every cabinetmaker has learned: It's much cheaper to make mistakes on paper. Draw to-scale sketches of 4x8-foot sheets of material, and experiment with various layouts to fit as many parts as possible on each sheet with a minimum of waste. Then make a list of the materials and hardware you'll need.

Tool and Skill Considerations

Although you won't need a shop full of power tools to build this pantry, you will need either a table saw or a radial arm saw to cut the melamine panels accurately and without chipping. Use a fine-tooth carbide-tip blade to make clean cuts in the two-sided melamine particleboard.

Though not absolutely necessary, a router will also come in handy. A self-centering Vix bit will simplify hardware installation, and a 35 mm Forstner bit will help you mount the hinges.

This cabinet is screwed together with drywall screws. There are no rabbets or dadoes, no joints of any kind to cut, and no gluing involved in the frame construction. If you make a mistake, you can simply unscrew the cabinet to fix it.

This method of assembly also means that if you cut the back piece perfectly square and attach it flush with the edges of the sides, the entire cabinet becomes self-squaring (Photo 4). The same is true of the roll-out trays; if you cut each bottom piece square, the entire tray will become square when you attach it to its frame.

Despite the fact that screw joinery makes this pantry simple to assemble, this is definitely a project for intermediate to advanced woodworkers only. The cabinet itself is relatively easy to build but, because of its scale, installing it and modifying your kitchen to accommodate it can be tricky. If you're unsure of your skills, consider hiring a cabinetmaker or professional remodeler to help you plan and install the pantry.

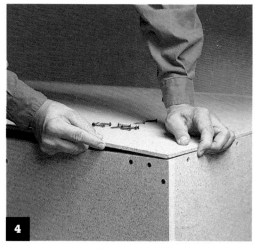

Screw joinery means the cabinet back can simply be screwed to the frame. The cabinet is automatically squared up when you align the edges.

Prepare the Frame Pieces

You can prepare the side, bottom, and top particleboard pieces, the edging, and drill the hinge and guide holes now. Other cutting and drilling will come later.

Cutting the Sides, Bottom, and Top

Slowly and carefully cut the particleboard pieces to the sizes shown in your cutting list (Photo 5). See the tip on page 147 for more information on cutting melamine-coated particleboard. Don't cut the end panel or panels yet, or the 1/4-inch particleboard for the back. Check that the top, bottom, and shelf are all the same size.

Cutting and Gluing the Edging

Cut the solid-wood edging at least 1/16 inch wider than the particleboard edge. Glue it to the front edges of the particleboard; use clamps or masking tape to hold it in place until the glue dries (Photo 6). You can plane off the excess, but be especially careful; if you make just one cut too deep, you'll cut through the melamine and ruin the piece. It's easier to use a router and a flush-trimming bit instead. Stain and finish the edging now.

Drilling Hinge Mortises and Glide Holes

Drill flat-bottom mortise holes in the cabinet sides for the hinges with a 35 mm Forstner bit. Secure this bit in a drill guide to make these holes. Then use the drill guide or a drill press when you drill hinge mortises in the doors (Photo 7). Place a hinge in each mortise to mark the positions of the mounting holes. Drill pilot holes at those marks. Do not mount the hinges yet; you'll need room to mark and mount the tray glides.

Consult your plans for the positions of the roll-out trays. Be sure that they will not interfere with the hinges. Measure and mark the tray positions, then use a drawer glide at each position to mark the mounting holes for the glides. Leave a 7/8-inch space between the glide and the front of the cabinet to accommodate the tray front. Drill pilot holes for the drawer glides at the marks. Finally, screw the hinges to the cabinet sides.

PREPARE THE FRAME PIECES

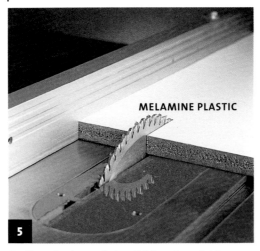

5

Cut the melamine-coated particleboard on a table saw with a fine-tooth carbide-tip blade. Make the cut slowly to avoid chipping the thin plastic surface.

MELAMINE PLASTIC

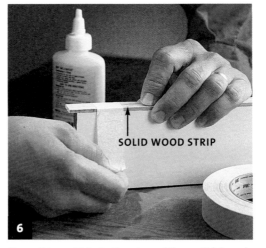

6

Glue solid-wood trim to the edges of the particleboard; hold it in position with masking tape. Trim the edging to width with a router.

SOLID WOOD STRIP

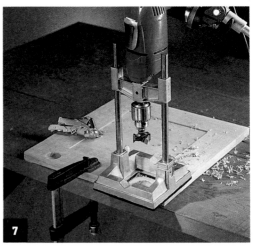

7

Drill mortise holes for the Euro-style hinges using a drill guide. Use a special 35 mm Forstner bit to make the flat-bottom holes that the hinges require.

Assemble the Frame

Use 2-inch drywall screws when you fasten the particleboard parts together.

Fasten the mounting strip to the top by driving screws through the top into the edge of the mounting strip.

Attach the shelf and the bottom to the center divider by driving screws through the shelf and bottom into the edges of the divider. Be sure the divider is exactly centered on them and is square to their front edges.

Screw one side of the cabinet to the edges of the top, shelf, and bottom. Make sure the bottom will be high enough above the floor to leave room for a toe kick to match that of the existing cabinets. Use a framing square to align the bottom, shelf, and top at right angles to the side. Clamp the pieces to hold them in position while you drill pilot holes and drive the screws (Photo 8). Countersink the screwheads. Attach the other side in the same way.

Measure the cabinet, then cut the 1/4-inch particleboard back. Check that it is square by measuring from corner to corner and verifying that the distances are the same. Drill pilot holes, and drive 1-inch drywall screws through the back into the frame (Photo 9). Fasten the back to the rear edges of the top and one side first, then screw it to the other side, the shelf, the divider, and the bottom. If you have cut the back square, it will pull the cabinet box into square.

Screw on the bottom mounting strips, one on each side of the center divider. Secure the mounting strips by screwing up through the bottom and in from the sides. Then cut a center support strip to go under the middle of the cabinet bottom. Offset it to one side of the divider, and drive screws down through the bottom into the support's top edge.

If your plan calls for it, cut and attach a scribing strip to the side of the cabinet along the wall (see the Cross-Section Detail, page 143). Directions for cutting a scribing strip to obtain a snug fit against the wall are found on page 73.

Screw on the levelers, and drill the access holes for the adjustment screws (Photo 10).

Cutting Tip

When cutting melamine-coated particleboard, minimize chipping by placing the melamine side face up if you use a table saw. Use a fine-tooth carbide-tip blade and feed the work slowly. If you have trouble with two-sided melamine pieces, cut them slightly oversize, then use a straightedge and a router with a straight carbide bit to clean up the edges.

ASSEMBLE THE FRAME

Assemble the main cabinet parts with drywall screws. With a pipe clamp, secure the parts in position while you drill the pilot holes.

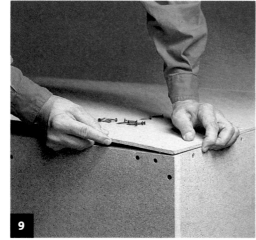

Line up the back and the cabinet edges carefully before screwing the back in place. A square-cut back will automatically true up the entire frame.

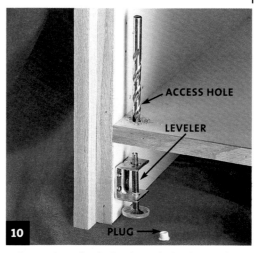

Drill access holes for the levelers, which adjust with a screwdriver from inside the cabinet. Put removable plugs in these holes later.

Cut the End Panel

Cut the end panel (or panels, if you're building a freestanding pantry). Make the panel 1/4 inch wider than the depth of the cabinet if you want to scribe it against the back wall during installation. (For more information on how to scribe for a tight fit, see page 73.) Otherwise, cut it straight, and cover any gap at the back wall with molding. Attach edging to the front lip as you did with the particleboard edges. Stain and finish the panel to match your kitchen, but don't attach it to the side of the cabinet yet. If you're planning to make doors, do so now. See "Making Your Own Doors," opposite.

Make the Roll-out Trays

Cut the frames for the trays from 1/2-inch birch plywood. Cut the plywood into strips 1-1/2 inches wide, then cut the strips to length for the sides, fronts, and backs of the frame. The sides are 7/8 inch shorter than the interior depth of the cabinet to allow for a facing piece across the front. The frame fronts and backs are 2 inches smaller than the interior width between the center divider and one side. When they are fastened between the frame sides, the outside dimension must be 1 inch less than the width of the cabinet section to provide clearance for the glides that support the trays. Glue and nail the frames together with 4d finish nails (Photo 11).

Measure the outside dimensions of the trays and cut the tray bottoms from 1/4-inch plywood. Cut the bottoms square, and attach them to the tray frames with glue and 4d finish nails. This will square up the frames.

Screw the drawer glides into the holes you drilled for them earlier (Photo 12). Then screw the drawer glides to the tray frames and test-fit the trays in the cabinet (Photo 13). Adjust the fit as you think necessary, either by sanding the tray side or by shimming out the drawer glide with tape or washers.

Cut, sand, and then stain and finish the solid-wood facings for the trays. Fasten them in place by driving short screws through the plywood tray frames into their facings.

Position the Cabinet

Place the cabinet in position in your kitchen. If you're building a freestanding pantry, attach the finished end panels first by driving 1-1/4 inch wood screws through the cabinet sides and into the backs of the panels.

If one side of the cabinet has a scribing strip to fit against a wall, do not attach the end panels to the other side yet. Instead, put the cabinet into position with that side tight against the adjacent counter and cabinets. Adjust the levelers until the cabinet sides are plumb; check for plumb with a level.

Set a compass to 3/4 inch wide. Scribe a line conforming to the shape of the wall down the scribing strip (Photo 14).

MAKE THE ROLL-OUT TRAYS

11

Assemble the tray frames with glue and 4d finish nails. Clamp the pieces in position while nailing. Glue and nail the bottoms, too.

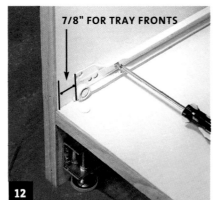

7/8" FOR TRAY FRONTS

12

Attach drawer guides inside the cabinet, set back to allow room for the tray fronts. Drill pilot holes before driving the screws.

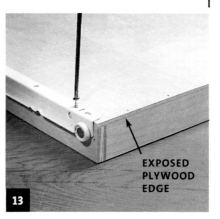

EXPOSED PLYWOOD EDGE

13

Attach drawer glides to the trays. Notice how this type of glide covers the exposed side edge of the plywood tray bottom.

Move the cabinet out again to plane or sand the scribing strip down to the scribed line. This will ensure a snug fit against the wall when you position the cabinet.

While the cabinet is out of position, use a stud finder to locate the studs in the wall behind it. Measure the distance of the studs from a common point—the nearest corner, for instance.

Slide the cabinet back in place and make sure that it is plumb and level. Measure and mark the stud positions on the mounting strips in the back of the cabinet. Screw through the mounting strips into the studs behind the cabinet with 3-inch drywall screws (Photo 15). If the cabinet is not tight against the back wall, add shims behind the mounting strips before driving screws into the studs.

Slide the finished end panel into place over the exposed cabinet side. Fasten it in position with 1-1/4 inch wood screws driven from the inside (Photo 16).

Final Touches

Mount the doors on the cabinet, adjusting them so there is a uniform gap and a flush fit, using the screw adjustments on the hinges. Then attach the door pulls.

Cut and finish the toe kick, nail it in place, set the nailheads below the wood surface, and fill the nail holes with wood putty. If you would like to make your own wood putty that matches the color of the wood, save some of the sanding dust and mix it with white glue.

Making Your Own Doors

The doors consist of panels of 1/4-in. oak-veneer plywood set into grooved frames made of 3/4- x 3/4-in. oak (see the photo at right). The frames are doweled and glued together. Stain and finish the completed doors to match the side panel and the rest of your kitchen cabinets.

FRAME
PLYWOOD

Make the doors with glued-and-doweled frames and 1/4-in. plywood panels set into grooves routed or sawed in the frame edges.

POSITION THE CABINET

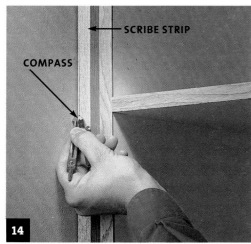

SCRIBE STRIP

COMPASS

14

Use a compass to mark wall irregularities on a scribing strip on the cabinet. For a tight fit, plane or sand the strip to the marked line.

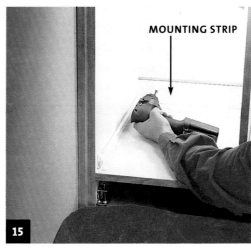

MOUNTING STRIP

15

Fasten the cabinet to the back wall. Drive 3-in. drywall screws through the top and bottom mounting strips into the wall studs.

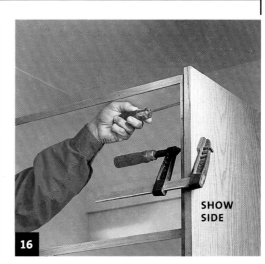

SHOW SIDE

16

Screw on the finished end panel from inside the cabinet. The panel is cut from 3/4-in. plywood and trimmed with solid-wood edging.

Bathroom Medicine Cabinet

Grace your bathroom with this spacious double-door medicine cabinet in warm natural oak.

An eye-catching new medicine cabinet can often be one of the most attractive ways to improve your bathroom storage. If you are familiar with routing simple beading and rabbet joints, you should find this project well within your skills.

When replacing an older medicine cabinet having a single center-mounted light over it, it may be best to use the same light or another of the same type, to avoid running new electrical supply lines. However, if electrical work doesn't bother you, consider a light on each side of the mirrors. Many find that this arrangement provides the best illumination.

Lend a touch of country to your bath with this mirrored medicine cabinet featuring a gracefully scrolled top, decorative edge beading, and a full-width shelf for your most-used items.

Construction Plan

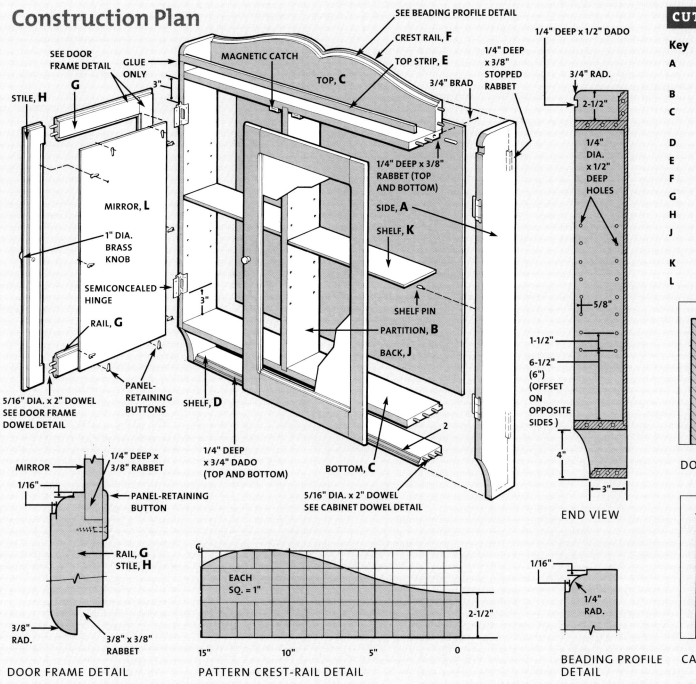

SEE DOOR FRAME DETAIL

GLUE ONLY

STILE, **H**

G

3"

MAGNETIC CATCH

SEE BEADING PROFILE DETAIL

CREST RAIL, **F**

TOP STRIP, **E**

TOP, **C**

3/4" BRAD

1/4" DEEP x 3/8" STOPPED RABBET

1/4" DEEP x 3/8" RABBET (TOP AND BOTTOM)

SIDE, **A**

SHELF, **K**

MIRROR, **L**

1" DIA. BRASS KNOB

SEMICONCEALED HINGE

RAIL, **G**

SHELF PIN

PARTITION, **B**

BACK, **J**

5/16" DIA. x 2" DOWEL SEE DOOR FRAME DOWEL DETAIL

PANEL-RETAINING BUTTONS

3"

SHELF, **D**

1/4" DEEP x 3/4" DADO (TOP AND BOTTOM)

BOTTOM, **C**

5/16" DIA. x 2" DOWEL SEE CABINET DOWEL DETAIL

Cutting List

Key	Qty.	Size and Description
A	2	3/4" x 4-1/2" x 32-1/2" oak (cabinet sides)
B	1	3/4" x 4-1/4" x 25" oak (partition)
C	2	3/4" x 4-1/2" x 28-1/2" oak (top and bottom)
D	1	3/4" x 3" x 28-1/2" oak (shelf)
E	1	1/4" x 1/2" x 30" oak (top strip)
F	1	3/4" x 5" x 28-1/2" oak (crest rail)
G	4	3/4" x 2-1/2" x 10-3/8" oak (door rails)
H	4	3/4" x 2" x 25" oak (door stiles)
J	1	1/4" x 25-1/4" x 29-1/4" oak plywood (back)
K	4	1/4" x 4" x 13-3/4" oak
L	2	1/4" x 11-1/16" x 20-11/16" mirror

1/4" DEEP x 1/2" DADO

3/4" RAD.

2-1/2"

1/4" DIA. x 1/2" DEEP HOLES

5/8"

1-1/2"

6-1/2" (6") (OFFSET ON OPPOSITE SIDES)

4"

3"

END VIEW

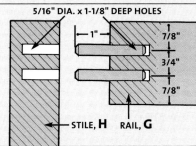

5/16" DIA. x 1-1/8" DEEP HOLES

1"

7/8"

3/4"

7/8"

STILE, **H**   RAIL, **G**

DOOR FRAME DOWEL DETAIL

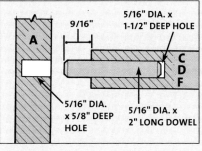

5/16" DIA. x 1-1/2" DEEP HOLE

9/16"

A

C D F

5/16" DIA. x 5/8" DEEP HOLE

5/16" DIA. x 2" LONG DOWEL

CABINET DOWEL DETAIL

MIRROR

1/4" DEEP x 3/8" RABBET

1/16"

PANEL-RETAINING BUTTON

RAIL, **G** STILE, **H**

3/8" RAD.

3/8" x 3/8" RABBET

DOOR FRAME DETAIL

EACH SQ. = 1"

15"   10"   5"   0

2-1/2"

PATTERN CREST-RAIL DETAIL

1/16"

1/4" RAD.

BEADING PROFILE DETAIL

Cut and Shape the Parts

Cut the sides (A), top and bottom (C), crest rail (F), and shelf (D) to the width and length specified in the Cutting List on page 151. Sand all the pieces smooth with medium (150 grit) sandpaper.

Using the grid shown in the Crest Rail Pattern in the plans on the preceding page, make a template out of heavy paper for the curves of the crest rail (F). Only half the crest rail is shown on the pattern, so you will need to flop the pattern to complete the shape.

Affix this template to the wood, then cut out the curved edges in the crest rail. Use a saber saw or a band saw (Photo 1). Also lay out and cut the curve in the sides (A). (See the End View in the plans.)

Smooth the cuts evenly by using a file, a scraper, or a small sanding drum mounted in an electric drill.

Chuck a self-piloting beading bit in a router, then cut the beaded edges on the crest rail (F) and shelf (D). For ease in making these cuts on narrow stock, mount the router in a table (Photo 2).

Now, using your table saw or radial arm saw, cut dadoes in both the top and bottom pieces (C) that hold the partition (B). Make your cuts so that the partition fits tightly. Later you can sand the partition for an easier fit. At this time also cut the small dadoes in the sides (A) for the top strip (E). Cut the top strip to the dimensions in the Cutting List and sand it smooth, but don't cut it to length yet.

Assemble the Parts

After checking that the bottom edge of the crest rail (F) is square with the sides, glue it to the top (C), aligning the ends with a straightedge. Locate and bore dowel holes in the ends of this assembly. Use dowel centers to transfer the locations of the holes to the sides (A). (See the Cabinet Dowel Detail on page 151.) Use brad-point drill bits for accuracy in boring the dowel holes. Then glue the dowels into the top and crest-rail assembly.

Drill dowel holes in the bottom and the shelf (D), using a doweling jig designed for corner and tee joints. Assemble the sides, shelf, bottom and top assembly to form the case (Photo 3). Before the glue dries, check that everything is square.

Use a self-piloting rabbeting bit to cut the rabbet for the back (J). You can either square up the rounded corners left by the router bit or round the corners of the back to fit. Cut the back to size, but don't install it yet. Trim the partition (B) to width, and cut its length to fit the dadoes exactly. Now sand the partition to size to fit the dadoes if necessary, and glue it in place.

To bore the shelf-pin holes, make a drilling jig from a narrow piece of scrap wood, placing 1/4-inch diameter holes 1-1/2 inches apart. Then clamp this jig to the inside of the cabinet to guide your drill. Notice in the End View on page 151 that the holes on the left and right sides of the case are offset by 1/2 inch (6 inches and 6 1/2 inches) so that they won't line up and penetrate the partition (B).

CUT AND SHAPE THE PARTS

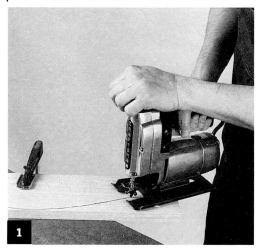

1

Cut the curved edges of the crest rail with a saber saw or a band saw. Smooth the edges with a file, a scraper, or a small sanding drum mounted in an electric drill.

2

Cut the beading on the front edge of the crest-rail curves with a self-piloting beading bit in your router. Mount the router in a router table for easier cutting.

After boring the holes for the shelf pins, install the back (J). Finally, cut the inner shelves (K) out of 1/4-inch oak.

Cut the door rails (G) and door stiles (H) to the sizes given in the Cutting List (page 151) and belt-sand the pieces smooth. Bore the rails and stiles for dowels and assemble them (see the Door Frame Detail in the plans). For frame joints like these, a self-centering doweling jig works very well (Photo 4). Shape the beaded inside edge of the frame with a self-piloting bit and your router table, then change to a rabbeting bit to cut the rabbets that will be used to hold the mirrors.

The router will make rabbets with rounded corners, so you'll need to square them up with a chisel to fit the square corners of the mirrors (Photo 5). Drill pilot holes on the inside of each door for the panel-retaining buttons to hold the mirrors in place (see the Door Frame Detail on page 151), then make pilot holes for the doorknobs.

Locate and drill holes for the hinges and mount them. Check that the doors fit properly, then remove them. Finish-sand all the components of the medicine cabinet with 320-grit sandpaper, and then apply three coats of moistureproof polyurethane

varnish. Between coats, sand the pieces with 320-grit sandpaper and wipe them clean with a tack cloth.

Once the last coat of varnish is dry, install the mirrors, rehang the doors, screw on the magnetic catches and pulls, and insert the shelves. Attach the cabinet to the wall by screwing through the crest rail (F) into wall studs with 3-inch screws. Drive two 2-inch screws through the bottom edge of the back, doing so from inside the cabinet.

ASSEMBLE THE PARTS

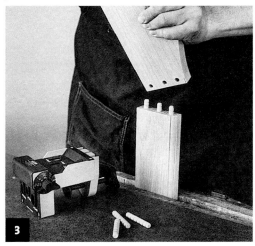

Drill dowel holes in the bottom and the lower shelf, using a jig. Assemble the sides, shelf, and bottom and top with glue and dowels to form the case.

Bore the ends for dowels after cutting the door rails and stiles to size. Use a self-centering doweling jig as shown to drill and assemble the frame joints.

Use a router to cut the door-frame rabbets to hold the mirrors. Square the rounded corners left by the rabbeting bit with a chisel to fit the mirror's corners.

Home Storage Projects

Utility Storage

Organize a jumbled attic, basement, garage, or workshop, or even construct a strong shed to house your utility-area overflow.

Utility Area Space Savers

Stack it, hang it, or stow it: store more with these quick and simple projects for attic, basement, or garage.

Modular Laundry Center

Cut the clutter of a laundry room with this simple-to-build workhorse of a cabinet and shelf system.

Simplified Workshop

Make your home workshop really work. Install this workbench and shelves in a corner of the garage or against a basement wall.

Sturdy Backyard Shed

Make room for your car in the garage at last. Let this handsome shed store your yard and garden gear.

Utility Area Space Savers

Stack it, hang it, or stow it: store more with these quick and simple projects for attic, basement, or garage.

Anyone can knock together a few boards into crude shelving. But to build a storage system that's cost effective, space efficient, and (why not?) even good looking requires a bit more thought.

You can easily build any one of these seven utility-storage units over a weekend. They all go together with simple butt joints and drywall screws or nails. If the plans call for screws, you'll save time if you use a combination drill and countersink bit in a 3/8-inch variable-speed drill. (For examples of this type of bit, see page 42 and the facing page.)

Either common pine boards or 3/4-inch plywood would be suitable to build any of these designs. Check your local prices for each, and then buy the least expensive material that will do the job and still look presentable.

For ease of construction and to minimize cutting, choose 1x10 or 1x12 pine boards. No. 2 common pine will contain small- to medium-size tight knots, but it is a cost-effective choice if you plan to paint your shelves anyway. If appearance is secondary to utility and you'll be leaving your shelving unfinished, choose the less-expensive No. 3 pine, which will contain loose knots and knotholes. In either case, select boards that don't show signs of twisting, bowing (end-to-end arcing), or cupping (side-to-side center depression).

Adjustable Shelving

This wonderfully versatile yet simple system of shelving is suitable for a storage shed or garage. In fact, you might choose to build several of these units to serve all around the house.

Use the plans shown here as a springboard to design and build a shelf system that will fit your own home's needs. To simplify construction, choose an appropriate grade of 1x10 or 1x12 pine. If your plans call for shelves wider than 11-1/4 inches, which is the actual width of a 1x12, select a suitable grade of 3/4-inch plywood instead.

▶ After cutting the case pieces to size with a circular saw, table saw, or radial arm saw, butt-join the unit with 2-inch drywall screws. Use a combination drill-and-countersink bit like the one shown at right or on page 42 to simplify the drilling of pilot, shank, and countersink holes. If you like, attach 1/4-inch thick plywood backs to the two outer units and add 1x3 lips to the front edges of their permanent bottom shelves.

▶ Allowing for the length of the open center shelves, secure the two end framed sections to wall studs by driving screws through the 1x3 strips at top and bottom.

▶ Finally, attach shelf standards to all but the outside faces of the end vertical supports. Level the holes in the standards front to back and left to right so that the shelves won't wobble.

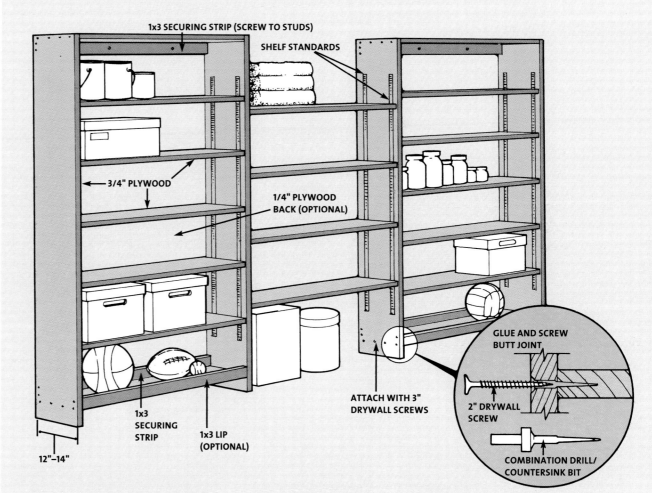

1x3 SECURING STRIP (SCREW TO STUDS)

SHELF STANDARDS

3/4" PLYWOOD

1/4" PLYWOOD BACK (OPTIONAL)

1x3 SECURING STRIP

1x3 LIP (OPTIONAL)

12"–14"

ATTACH WITH 3" DRYWALL SCREWS

GLUE AND SCREW BUTT JOINT

2" DRYWALL SCREW

COMBINATION DRILL/ COUNTERSINK BIT

TOOLS

HAND TOOLS
Carpenter's level
Carpenter's square
Screwdrivers
Tape measure

POWER TOOLS
Circular saw
Drill; driver bit; combination drill/countersink bit

OPTIONAL
Table saw or radial arm saw

MATERIALS

3/4" plywood or 1x10 pine* or 1x12 pine* for sides and shelving

1/4" plywood backing (optional)

* No. 2 common (better) or No. 3 common (see page 156)

1x3 pine front edging (optional)*

2" drywall screws

Shelf standards

Z-Bracket Shelving

When you need wall-mounted light-duty utility shelves in a hurry and appearance can take a back seat to function, you can't do better than to build a simple system around Z-bracket supports.

Z-brackets are inexpensive, readily available at most home centers, and versatile. These brackets come in three-shelf units capable of supporting shelves up to 14 inches wide. You can cut off part of the brackets with a hacksaw if you need only one or two shelves, or combine units if you need more.

Select the material for your shelves based on how much you want to spend and how you'd like your shelves to look.

▶ Install the brackets by driving 2-inch drywall screws into wall studs. Attach one bracket and then, with a helper, determine the position of the opposite one by setting a shelf board with a carpenter's level on it across the supports of both brackets. When the shelf board is level, your second bracket is in the correct position.

▶ Finally, cut the shelves to size and attach them to the bracket supports with 1/2-inch flathead wood screws, driving the screws from below.

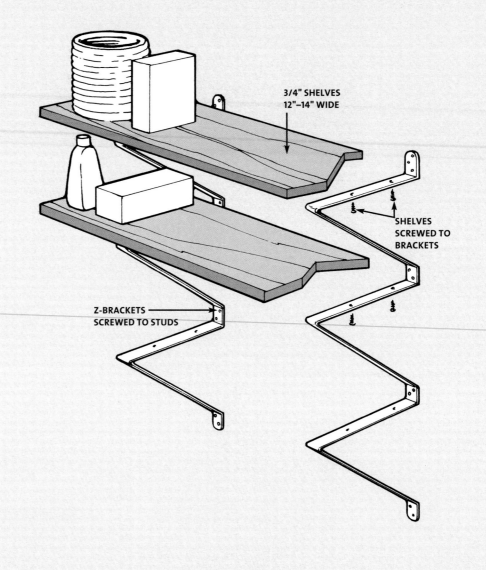

3/4" SHELVES 12"–14" WIDE

SHELVES SCREWED TO BRACKETS

Z-BRACKETS SCREWED TO STUDS

TOOLS

HAND TOOLS
Carpenter's level
Carpenter's square
Handsaw
Screwdrivers
Tape measure

OPTIONAL
Circular saw
Hacksaw

MATERIALS

3/4" plywood shelving
2" drywall screws
1/2" flathead wood screws
Z-bracket supports

Stacking Cases

Utility shelving that consists of any number of unattached stacking cases allows you to rearrange or add to the storage system as your needs change.

You may choose to build only the 1 x 2-foot cases shown stacked in the plans. Or you may prefer to design a system that combines 1 x 2-foot and 2 x 2-foot cases. If you build both sizes, you can combine them in modular fashion, stacking the smaller units vertically if you prefer.

▶ Build the cases by cutting the boards to your specifications, then butt-joining them using glue and 6d finish nails. Screw joinery really isn't necessary here, because the design doesn't put a lot of stress on the joints.

▶ If you like, use 1/4-inch plywood for the backs of the cases. And if you'll use the cases in a basement or a detached garage or shed where moisture may be a problem, support the units on 2x2 spacers to raise them off the floor.

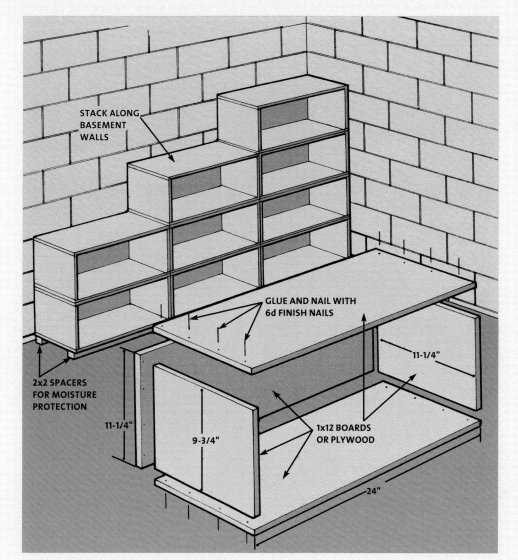

STACK ALONG BASEMENT WALLS

GLUE AND NAIL WITH 6d FINISH NAILS

2x2 SPACERS FOR MOISTURE PROTECTION

11-1/4"

11-1/4"

9-3/4"

1x12 BOARDS OR PLYWOOD

24"

TOOLS

HAND TOOLS

Carpenter's square

Hammer

Nail set

Tape measure

POWER TOOLS

Circular saw

MATERIALS

1/4" plywood backing (optional)

3/4" plywood shelving, or 1x12 pine shelving*

2x2 pine* (2 per base unit)

6d finish nails

Woodworker's glue

* No. 2 common (better) or No. 3 common (see page 156)

Under-Eave Storage

When you think you're completely out of storage space, look up. There's probably plenty of underutilized space beneath unfinished eaves in your attic. Under-eave attic storage is perfect for items you wish to keep over the long term but won't use frequently. And because these shelves are tucked well out of sight, you can build them with scrap lumber and sheet goods you may already have on hand.

▶ Cut 2x2 uprights to size, angle-cutting the tops to match the slope of the rafters. Then attach the uprights to the rafters with 2-inch drywall screws.

▶ Brace the uprights across to the rafters and to each other with 1x2 shelf cleats at the heights you plan for your shelves. Level the cleats and secure them to the uprights and the rafters with 2 inch drywall screws.

▶ Now cut your shelves to widths that will let them fit snugly between the uprights and the rafters. Because of the roof's slope, the bottom shelves will be deeper than the top ones.

▶ Finally, attach the shelves to the cleats with 4d finish nails driven from above. Near the shelves' ends, drill pilot holes for the nails to avoid splitting the wood.

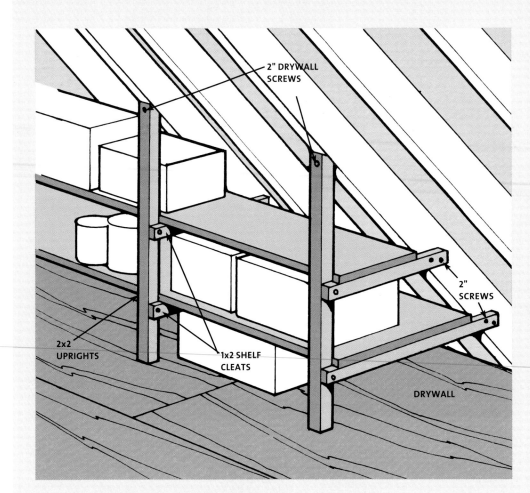

2" DRYWALL SCREWS

2" SCREWS

2x2 UPRIGHTS

1x2 SHELF CLEATS

DRYWALL

Overhead Bins

These overhead storage bins are the most complicated to build of all the projects in this chapter. But the extra time to add them to your basement or garage will repay itself many times over with versatile storage in "found" space near the ceiling.

Each bin is basically a simple box constructed of 3/4-inch plywood, with adjacent boxes sharing a common end board. Each end board extends above the top of the bin to attach to an overhead joist. The adjacent bins are screwed together in a build-as-you-go fashion, to the joists on top and ledger boards below (the front end of one is just visible in the drawing at right). This arrangement makes it simple to determine the length of the various bin components: just measure the spacing of the ceiling joists.

▶ Referring to the plan and inset drawings, build the basic bins, then attach the doors with butt hinges so that they fit neatly into the 3/4-inch recesses in the tops and bottoms.

▶ Hang screw hooks from the joists to support the doors in their open positions as follows: Open the doors, install a screw hook on the joist above the edge of each door, then use the hooks to help you locate the mating screw eyes on the door faces.

▶ If you'd like to outfit some or all of the bins with interior shelves, mount them with screws driven directly through the sides of the bins.

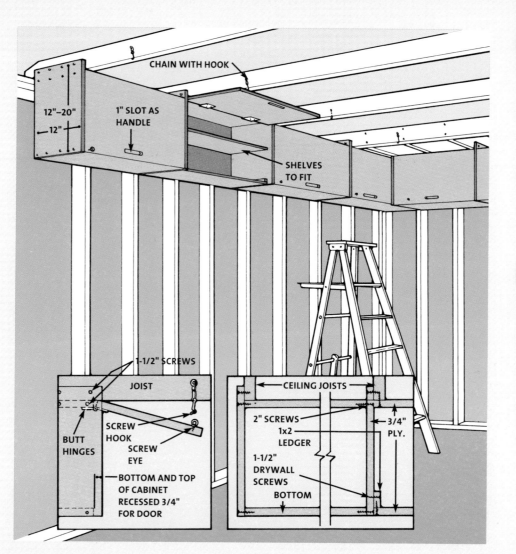

TOOLS

HAND TOOLS
Adjustable wrench
Carpenter's level
Framing square
Screwdrivers
Tape measure

POWER TOOLS
Circular saw
Drill; driver bit

MATERIALS

3/4" plywood
1x2 pine ledger
2x3 pine framing
2" drywall screws
1-1/2" drywall screws
2-1/2" lag bolts
Butt hinges
Screw hooks and screw eyes

Bicycle Hanger

Few things are more successful at eating up valuable space in your garage than a bevy of bicycles. And bikes leaned haphazardly against garage walls are susceptible to damage from inadvertent spills; the family car is in danger too.

The ingeniously simple bicycle hanger shown here moves the storage problem up off the floor yet leaves the family's bikes readily accessible.

▶ First cut two 2x4 arms about 15 inches long. Then groove out a 1-1/2 inch diameter half-round slot with a saber saw, or a hole saw if you have one, near one end of each support.

▶ Temporarily tack the arms to neighboring wall studs with finish nails. Test-fit a bike on the supports without putting its full weight on them. Check that there's ample room for the handlebars and pedals in the spaces between studs.

▶ Adjust the length and spacing of the two support arms as necessary, then permanently attach them to the studs with 3/8 x 4-inch bolts.

TOP OF GARAGE WALL

2x4 ARMS

DIMENSIONS TO FIT BIKE

1-1/2" DIA.

3/8" x 4" BOLTS, NUTS, AND WASHERS

WALL STUD

Garage Rack

This straightforward garage rack, like the preceding Bicycle Hanger, also takes advantage of a wasted area near the ceiling, but this time it's space over the hood of your car.

▶ Build the two 2x3 end support frames first (see the plans), determining the shelf width and vertical spacing needed to suit your space.

▶ Then hang these frames from overhead beams with 2-1/2 inch lag bolts. If you build the rack in a corner, construct just one end support frame, then mount the opposite 2x3 shelf ledgers directly to the side wall of the garage with 2-1/2 inch drywall screws.

▶ Measure and cut 3/4-inch plywood shelves. Attach them to the shelf ledgers with 1-1/4 inch drywall screws.

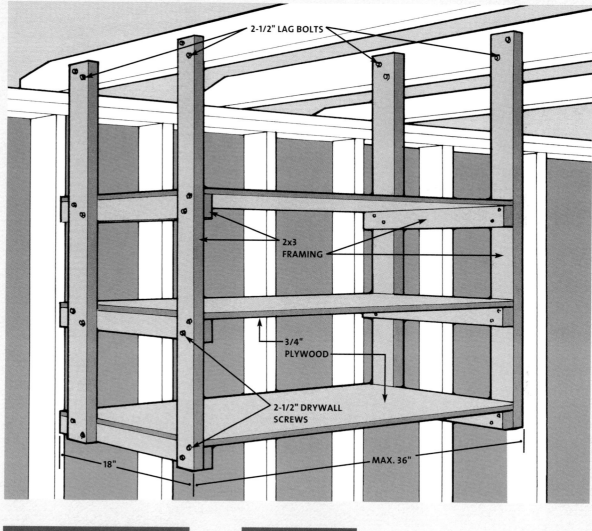

2-1/2" LAG BOLTS

2x3 FRAMING

3/4" PLYWOOD

2-1/2" DRYWALL SCREWS

18"

MAX. 36"

TOOLS

HAND TOOLS

Adjustable wrench

Carpenter's level

Carpenter's and framing square

Screwdrivers

Tape measure

POWER TOOLS

Circular saw

Drill; driver bit

MATERIALS

2x3 pine framing

3/4" plywood shelving

2-1/2" drywall screws

1-1/4" drywall screws

2-1/2" lag bolts

Modular Laundry Center

Cut the clutter of a laundry room with this simple-to-build workhorse of a cabinet and shelf system.

White melamine-coated particleboard makes it a breeze to clean this bright, spacious, easy-to-build laundry center.

The modular design of this versatile, roomy shelf system lets you build it one piece at a time. And because it's made from particleboard that you can buy already laminated with melamine—a thin layer of protective plastic—you can achieve the sleeker look of more expensive plastic-laminated shelves.

These shelves are the perfect project for the do-it-yourselfer who has limited wood-working experience but feels ready for a new challenge. To build them you'll need just a few basic tools: a circular saw, a drill, a tape measure, a framing square, a stapler, a level, and a few bar clamps.

Materials You'll Need

All the materials you'll require to make this shelf system are inexpensive and readily available at home centers:

▶ Stock 1x4 boards for the hanger rails. Home centers often carry several grades of these. You can save money by using a less-expensive grade, but because some of these boards will show in the finished project, pick out straight ones that have as few knots as possible.

▶ Plastic-coated hardboard, sometimes called tileboard, available in 4 x 8-foot sheets, for the back panels of the shelf units. This type of surface is brighter and easier to clean than regular hardboard.

▶ Melamine-coated 3/4-inch particle-board. Buy 4 x 8-foot sheets for large sections like the base units. For the shelves themselves, choose boards in 12- and 16-inch widths, which are available in 2-, 4-, and 8-foot lengths.

Many home centers stock two types of melamine-coated particleboard: one with rows of holes for adjustable shelf pegs (for the sides of the shelf units) and another without holes (for the actual shelves). White is the most popular color, but you can also find black and imitation wood-grain finishes.

Be aware that some coated shelving materials scratch more easily than others. To test the material you plan to buy, rub it with the edge of a coin. Good-quality coatings won't scratch away.

▶ Edge banding. The shelf material you buy will come banded, or covered with a strip of plastic on one edge. Larger pieces, like 4 x 8-foot sheets, usually aren't banded, so after cutting them to size you'll need to cover the exposed edges with iron-on edge banding, which comes in rolls.

▶ Coarse-threaded 2-inch drywall screws. Use a No. 8 pilot bit to simultaneously drill a pilot hole for the screw and counter-sink the screwhead.

▶ RooClear glue. Most of the glues you'll find at a typical home center won't stick to melamine. For this project use only RooClear glue, which is sold by specialty retailers. (For the name of a dealer near you, contact Roo Imports, P.O. Box 13574, Salem, OR 97309; [503] 588-0788. In Canada, contact McKillican Distribution Ltd., 16420 118th Avenue, Edmonton, ALTA T5V 1C8; [403] 453-3841.)

TOOLS

HAND TOOLS

Bar clamps

Framing square

Hammer

Level

Screwdrivers

Stapler

Stud finder

Tape measure

POWER TOOLS

Circular saw; carbide-tip blade

Drill; No. 8 pilot bit

OPTIONAL

Radial arm saw or table saw

Masonry bit

MATERIALS

3/4" melamine-coated particleboard

1x12 and 1x16 melamine-coated boards

Plastic-coated hardboard panels for backing

1x4 boards for hanger rails

1/2" screws

1-1/4" screws

2" drywall screws

3" flathead or masonry screws

Closet rod

Drawer glides

Edge banding (by the roll)

Latex paint to match melamine color

Masking tape

RooClear glue

Shelf pegs

Construction Plan

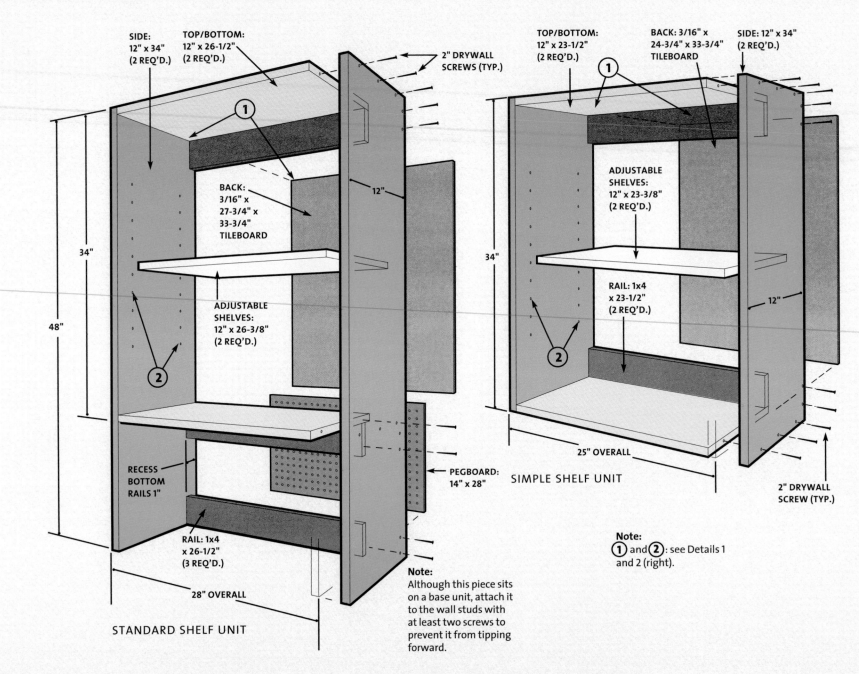

SIDE:
12" x 34"
(2 REQ'D.)

TOP/BOTTOM:
12" x 26-1/2"
(2 REQ'D.)

2" DRYWALL
SCREWS (TYP.)

①

12"

34"

48"

②

BACK:
3/16" x
27-3/4" x
33-3/4"
TILEBOARD

ADJUSTABLE
SHELVES:
12" x 26-3/8"
(2 REQ'D.)

RECESS
BOTTOM
RAILS 1"

RAIL: 1x4
x 26-1/2"
(3 REQ'D.)

PEGBOARD:
14" x 28"

28" OVERALL

STANDARD SHELF UNIT

TOP/BOTTOM:
12" x 23-1/2"
(2 REQ'D.)

BACK: 3/16" x
24-3/4" x 33-3/4"
TILEBOARD

SIDE: 12" x 34"
(2 REQ'D.)

①

ADJUSTABLE
SHELVES:
12" x 23-3/8"
(2 REQ'D.)

34"

②

RAIL: 1x4
x 23-1/2"
(2 REQ'D.)

12"

25" OVERALL

SIMPLE SHELF UNIT

2" DRYWALL
SCREW (TYP.)

Note:
① and ② : see Details 1
and 2 (right).

Note:
Although this piece sits
on a base unit, attach it
to the wall studs with
at least two screws to
prevent it from tipping
forward.

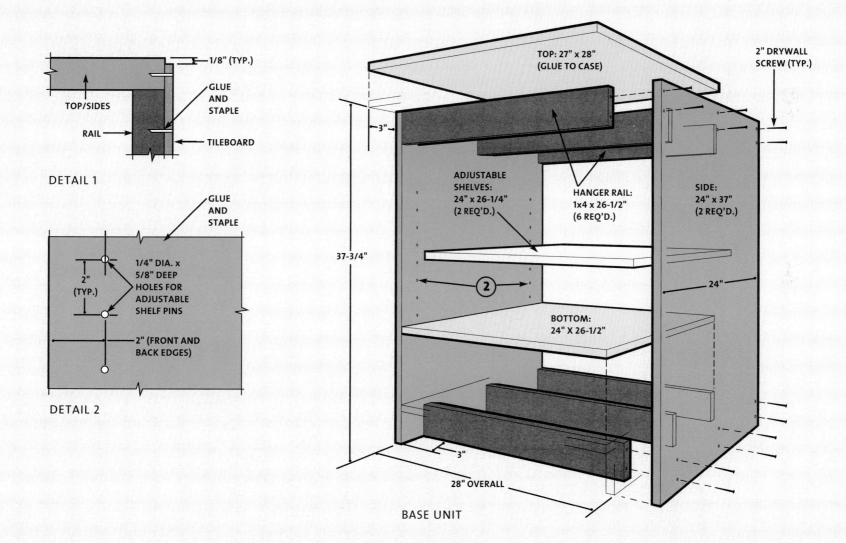

1/8" (TYP.)

GLUE
AND
STAPLE

TOP/SIDES

RAIL

TILEBOARD

DETAIL 1

GLUE
AND
STAPLE

1/4" DIA. x
5/8" DEEP
HOLES FOR
ADJUSTABLE
SHELF PINS

2"
(TYP.)

2" (FRONT AND
BACK EDGES)

DETAIL 2

TOP: 27" x 28"
(GLUE TO CASE)

2" DRYWALL
SCREW (TYP.)

3"

ADJUSTABLE
SHELVES:
24" x 26-1/4"
(2 REQ'D.)

HANGER RAIL:
1x4 x 26-1/2"
(6 REQ'D.)

SIDE:
24" x 37"
(2 REQ'D.)

37-3/4"

2

24"

BOTTOM:
24" X 26-1/2"

3"

28" OVERALL

BASE UNIT

Installing a Pull-out Closet Rod

A pull-out closet rod makes a handy addition to laundry-room shelving units. You could, for instance, install one over a sink tub to let clothes drip dry there.

With 1/2-in. screws, mount a pair of drawer glides to the inside surfaces of the unit's side panels. (If your shelving unit is only 12 inches deep, you may need to go to a specialty woodworking store to find shorter drawer glides to fit it.) Then cut a piece of closet rod and a scrap of 1x4 the same length to fit between the glides. Attach the closet rod toward the front of the glides and the 1x4 piece at the back—and that's it.

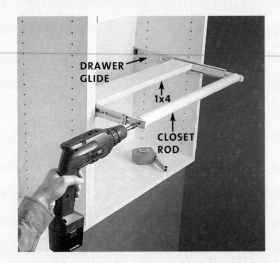

DRAWER GLIDE

1x4

CLOSET ROD

Design Considerations

Use these plans and instructions as suggestions for designing a laundry shelf system that fits the available space and your own storage requirements. As you design your system, consider these points:

▶ To give your shelf system pleasing proportions, build it the same width as your washer and dryer.

▶ Size your shelves carefully. Don't make them extend so far out over the washer that you can't see inside. And don't hang them so low that you can't open the washer lid. If your washer and dryer rest directly against a wall, you'll probably have to use 12-inch wide shelving material. But if they sit a few inches away from the wall, to allow room for plumbing and exhaust connections, you may be able to use wider 16-inch boards.

▶ Avoid wasting material by sizing your shelf units carefully. For example, if you'd like your shelf units to be 33 inches tall, consider making them 31-7/8 inches high instead. This allows you to cut three side pieces instead of just two from an 8-foot long piece of material.

As you lay out your pieces, don't forget to allow for the kerf—the width of the saw blade—which is about 1/8 inch. If you cut a 4-foot long piece exactly at its center, you'll end up with two pieces that are both slightly less than 2 feet long. In the example in the preceding paragraph, the 31-7/8 inch length provides the 1/8 inch needed for the kerf.

▶ Remember to cut the top and bottom panels 1-1/2 inches shorter than the overall width of the individual units, to allow for the thickness of the side panels.

▶ For ease of assembly, cut the back panels 1/4 inch smaller each way than the overall size of each individual unit.

▶ To make repositioning the adjustable shelves easy, design the shelves to be 1/8 inch shorter than the top and bottom panels of the cabinet.

▶ Particleboard isn't as strong as other shelf materials, and long shelves will gradually sag under a heavy load. To prevent sagging, size your shelves no longer than 26 inches. If you notice a shelf starting to sag, simply flip it over. For sizable loads, reinforce the shelves with edging strips along the back edge, sized as needed. (See the tip on page 171.)

▶ Finally, you'll speed your work and minimize mistakes if you begin by compiling a cutting list based on your plans. List on it all the parts you'll need, the quantity for each, and their exact size and description.

Cut Out the Parts

The ultimate success of any project like this begins with cutting out the parts accurately. Here are some tips that will help you achieve smooth, precise cuts.

▶ A radial arm saw would be perfect for this project, but you can achieve good results with a circular saw too. For the smoothest cuts with either tool, use a carbide-tip saw blade. The more teeth on the blade, the smoother the cuts will be.

▶ For accurate cuts with a circular saw, make yourself a saw guide (Photo 1). Build it from two pieces of scrap plywood or particleboard, with one piece cut to about 1 foot wide and the other 2 inches wide with a straight factory edge. The length of these pieces isn't critical, but they must both be at least 6 inches longer than the width of the largest piece you'll want to cut using this homemade guide.

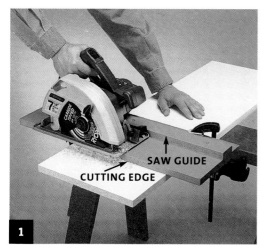

Mark the location of the cut using a framing square. Then clamp both ends of the saw guide across the workpiece with the cutting edge of the guide firmly against the pencil line.

To assemble the saw guide, screw the two pieces together so that the narrow strip is inset 2 inches from one edge of the wide strip. This flange provides a clamping surface. Now cut the saw guide to its final width by running your saw along the other side of the narrow strip and cutting off part of the wide piece. To use the saw guide, simply align this cut edge on your cutting line and clamp the guide in place. When the base of your saw is against the narrow guide strip, the saw blade will be correctly positioned.

▶ For easier assembly later, label each part with a soft pencil as soon as you cut it out. After assembly, you can easily wipe away these pencil marks.

▶ You can expect the melamine coating to chip along the edges of cuts. Although you can minimize chipping by covering the cut line with masking tape, you can't eliminate it altogether. The melamine coating will chip on the side of the material where the saw teeth exit, leaving a piece that's cut cleanly on one side but chipped on the other. If you're using a circular saw, the side of the material facing up will chip. With a radial arm saw or table saw, the underside will chip.

▶ By planning ahead, you can build your units so the chipped edges will be hidden. For example, if you're cutting with a circular saw, trim the side panels to length with the predrilled holes facing up. That way the chipped areas will be covered by the top and bottom panels.

▶ To hide any chipped areas that are still visible after you assemble the units, wipe latex paint over the chipped sections with a rag. The paint will adhere to the exposed particleboard but will wipe off the melamine easily.

▶ Remember that your shelf boards are prebanded on one edge only. Plan your cuts so that this edge will face out when you assemble the units.

▶ Finally, if you're working with melamine-coated particleboard that's been predrilled for shelf supports, be sure to cut the side panels so their holes will align front to back and side to side when you assemble them. Otherwise your shelves will slant or wobble.

Assemble the Units

This shelving system is basically just an arrangement of boxes assembled with simple butt joints. Refer to the Construction Plan on pages 166–167 for specifics on building the boxes. Keep these guidelines in mind:

▶ Paint the 1x4 hanger rails to match the melamine before assembly. Touch up any nicks or chips after hanging the units.

▶ If you need to drill holes for the adjustable shelf pegs in the side panels, do this before assembling the units. Make a drill jig from a piece of scrap 1x4 in which you've drilled a row of holes spaced an even 2 inches apart. Or clamp a strip of pegboard to the side panels and use its holes as a jig. Make the holes 1/2 inch deep and 1/4-inch or 3/16-inch wide, depending on the type of shelf pegs you'll

use. (For information about the various types of adjustable shelf hangers available, see the box on page 21.) Use a depth gauge or wrap your bit with a strip of masking tape at the 1/2 inch mark as a warning flag so you won't accidentally drill through a side panel (Photo 2).

▶ Drill pilot holes to prevent the material from splitting when you drive the screws (Photo 3). Using a No. 8 pilot bit, make the first hole and apply glue to the joint. Then drill the remaining pilot holes and drive the other screws.

▶ Use glue liberally wherever two surfaces join. Immediately wipe away any excess glue that squeezes out after you drive the screws.

▶ Tighten the screws only until the parts are snug, not so firmly that the screwheads dig into the particleboard.

Overtightening will also contribute to weaker joints by squeezing out too much glue. If necessary, practice with scrap wood until you've mastered the technique.

▶ Square-drive screws are the easiest to use, because they lock the screwdriver bit firmly into the screwhead.

▶ Assemble the individual units in this order: First attach the top and bottom panels to a side panel. Then secure the hanger rails, followed by the second side panel (Photo 4).

▶ Finally, square up the unit by measuring the diagonals from corner to corner. With a helper or a long bar clamp, adjust the sides until the measurements are equal. Then apply a bead of glue and staple the back panel in place (Photo 5).

ASSEMBLE THE UNITS

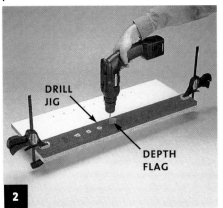

Before assembly, drill 1/2-in. deep shelf-peg holes in the side panels. Wrap the bit with a masking tape flag at the correct depth to avoid drilling too deep and penetrating the panels.

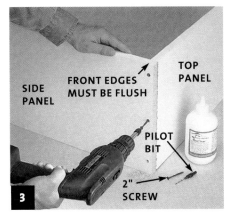

Assemble the top and first side panel. Use a No. 8 bit to drill a pilot hole, then apply glue, drive a 2-in. screw, wipe off excess glue, and proceed in order for the other screws.

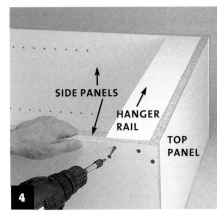

Attach the second side panel after securing the top and bottom panels and the hanger rails to the first side panel. Be careful not to overtighten the screws.

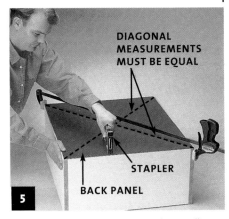

Square up the unit by measuring diagonally from corner to corner and adjusting the unit until the two measurements are equal. Then apply glue and staple on the back panel.

Hang the Units

Hang the units by driving screws through the hanger rails into the wall. Use at least two screws in each hanger rail. Then secure adjoining units to each other by clamping them together and driving 1-1/4 inch screws through the side panel of one unit into that of the next (Photo 6). This is a two-person job; you'll need a helper to hold the unit in place while you level it, drill pilot holes, and drive the screws.

If your walls have wood studs, drive the hanger-rail screws directly into them. Use screws that are at least 3 inches long for the best penetration.

To find the stud locations, either use a stud finder or drive a nail on a part of the wall that will be covered by a shelf unit. If you don't hit wood, move the nail and keep trying until you find the center of a stud. Then use a tape measure to find the next studs. The center of a new stud will usually be 16 inches (but sometimes 24) from the center of the last one.

If you have concrete-block or solid-concrete walls, drill pilot holes with a masonry bit and hang the shelves using 3-inch masonry screws. For the various options available in wall fasteners, see pages 186–189.

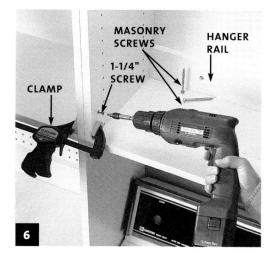

MASONRY SCREWS

1-1/4" SCREW

HANGER RAIL

CLAMP

6

Hang the units on the wall by driving at least two screws through both the top and bottom hanger rails. Clamp adjoining units together and attach them with 1-1/4 in. screws.

Particleboard Tip

To add support to the particleboard back, nail or screw an edging strip along the back edge. Make the edging strip about twice as wide as the shelf is thick. A 1x3 strip board should normally be adequate.

Simplified Workshop

Make your home workshop really work. Install this workbench and shelves in a corner of the garage or against a basement wall.

This workbench has a generous work surface over two spacious shelves for tool and material storage. And the shop vacuum niche can be vacated to let you pull up a comfortable stool for close-up work like winter fly-tying. The wall studs near the bench can support many more handy shelves.

The design of this workbench is both functional and cost effective. All of the legs, shelf supports, and frame components are cut from just five 12-foot 2x4's, with only a few inches of waste per board. The shelves, end panels, and top are sawed out of two 4 x 8-foot sheets of 1/2-inch thick sanded A-C grade fir plywood. As you can see from the color-keyed Cutting Guide at the right, the sheet-goods waste is also minimal.

This is by no means a complicated workbench to build, but the job will go more smoothly if you heed these tips:

▶ Use a circular saw with a sharp blade to cut the lumber and plywood, and an electric drill with a screwdriver bit to do the joinery. A 3/8-inch variable-speed reversible drill with a Phillips-head bit will save time and effort.

▶ You will probably need a helper during several of the assembly steps, such as attaching the legs and installing the 2x4 shelf pieces.

▶ To simplify assembly, drill pilot holes for the screws before joining the 2x4 components. This keeps the lumber from splitting and creates tighter joints.

Cutting Guide

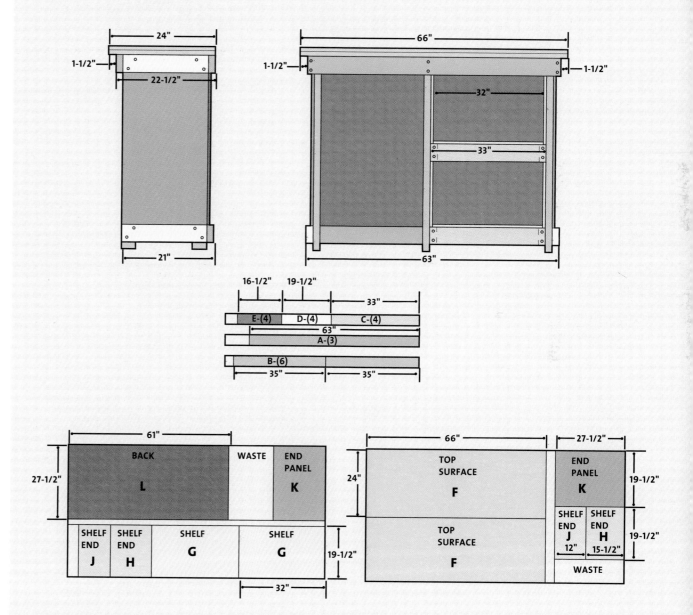

Construction Plan

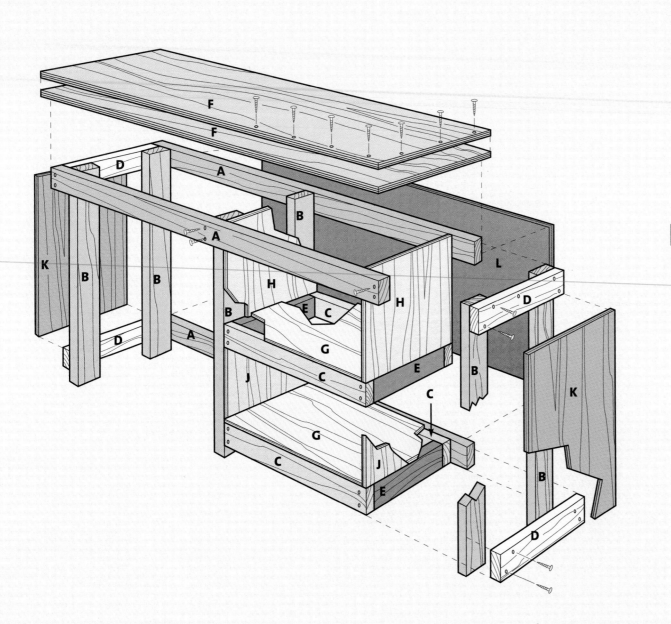

TOOLS

HAND TOOLS

File

Framing square

Hammer

Handsaw

Screwdrivers

Tape measure

Torpedo level

POWER TOOLS

Circular saw

Drill; Phillips-head bit

MATERIALS

Qty.	Size and Description
2 sheets	1/2" A-C grade fir plywood
5	12' 2x4's for workbench
	2x4 boards for wall brackets
	1x4 boards
	2x6 boards
	1x12 boards
	4d and 6d nails
	1-1/2" drywall screws
	2-1/2" drywall screws
	Sandpaper
	Woodworker's glue

Build the Base

After you've laid out and cut all the parts, referring to the Cutting Guide on page 173, build the base. Once the base is constructed, attaching the top is easy.

To build the base, assemble the three 63-inch long main frame components (A), the four 19-1/2 inch frame members (D), and the four outer pairs of legs (B), using butt joints and 2-1/2 inch drywall screws (Photo 1). Then add the bottom-shelf frame members (C and E) and the inner pair of legs (B).

Now install the top-shelf frame members (C and E) (Photo 2). You can locate the top shelf wherever you like, as long as you remember to alter the sizes of the inner shelf end panels (H and J) accordingly. Test-fit whatever you anticipate storing on the top shelf. For instance, if you plan to keep a large tool box there, measure the height you'll need to clear its lid in the fully opened position before you decide on the shelf's height.

Next, attach the end panels (K) and back (L) (Photo 3). These panels, along with the inner shelf end panels, will both stabilize the bench and prevent tools and equipment from falling off the shelves.

Secure the inner shelf end panels (H and J) with 4d nails. Then fasten the bottom and top shelves (G).

BUILD THE BASE

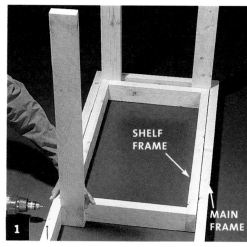

1

Assemble the three 63-in. long main frame components (A), four 19-1/2 in. frame members (D), and outer pairs of legs (B), using butt joints and 2-1/2 in. screws.

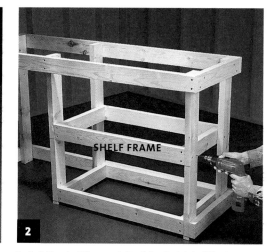

2

Install the shelf frame. Adjust the height of the top shelf to fit your needs, remembering to alter the size of the inner shelf end panels accordingly.

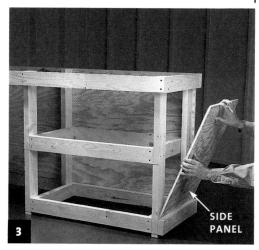

3

Attach the end panels (K) and back panel (L). These sections will help stabilize the workbench and prevent tools and equipment from falling off the shelves.

Make the Top

Complete the workbench by tacking the bottom panel of the workbench top (F) to the frame with 4d or 6d nails (Photo 4). Align this panel flush with the back edge of the workbench's frame and leave a 1-1/2 inch overhang at each end as shown in the Cutting Guide on page 173.

Sand the top (working) surface of the top panel, and set it aside for the moment. Now apply woodworker's glue to the entire top surface of the bottom panel, using a short length of scrap wood to spread it evenly (Photo 5). This glue helps prevent gaps between the two 1/2-inch plywood panels that form the workbench's top.

Before the glue sets, place the top plywood panel, sanded side up, onto the freshly glued bottom one. Make sure all the panels' edges are flush with each other, then attach the top with 2-1/2 inch drywall screws driven through both panels into the frame (Photo 6). This completes the workbench except for applying a finish if you like. A clear polyurethane coating will provide a long-wearing surface that's spillproof and easy to clean.

M A K E   T H E   T O P

BOTTOM SHEET

4

Tack the bottom panel of the workbench's top to the frame with 4d or 6d nails. Make sure the panel is flush with the back edge of the frame and that it overhangs each end by 1-1/2 in.

WOOD GLUE IS COLORED FOR CLARITY

5

Sand the top surface of the top panel, then apply wood glue to the entire top surface of the bottom plywood panel, spreading it evenly with a short length of scrap wood. The glue prevents gaps between the panels.

6

Place the top panel onto the glued bottom panel, with its sanded side up. Align all the panel edges, then attach the top to the workbench frame using 2-1/2 in. drywall screws.

Add Wall Shelving

If your shop area has an open-stud wall, you can take advantage of some often-overlooked storage space. The cavities between adjacent wall studs are perfect for mounting brackets and shelves.

To make brackets and shelves, cut 15-inch long 2x4 horizontal brackets, level them, and attach them to the wall studs with 2-1/2 inch drywall screws (Photo 7). Then lay out and cut diagonal 2x4 braces and attach them to the studs and horizontal brackets as shown, again with 2-1/2 inch drywall screws. Drill pilot holes for screws to join the diagonal braces to the horizontal brackets. If you like, use a handsaw to angle-cut the bottom ends of the horizontal brackets to match the angle of the braces, as shown.

You can cut a 1x12 shelf to any length you wish, but don't extend it more than 18 inches beyond the shelf brackets. A shelf up to 4 feet long can be supported with two brackets, but for longer shelves you'll need to add intermediate brackets to prevent sagging. Drill pilot holes, then attach the shelves to the horizontal brackets with 1-1/2 inch drywall screws (Photo 8).

To attach shelves between studs, cut the shelves from 1x4 or 2x6 boards to fit inside the stud spacing. Secure them with 2-1/2 inch drywall screws into pilot holes through the studs and into the shelf ends (Photo 9). For 2x6 shelves, round the protruding front corners as shown to reduce the chance of injury. Cut them off at a 45-degree angle, then file or sand them before you install the shelves.

For safety's sake, position your shelves so that you can't stack spillable items such as paint cans more than one row high. It's better to add more rows than to overload between-stud shelves. A 1x4 shelf will safely hold quart-size cans and most aerosol cans. A 2x6 shelf will comfortably hold two one-gallon cans (Photo 10).

ADD WALL SHELVING

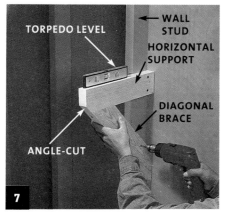
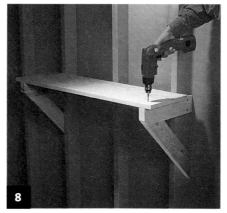
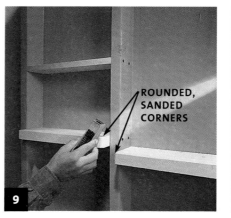

7 — **Attach 15-in.** long horizontal brackets to the wall studs. Then secure diagonal braces to the bottoms of the brackets and the wall studs with 2-1/2 in. drywall screws.

8 — **Position the shelves** on the horizontal brackets and attach them with 1-1/2 in. drywall screws. Drill pilot holes first to prevent splitting the shelves close to the ends.

9 — **Install 2x6** and 1x4 boards between studs with 2-1/2 in. drywall screws. On 2x6 shelves, cut protruding front corners at a 45-degree angle, then round them off with a file or sandpaper.

10 — **Stagger the heights** of adjacent shelves for easier installation. When storing items such as paint cans, don't stack them more than one row high.

Sturdy Backyard Shed

Make room for your car in the garage at last. Let this handsome shed store your yard and garden gear.

This sturdy 8 x 12-foot storage shed is much better looking than a commercially available kit, and almost as easy to build.

Anyone with average carpentry skills and some tools—rented or owned—should be able to complete this project in a few weekends. You'll need a helper for a few of the steps, but the most complicated task—framing the roof—is simplified by using a jig to cut and assemble the trusses.

Even if your own shed doesn't include the vents, skylights, and roll-up steel door shown here, you'll appreciate this shed's fully framed walls, snow-supporting roof, and long-lasting flooring, all designed to meet most building codes.

Even though you can buy off-the-shelf storage sheds for about the same cost as the materials for this project, this design has several advantages that make it worth the extra time to build.

▶ This storage shed is designed to meet most building codes and is built to last. The floor and everything below it are made of rot-resistant, pressure-treated material. This shed's fully framed walls won't shake in a stiff wind, and its roof won't sag under a heavy weight of snow.

▶ The standard stud-wall construction technique that's outlined here lets you easily mount shelves, brackets, and storage hooks on the walls.

▶ This shed includes features that many kits don't, such as vents, skylights, and a steel roll-up door for extra security.

Build the Foundation

To build this shed, you'll have to start with a perfectly level site. If your back-yard slopes or is uneven, fill an area in with pea gravel to form a flat base. You could also use sand or clean fill dirt, but they're not as stable in wet areas. Pack down the fill material using a 6-foot long 4x4 held vertically as a tamping tool. If you are making a shed larger than the one shown here and have a big area to tamp, you could rent a plate vibrator to save time and effort.

You could build this shed right on a platform of leveled pea gravel, but a foundation of treated 5x6 timbers will be more rigid, and it will make the rest of the project simpler.

First cut two 5x6's to 12-foot lengths. Lay these 12-foot timbers parallel to each other so that their outside edges are 8 feet apart. Then measure the distance between their inside edges at each end and cut the other 5x6's to fit. Nail these timbers together with 10-inch spikes.

Square up the foundation by measuring it diagonally from corner to corner in both directions (Photo 1). Adjust the timbers and keep remeasuring until the two distances are equal.

Now make sure all four foundation timbers are level. Set one of the 14-foot 2x6 fascia boards on edge across the timbers at various points and rest a level on its top edge.

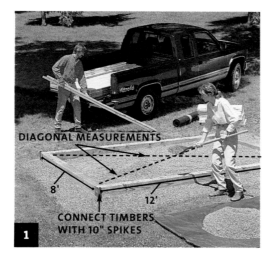

DIAGONAL MEASUREMENTS

8'   **12'**

1

CONNECT TIMBERS WITH 10" SPIKES

Level and tamp the shed site, then square up the timber foundation by adjusting it until its diagonal, corner-to-corner measurements are equal.

Design Options

The measurements and materials shown in the Construction Plan (pages 180–181) are based on an 8 x 12-foot floor plan, but you could easily build a longer shed by adding trusses. For simplicity and economy, add length in increments of 2 feet. First calculate what you'll need by way of extra nails and roofing materials, longer treated timbers, treated 2x6 rims, and 2x6 soffit boards. Then, for every additional 2 feet of length, add the following to your materials list:

▶ One treated 8-foot 2x6

▶ Six 7-foot 2x4's

▶ A half sheet of treated 3/4-inch plywood (probably available only as a full sheet)

▶ One sheet of siding

▶ One sheet of 5/8-inch plywood.

To keep the same floor plan but reduce costs, omit some of these features:

▶ The timber foundation. Timbers make the foundation firmer and assembly easier but aren't absolutely necessary.

▶ One or both skylights.

▶ One or both gable vents, which are primarily to air out gasoline fumes from small engines. This shed is not airtight, so if you don't live in a wet or humid climate and won't be storing small-engine-powered equipment in the shed, you can omit these vents.

▶ Finally, use less-expensive siding material and 1/2-inch treated plywood for the floor instead of 3/4-inch sheets. The thinner flooring will cause the floor to feel slightly spongy underfoot.

Construction Plan

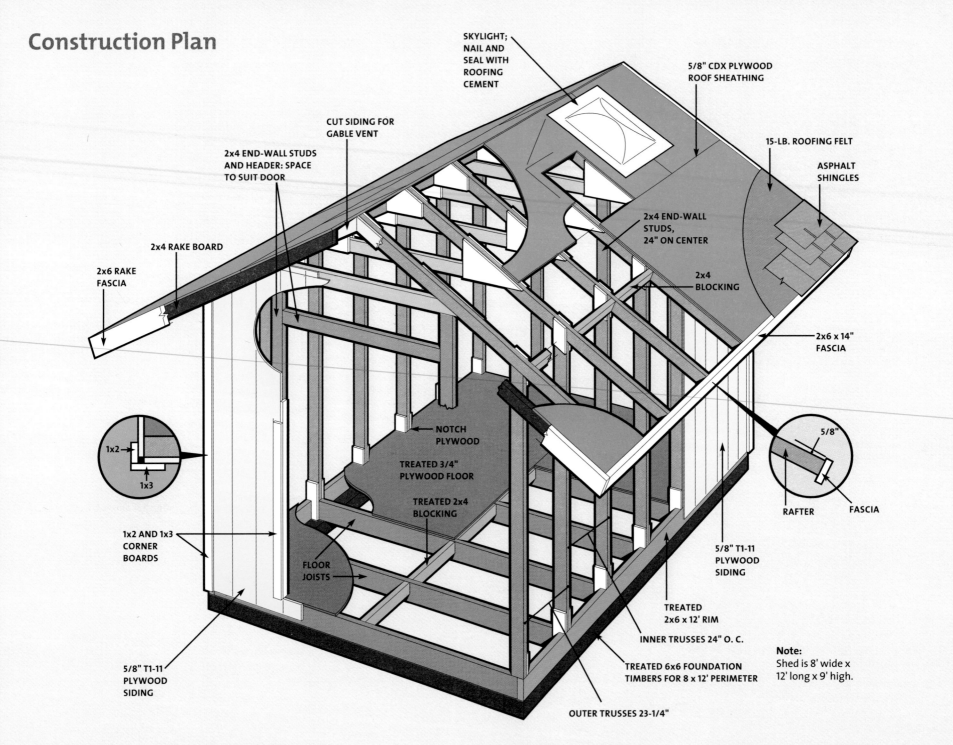

SKYLIGHT; NAIL AND SEAL WITH ROOFING CEMENT

5/8" CDX PLYWOOD ROOF SHEATHING

15-LB. ROOFING FELT

ASPHALT SHINGLES

CUT SIDING FOR GABLE VENT

2x4 END-WALL STUDS AND HEADER: SPACE TO SUIT DOOR

2x4 END-WALL STUDS, 24" ON CENTER

2x4 RAKE BOARD

2x4 BLOCKING

2x6 RAKE FASCIA

2x6 x 14" FASCIA

1x2

1x3

NOTCH PLYWOOD

5/8"

TREATED 3/4" PLYWOOD FLOOR

RAFTER

FASCIA

TREATED 2x4 BLOCKING

1x2 AND 1x3 CORNER BOARDS

FLOOR JOISTS

5/8" T1-11 PLYWOOD SIDING

5/8" T1-11 PLYWOOD SIDING

TREATED 2x6 x 12' RIM

INNER TRUSSES 24" O. C.

Note:
Shed is 8' wide x 12' long x 9' high.

TREATED 6x6 FOUNDATION TIMBERS FOR 8 x 12' PERIMETER

OUTER TRUSSES 23-1/4"

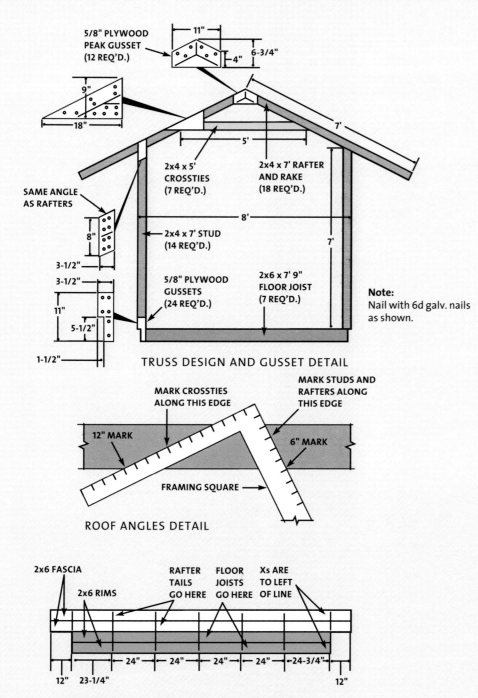

5/8" PLYWOOD PEAK GUSSET (12 REQ'D.)

11"

6-3/4"

4"

9"

18"

SAME ANGLE AS RAFTERS

8"

3-1/2"

3-1/2"

11"

5-1/2"

1-1/2"

2x4 x 5' CROSSTIES (7 REQ'D.)

2x4 x 7' RAFTER AND RAKE (18 REQ'D.)

5'

7'

2x4 x 7' STUD (14 REQ'D.)

8'

7'

5/8" PLYWOOD GUSSETS (24 REQ'D.)

2x6 x 7' 9" FLOOR JOIST (7 REQ'D.)

Note:
Nail with 6d galv. nails as shown.

TRUSS DESIGN AND GUSSET DETAIL

MARK CROSSTIES ALONG THIS EDGE

MARK STUDS AND RAFTERS ALONG THIS EDGE

12" MARK

6" MARK

FRAMING SQUARE

ROOF ANGLES DETAIL

2x6 FASCIA

2x6 RIMS

RAFTER TAILS GO HERE

FLOOR JOISTS GO HERE

Xs ARE TO LEFT OF LINE

24" 24" 24" 24" 24-3/4"

12" 23-1/4" 12"

RIM AND FASCIA MARKING PATTERN DETAIL

TOOLS

HAND TOOLS
Caulking gun
Framing square
Hammer
Handsaw
Level
Nail set
Screwdrivers
Tape measure

POWER TOOLS
Circular saw
Saber saw
Power miter box (rented)
Reciprocating saw (rented)
Table saw

OPTIONAL
Bar clamps
Air compressor (rented)
Power air nailer (rented)
Plate vibrator tamper (rented)

MATERIALS

Qty.	Size and Description
2	Treated 5x6's x 8' for foundation
2	Treated 5x6's x 12' for foundation
7	Treated 2x6's x 8' for floor joists
2	Treated 2x6's x 12' for perimeter rims
40	2x4's x 7' for studs, rafters, crossties, rake boards, and door header*
8	2x4's x 8' for end-wall studs and blocking between rafters
4	2x6's x 8' for rake fascia
2	2x6's x 14' for fascia
3 sheets	Treated 3/4" plywood for floor
10 sheets	Plywood siding
8	5/8" CDX plywood for roof and gussets**
5	1x2's x 8' for corner boards and door casing
5	1x3's x 8' for corner boards and casing
2	Adjustable-pitch gable vents
2	Skylights
4	10" spikes for foundation timbers
5 lbs.	16d galvanized nails for framing
5 lbs.	8d galvanized nails for roof deck, floor, and siding
5 lbs.	6d galvanized nails for gussets
1 lb.	3" drywall screws for end-wall studs
200 sq. ft.	15-lb. roofing felt and shingles
7	10' pieces of drip edge
5 lbs.	1/2" roofing nails
2 tubes	Roofing cement to seal skylights
	Pea gravel

* The 2-ft. leftovers from the crossties can be used for blocking between floor joists.

** Cut four of the 5/8-in. sheets of plywood to 3 ft. wide to fit the roof. Use the leftover 1 ft. x 8 ft. pieces for gussets.

Make the Roof Trusses

To align and assemble the shed's roof trusses, you'll need to have a power miter box (rentable), a circular saw, and a framing square.

Cutting Tip

When cutting lumber thicker than the reach of your circular saw's blade, cut from one side, flip the piece over, and cut from the other side. If that doesn't complete the cut, make similar kerfs on the other two sides and finish up with a handsaw.

The seven trusses to be built have 126 individual parts, but even so, this phase of the project isn't as difficult as conventional roof framing. To save time and effort, rent an air compressor and power air nailer. Here are some further suggestions to speed your work.

▶ Mark and cut just one of each component—the trusses, rafters, crossties, floor joists, and gussets (see the Roof Angles Detail on page 181 and Photo 2). Use these pieces as patterns for marking the remaining parts.

▶ You won't use them right away, but now is a good time to cut the twelve 22-1/2 inch 2x4 and six 21-3/4 inch 2x4 blocking pieces to go against the end walls. By using the 2-foot scraps left over from cutting the crossties, you can cut the rest of the blocking from just three 8-foot 2x4's.

▶ Build a jig to help assemble the trusses accurately (Photo 3). Nail three full sheets of 5/8-inch plywood across 14-foot 2x6's. Then nail blocks of scrap 2x4's to the jig's platform and sides to help you locate the truss components and hold them in place while you nail on the gussets.

▶ Nail all seven gussets to one side of the truss (see the Truss Design and Gusset Detail on page 181). Then, with a helper, flip the truss over and nail the gussets to the other side (Photo 4). Note that the two end-wall trusses will have gussets on one side only, because siding will cover their outer surfaces.

MAKE THE ROOF TRUSSES

2

Mark and cut one of each component, then use it as a pattern for the rest. This will let you quickly cut the rafters, wall studs, crossties, floor joists, and gussets.

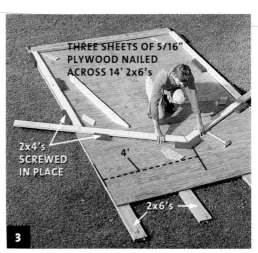

3

Build a truss jig from 2x4 scraps and 5/8-in. plywood you'll use later for the roof. Use this jig to hold the truss parts in place while you connect them with gussets.

Nail gussets to one side of the truss, flip it over, and nail the gussets to the other side. The two end-wall trusses need gussets on their insides only.

Frame the Shed

To erect the trusses, cut two 2x6's to exactly 12 feet each and two more to precisely 14 feet. Then mark the four 2x6's 2 feet on center (O. C.) so that when you center the trusses on the lines you've drawn they will be exactly 2 feet apart (see the Rim and Fascia Marking Pattern Detail on page 181 and Photo 5). The distance between the outermost trusses will be 23-1/4 rather than 24 inches.

With a helper, erect the center truss (Photo 6). Position one of the marked rim pieces on the foundation timber. Use a level to plumb the truss while your helper drives three 16d nails through the rim and into the floor joist. Then toenail the floor joist to the foundation timber.

Next, erect one of the end-wall trusses, facing the side without gussets toward the outside. Plumb and secure it to the foundation timber as you did the center truss. After two trusses are up, nail a 14-foot fascia board to their rafter tails so that the top edge of each fascia is 5/8 inch above the top edges of the rafter tails (see the inset at center right on page 180). Use a scrap of 5/8-inch plywood as a spacer.

Now position and attach the remaining trusses, using the center-line marks you made on the rim and fascia boards as guides (Photo 7).

When the trusses, rims, and fascias are in place, add treated 2x4 blocking between the floor joists, centered on the width of the joists, and do the same between the rafters, just beyond the wall studs.

FRAME THE SHED

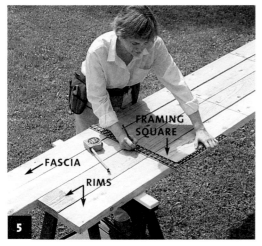

5

Mark the truss locations carefully on the fascia and rim boards, using a framing square; this isn't difficult but is important for proper framing.

6

Hold the truss perfectly vertical while a helper drives three 16d nails through the rim into the floor joist. Toenail through the joist into the foundation timber.

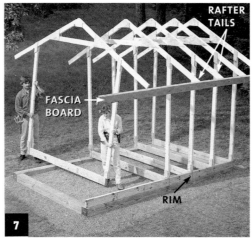

7

Set the other trusses, nail them through the rim and fascia, toenail the floor joists to the foundation, and attach the opposite rim and fascia boards.

Add the Flooring and Final Framing

Cover the floor with 3/4-inch treated plywood (see the Construction Plan on pages 180–181 and Photo 8). Using a framing square, lay out the locations of the trusses and notch the plywood for them with a saber saw. Fit the notched panels around the trusses and attach them to the joists and blocking with 8d galvanized nails every 6 inches.

Complete the skeleton by adding framing to the trusses that form the end walls (Photo 9). Screw three 2x4 studs along the back wall, spacing them 2 feet apart. On the front wall, add two studs, to frame the opening for the type of door you'll be using. Attach a 2x4 header between the two front-wall studs at the height required.

Side and Straighten the Shed

Cut the siding sheets to length and nail them on. To avoid water damage, don't let the siding extend closer than 6 inches to the ground (Photo 10).

Cut about 10 inches off the length of each of the six sheets of siding used on the side walls. On the end walls, set a sheet of siding on nails driven partway into the rim board. Hold it in place against the wall while your helper marks the diagonal cuts and identifies the door opening on the front wall.

By now, the shed's frame will probably have tilted slightly out of square and plumb since the time when you erected the trusses. Use the following steps to straighten out the frame while you are siding the shed.

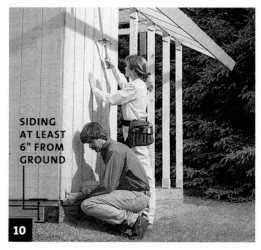

10

Nail siding sheets to the side-wall and end-wall studs. At the corners, fit the sheets so they're flush with the corners of the studs and not overlapping each other.

▶ Starting at a corner, nail a sheet of siding to the end-wall truss only.
▶ Hold a level against one of the end walls. If the wall is plumb, finish nailing on the sheet.
▶ If the wall isn't plumb, ask your helper to nudge the end wall one way or the other until it's perfectly vertical. Then complete the nailing on of the sheet.
▶ Repeat this procedure with another sheet of siding on the other side wall.
▶ Finally, nail the cut sheets of siding to the side-wall and end-wall studs with 8d galvanized nails. At the corners, align the sheets so they're flush with each other and not overlapping.

ADD THE FLOORING AND FINAL FRAMING

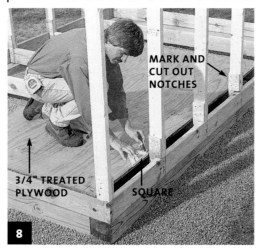

8

Mark the truss locations on the plywood floor and cut notches for them with a saber saw. After the notches are cut, fit the plywood into the gaps between trusses.

9

Add the blocking and end-wall studs. Locate the front-wall studs to fit your shed door. Screwing these pieces in place is easier than toenailing them.

Finish the Roof

Cover the gables with four triangular pieces of siding, each covering half a gable. Before you nail on the gable siding, lay the matched pieces together, center the gable vent over them, and mark and cut out the vent opening.

Sheathe the lower ends of the roof with four 4-foot wide sheets of 5/8-inch plywood. Cut them to 7 feet long so that one end will be flush with the end of the rake fascia (not yet installed) and the other will fall on the center of the middle rafter. Use 3-foot wide sheets to finish sheathing the roof. Center an 8-foot long sheet in the middle of the roof and cut 3-foot long pieces for each end above the gables.

When the sheathing is complete, cut openings for the two skylights (Photo 11).

A 2x4 cleat temporarily nailed to the roof will keep you from slipping. Now attach the rake boards (Photo 12). Cut 2x6 rake fascias 85-1/2 inches long and to the same angle as the rafters. Nail the rake fascias to the rake boards. Now lay the roofing felt and shingles, following the shingle manufacturer's instructions, and fit the skylights (Photo 13). Then install the drip edge.

Install the Door

Trim the door opening with 2x3's, then cover the corners of the shed with corner boards made from one length of 2x2 and a length of 2x3.

Install the door you've selected, following the manufacturer's instructions, and prime and paint the shed to match your house if you like.

FINISH THE ROOF

11 SKYLIGHT — 2x4 CLEAT NAILED TO ROOF

Cut openings for the skylights between the rafters, being careful not to cut into the rafters themselves. For safety, nail 2x4 cleats to the roof for footing.

12 ROOF SHEATHING — RAKE BOARD — CLAMP — ATTACH 2x6 RAKE FASCIA OVER RAKE BOARD

Nail or screw the rake boards to the underside of the roof sheathing, clamping the boards in place. Then cover these boards with 2x6 rake-fascia boards.

13 FELT — SKYLIGHT — ROOFING CEMENT

Nail the skylights in place after the roofing felt is attached. A skylight's lip goes over the shingles on its lower edge but under shingles at the sides and top.

Wall Fasteners

These handy fasteners let you hang light or heavy items on drywall or lath-and-plaster walls without locating studs. Some even make it possible to attach objects to masonry and concrete.

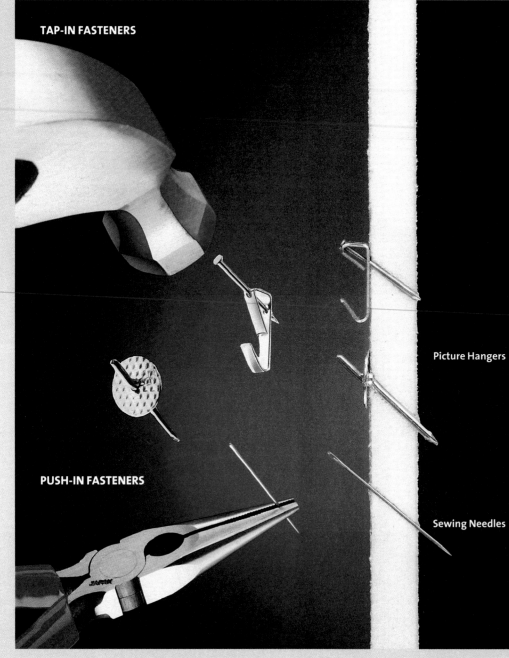

TAP-IN FASTENERS

PUSH-IN FASTENERS

Picture Hangers

Sewing Needles

TAP-IN FASTENERS

Picture Hangers. Tap either of these two common types of picture hangers directly into drywall. They come in several sizes. The thicker the nail, the heavier the weight it will support—up to about 40 pounds.

PUSH-IN FASTENERS

Sewing Needles. Push a sewing needle into drywall with a pair of needle-nose pliers, working it in slowly so it won't break. Needles work well as picture hangers and leave only a tiny hole when removed.

Drywall: Heavy Objects

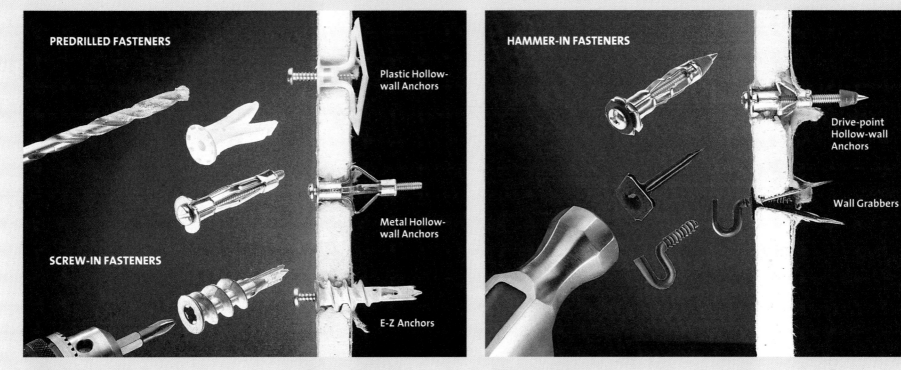

PREDRILLED FASTENERS

Plastic Hollow-wall Anchors

Metal Hollow-wall Anchors

E-Z Anchors

SCREW-IN FASTENERS

HAMMER-IN FASTENERS

Drive-point Hollow-wall Anchors

Wall Grabbers

PREDRILLED FASTENERS

Plastic Hollow-wall Anchors.
Drill a hole as large in diameter as the plastic anchor, then squeeze the anchor's wings together and insert it into the hole. Separate the anchor's wings with a nail or the supplied peg. These fasteners, available in several sizes, remain permanently fixed in the wall.

Metal Hollow-wall Anchors.
Drill a hole the same diameter as the anchor's shank, insert the anchor into the hole, and then tighten the screw to expand the anchor inside the wall. These anchors, which also stay in the wall after the screw is removed, are available in several sizes and shank lengths for different wall thicknesses.

SCREW-IN FASTENERS

E-Z Anchors.
Drive these anchors directly into the wall with a Phillips-head screwdriver bit in a variable-speed drill. Then drive a No. 8 screw into the anchor. This type of fastener, which is removable, also comes in a plastic version called Zip-It anchors.

HAMMER-IN FASTENERS

Drive-point Hollow-wall Anchors.
Drive these anchors completely through the drywall with a hammer, then tighten the screw to expand the shank. The shattered drywall on the back side of the wall makes this fastener weaker than a regular hollow-wall anchor.

Wall Grabbers.
Drive these fasteners through the wall with a hammer, keeping the flat side parallel to the floor. Then insert a screw or hook to spread the fastener's legs and secure it. Although they're removable, wall grabbers can also weaken the back side of the drywall.

Plaster: Light and Heavy Objects

Masonry: Light and Heavy Objects

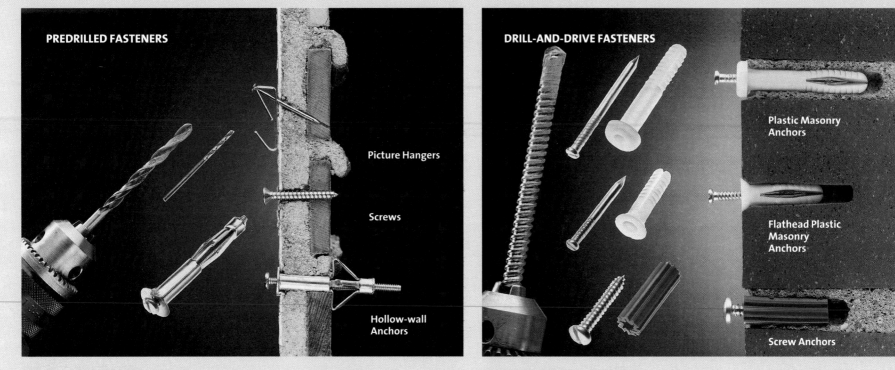

PREDRILLED FASTENERS

Picture Hangers

Screws

Hollow-wall Anchors

DRILL-AND-DRIVE FASTENERS

Plastic Masonry Anchors

Flathead Plastic Masonry Anchors

Screw Anchors

PREDRILLED FASTENERS

Picture Hangers.
Drill a pilot hole the same diameter as the nail, and then tap the picture hanger into the wall carefully so that you don't crack the plaster.

Screws.
Drill a shank hole for screws through the plaster only, then drive the screws into the 3/8-inch wood lath backing the plaster. If a screw happens to hit a gap between laths, relocate the hole.

Hollow-wall Anchors.
Drill a hole the same diameter as the shank and insert the anchor. Tighten the screw to expand the anchor. Use a long-shank anchor like the one shown to extend through a typical 7/8-inch thick plaster wall.

DRILL-AND-DRIVE FASTENERS

Plastic Masonry Anchors.
Drill a hole with a carbide-tip bit the same diameter as the anchor. Insert the anchor. The button top clamps the object you want to hang when you drive the special nail, which has a slotted head and a threaded shank for easy removal.

Flathead Plastic Masonry Anchors.
These anchors are similar to the ones above, except that they have a flat head that you can countersink and conceal. If you may want to remove the anchor later, drill into a mortar joint instead of into the side of a brick.

Screw Anchors.
Drill a hole the same diameter as the anchor, insert the plastic or lead anchor, and drive the proper-size screw. Be sure to match the size of the anchor to that of the screw.

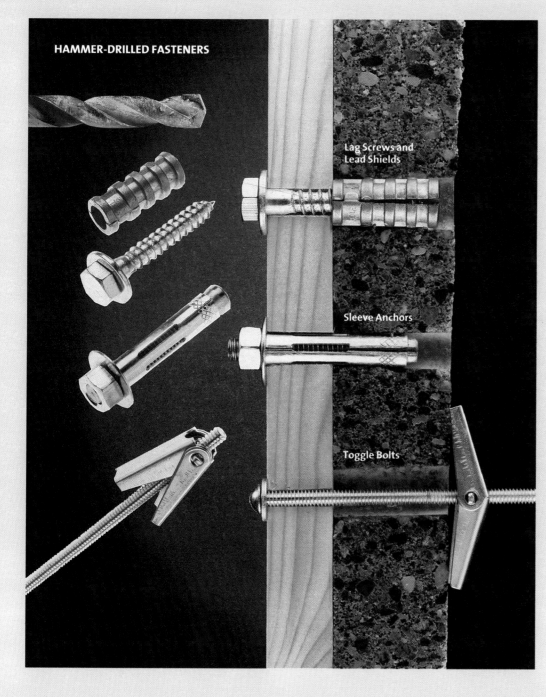

HAMMER-DRILLED FASTENERS

Lag Screws and Lead Shields

Sleeve Anchors

Toggle Bolts

HAMMER-DRILLED FASTENERS

Lag Screws and Lead Shields.
Using a carbide-tip bit rated for percussion in a hammer drill like that shown, bore the proper-size hole. Then insert the lead shield and drive a lag screw with a wrench. Match the shield's size to that of the screw.

Sleeve Anchors.
Again, use a hammer drill to make a hole the same diameter as the anchor. Insert the anchor, then tighten the screw with a wrench to expand the sleeve and clamp it against the sides of the hole. These fasteners come in many sizes.

Toggle Bolts.
Drill a hole just large enough to pass the bolt's wings when they are compressed. The wings will open loosely in the hollow wall space to hold the bolt until you can tighten the screw. This fastener, which is available in many sizes, also works well in drywall and plaster hollow walls. Its only disadvantages are that you must drill a larger hole for the wings than for some other anchors and you can't remove it without losing the wings inside the wall.

Index

Acknowledgments:

Diana Berndt, Ron Chamberlain, Ken Collier, Carl De Groote, John Emmons, Bill Faber, David Farr, Hope Fay, Mary Flanagan, Roxie Filipkowski, Charles Frizzell, John Frost, M. Bernadette Goering, Barb Herrmann, Al Hildenbrand, Shelley Jacobsen, Duane Johnson, Bruce Kieffer, Mike Krivit, Phil Leisenheimer, Gerry Lofland, Terry McMickle, Susan Moore, Doug Oudekerk, Deborah Palmen, Mary Jane Pappas, Don Prestly, Dave Radtke, Don Raymond, Art Rooze, Jessica Sia, Sudi Scull, Mike Smith, Marvin Stehr, Dan Stoffel, Eugene Thompson, Mark Thompson, Bob Ungar, Alice Wagner, Gregg Weigand, Mac Wentz, Michaela Wentz, Gordy Wilkinson, Marcia Williston, Donna Wyttenbach, Bill Zuehlke.

This book was produced by Roundtable Press, Inc.,
for the Reader's Digest Association
in cooperation with *The Family Handyman* magazine.

If you have any questions or comments, please feel free to write us at:

The Family Handyman
7900 International Drive
Suite 950
Minneapolis, MN 55425

Measuring the Metric Way

Use these guides and tables to convert between English and metric measuring systems.

Fahrenheit and Celsius

The two systems for measuring temperature are Fahrenheit and Celsius (formerly known as Centigrade). To change from degrees Fahrenheit to degrees Celsius, subtract 32, then multiply by $5/9$. For example: $68°F - 32 = 36$; $36 \times 5/9 = 20°C$. To convert degrees Celsius to degrees Fahrenheit, multiply the degrees by $9/5$, then add 32 to that figure. For example: $20°C \times 9/5 = 36$; $36 + 32 = 68°F$.
(See also Some Rules of Thumb.)

Some Rules of Thumb

Temperature:

If the Fahrenheit temperature is between 0° and 100° and you want to know the approximate degrees Celsius, subtract 30 from the number of degrees Fahrenheit, then divide by 2.
For example: $70°F - 30 \div 2 = 20°C$.

In fact, 70°F is slightly more than 21°C.

The "10 Percent and Up" Rule:

1 meter is 10% longer than 1 yard
1 liter is 10% less than 1 quart
1 kilogram is 10% more than 2 pounds
1 tonne is 10% more than 1 short ton (2,000 pounds)
1 square meter (m^2) is 20% greater than 1 square yard
1 cubic meter (m^3) is 30% greater than 1 cubic yard

The "30" Rule:

1 foot is slightly more than 30 centimeters
1 ounce is just under 30 grams
1 fluid ounce is almost 30 milliliters

The "About" Rule:

1 inch is about 25 millimeters or 2.5 centimeters
4 inches are about 10 centimeters
A 2-inch by 4-inch piece of lumber (a 2x4) is about 5 centimeters by 10 centimeters
3 feet are about 1 meter
10 yards are about 9 meters
100 yards are about 90 meters
1 mile is about 1.5 kilometers
5 miles are about 8 kilometers
1 pound is about 0.5 kilogram
1 imperial gallon is about 4.5 liters (1 U.S. gallon is about 4 liters)
1 quart is about 1 liter (the imperial quart is 1.136 liters; the U.S. quart is 0.946 liter)
1 pint is about 0.5 liter (the imperial pint is 0.568 liter; the U.S. pint is 0.473 liter)